PROMISES, MORALS, AND LAW

PROMISES, MORALS, AND LAW

PROMISES, MORALS, AND LAW

===

BY

P. S. ATIYAH, F.B.A.

*Professor of English Law in the
University of Oxford*

CLARENDON PRESS · OXFORD

Oxford University Press, Walton Street, Oxford OX2 6DP

London Glasgow New York Toronto
Delhi Bombay Calcutta Madras Karachi
Kuala Lumpur Singapore Hong Kong Tokyo
Nairobi Dar es Salaam Cape Town
Melbourne Auckland

and associates in
Beirut Berlin Ibadan Mexico City Nicosia

Published in the United States by
Oxford University Press, New York

British Library Cataloguing in Publication Data
Atiyah, P. S.
  Promises, morals and law.
  1. Promises
  I. Title
  170   BJ1025
  ISBN 0-19-825377-X
  ISBN 0-19-825479-2 (pbk.)

Library of Congress Cataloging in Publication Data
Atiyah, P. S.
  Promises, morals, and law.
  Reprint. Originally published: Oxford:
Clarendon Press, 1981.
  Includes bibliographical references and index.
  1. Promises.   2. Promise (Law)
  3. Law and ethics.   I. Title.
[BJ1500.P7A84 1983]   174'.3   82-14412
ISBN 0-19-825377-X
ISBN 0-19-825479-2 (pbk.)

First published 1981
Reprinted (New as Paperback) 1982

Printed in Hong Kong

Preface

This is not the work on Modern Contract Theory which I foreshadowed in *The Rise and Fall of Freedom of Contract*. But it is a by-product of my continuing work on the theory of contractual and promissory obligation.

The present book is addressed to philosophers, and especially to moral and linguistic philosophers interested in the topic of promising, on the one hand, and to lawyers with a taste for theory, on the other. This explains why the work contains a number of elementary explanations of some basic legal and philosophical issues. I hope that readers of both disciplines will nevertheless find sufficient to interest them in this attempt to bring legal and moral theory into one intellectual discussion.

I am deeply indebted to a number of colleagues and friends for reading the first draft of the book and offering me much valuable criticism; in particular I am glad to express my thanks to John Dwyer, Joseph Raz, Gordon Baker, Robert Summers, Colin Grant, Neil MacCormick, and Richard Bronaugh.

St. John's College,
Oxford

P.S.A.

CONTENTS

Chapter 1

Promising in Law and Morals

Promissory and contractual obligations raise many issues of common interest to philosophers and lawyers. For lawyers, it goes without saying that the nature and extent of contractual liabilities are matters of enduring professional concern. But because the nature of their discipline makes them more immediately interested in practical questions, lawyers tend to adopt theories of liability without testing them too rigorously for consistency with positive law. And for many years now English lawyers, including even academic lawyers, have shown little interest in the underlying rationale of the law of contract. They generally take it to be axiomatic that this branch of the law is founded upon the prima-facie enforceability of promises, subject only to compliance with some simple legal rules. There has been virtually no disposition to inquire into the nature of promises, or to probe into the reasons for their legal enforceability. It is almost always taken for granted by lawyers that prima facie promises are morally binding and that this is at least one, if not itself a sufficient, ground of legal liability.

For their part, philosophers have found the nature of promissory obligation of absorbing interest. For many years, the morally binding nature of a promise has been thought one of the strongest refutations of utilitarianism, on the ground that breach of a promise would not normally be condoned even though it seemed likely to produce more happiness (or more good) than keeping it. On the other hand, if utilitarianism is rejected, the moral obligation to keep a promise has seemed to some philosophers to be puzzling in the extreme. How, it is asked, can a person create an obligation by the mere process of wishing to have one, or perhaps, declaring that he has one? To some, ethical theory has centred on the concept of duty, irrespective of consequences, and the nature of these duties is a matter for internal reflection or intuition. The obligation to keep a promise has been treated by some writers as a paradigm example of a duty which is readily recognized by this intuitive process. More recently, promising has figured prominently in the work of linguistic philosphers.

Promising has been treated as an obvious illustration of a performative, a verb with the aid of which one can not merely say that one promises but actually *do* it. Yet another group of writers has used the rule that promises should be kept as a prime illustration of a constitutive rule; the 'practice of promising', it is said, is logically impossible without prior recognition of rules constituting the practice, and enabling obligations to be created by the mere act of promising. And there has, too, been controversy about whether it is possible to bridge the logical gap between 'is' and 'ought' by pointing to the binding nature of a promise.

With isolated and minor exceptions, most of this literature has, in recent years, proceeded in total disregard of the law. Just as the lawyer tends to think of the philosopher as an airy theorist having little contact with reality, so the philosopher tends to see the law as technical and abstruse, having little contact with morality. It was not always thus. Until Bentham and Austin wrought their work in setting apart legal and moral obligations, discussions of the nature and limits of promissory liability treated the two as though they were inextricably interwoven. In the works of the seventeenth-century Natural Lawyers, for example, positive law, natural law, and the moral law are all treated together in such a way as to suggest that it would be impossible to understand at least the latter two in isolation from each other. And even in the writings of moralists and philosophers in the British tradition, such as Hume and Paley, there is a much greater awareness of, and reference to, the law as itself of profound relevance to the moral issues involved in the subject of promises. With the common lawyers, too, particularly in the early formative period of the development of modern contract law, there are signs that lawyers tended to fashion the law of contracts broadly in accord with what they took to be moral principles. They tended to create the law in the image of morality as they understood it. No doubt, as the Natural Lawyers made explicit, positive law did sometimes diverge from morality. But in its central doctrines and ideas, law and morality were largely congruent.

Now the importance of this lies in the fact that the English common law has never treated the mere fact that a promise has been made as even prima facie a sufficient condition for the creation of a legal obligation. Even in the latter half of the sixteenth century, when common lawyers began to build the modern law of contract on new foundations, it is quite plain that they rejected the notion that prima facie a promise created a legal obligation. To them, it was of vital importance to ask *why* a promise had been given. A promise made for a good reason—a good 'consideration' as it came to be said—was prima facie enforceable; a promise made without reason—or consideration—was prima facie not enforceable.

Very roughly, it could be said that a promise was only legally actionable if the promise was to do something which the promiser ought to have done anyway.[1] As a matter of positive law, the doctrine of consideration crystallized in the reign of Elizabeth I into a number of rules which are still clearly recognizable by the modern common lawyer. First, if a person received a benefit at the hands of the promisee for which he promised to pay, the benefit was a sufficient consideration: in effect, the promise here was bought and paid for. Second, if the promisee acted to his detriment in reliance on the promise, so that the non-fulfilment of the promise would cause him actual pecuniary loss, the detriment was a sufficient consideration. And thirdly, if two parties exchanged mutual promises, each promise was a sufficient consideration for the other promise: here, as in the first case, an exchange of benefit was contemplated, though one party might be able to sue the other (for example where the latter's performance was due first) even though he had not himself yet performed, or even though the anticipated benefit turned out to be harmful rather than beneficial. Much has been written by modern lawyers and legal historians about this doctrine of consideration, but most of this literature has tended to take for granted the perspective of the modern lawyer who accepts the prima-facie binding nature of a simple promise. The doctrine of consideration has, therefore, often seemed in need of explanation; the assumption has nearly always been that the doctrine is somehow odd and perhaps unjust in rejecting the simple notion that prima facie a promise is binding. But in recent times it has been suggested that this is to read history through modern spectacles. The doctrine of consideration, it is now urged,[2] was a profoundly moral doctrine, reflecting the belief of the early common lawyers, not merely that a promise *per se* should not be legally enforceable, but also that a promise *per se* was not necessarily

---

[1] A. W. B. Simpson, *A History of the Common Law of Contract* (Oxford, 1975), p. 457.
[2] Ibid., p. 488.

morally binding. More acceptably to modern eyes, the doctrine of consideration itself showed what circumstances *were* conceived to render a promise morally binding, and hence legally deserving of protection. What has not so far been seriously canvassed is the possibility that the ideas underlying the doctrine of consideration are relevant also to the nature of a promise itself, the question whether a promise creates an obligation, the weight of that obligation, and, indeed, to the question whether a promise has ever been made at all.

I myself have written at length elsewhere[3] suggesting that the common lawyers' approach to these questions underwent a complete metamorphosis between about 1600 and 1800. By the latter date, the common lawyers had largely come round to the modern viewpoint, that promises *per se* are morally binding, and that insofar as the doctrine of consideration fails to give effect to this moral ideal, it is an anomaly, a technicality, a curiosity of legal history. During the greater part of the nineteenth century, I have argued, the result of this change in attitude reflected itself in a large number of ways in the development of the law. Although the doctrine of consideration could not be overthrown—it was too firmly embedded in the law for that—it could be downgraded into a subordinate role. Lawyers came to place an increasing emphasis on the notion that the law of contract was designed to give full effect to the intention of the parties: the distinction between liability on a bare promise (or an exchange of bare promises) on the one hand, and liability on paid-for, or relied-upon promises, on the other hand, became much less important. Lawyers tended increasingly to ignore the reasons for which promises were given, and to assume that promises were always made with a view to creating a binding future commitment.

During this period, it may be said that the morality underlying the law of contract fell largely into line with the writings of utilitarians and other moralists. From Paley at one end of the period[4] to Sidgwick[5] at the other, moral discussion about the nature and extent of promissory liability was closely in accord with the moral ideals prevailing in the Courts. There remained, of

---

[3] *The Rise and Fall of Freedom of Contract* (Oxford, 1979) (hereafter referred to as *Freedom of Contract*).

[4] Paley, indeed, was cited to the Courts on a number of occasions, and his views on the effect of ambiguous promises were largely adopted in *Smith* v. *Hughes* (1871) LR 6 QB 597.

[5] *Methods of Ethics* (London, 1907).

course, the problem of the gratuitous unilateral promise, binding in morals, no doubt, but still not legally enforceable. But cases of this nature only rarely came before the Courts, and when they did, it was not difficult for judges to find some implied counter-promise, or some act of detrimental reliance, or some element of benefit to the promisor, and thus uphold the binding nature of the promise. For example, in the well-known case of *Shadwell* v. *Shadwell*[6] an uncle promised his nephew (who was a barrister) £150 a year on hearing of the nephew's intended marriage. The Court decided that, on his marriage, the nephew acted to his detriment in the sense that he took upon himself the obligation of maintaining a wife, and that this rendered the promise legally enforceable.[7]

There were, of course, other legal rules (such as the requirement that certain legal contracts should be evidenced in writing) which sometimes compelled Courts to refuse legal validity to promises which would generally have been regarded as morally binding. Thus under the Statute of Frauds of 1677 (an Act which may well have been influenced by the then prevailing morality) various types of contract could not be enforced unless they had been partly performed, or were evidenced by some signed note or memorandum. In the mid-nineteenth century, judges made no secret of their dislike for this Statute, and to plead the Statute as a defence came to be thought a dishonourable and shabby thing to do.[8]

Since the end of the last century, and, more particularly, in the past twenty or thirty years, there have been (I have argued[9]) growing signs of a legal reversion to the moral ideals which were more in evidence before the nineteenth century. On the one hand, there are signs of an increasing reluctance to impose liability in wholly executory contracts, that is, on promises which have neither been paid for, nor relied upon. And on the other hand, there are many signs of an increasing tendency to regard the rendering of benefits and acts of justifiable reliance as more

---

[6] (1860) 9 CB (NS) 159.

[7] Many modern lawyers consider the decision was wrong, precisely because there appears to have been no 'real' detriment or benefit, and the Court was thus enforcing a bare gratuitous promise. Interestingly, Byles J., who dissented, is known to have been out of sympathy with the prevailing adherence to freedom of contract ideology, see my *Freedom of Contract*, pp. 380-3.

[8] See, e.g., Isaacs J. in *Charlick* v. *Foley Bros. Ltd.* (1916) 21 CLR 249. In 1885 Sir James Fitzjames Stephen argued for repeal of the Act in the first number of the *Law Quarterly Review*.

[9] *Freedom of Contract*, Part III.

important grounds for the imposition of legal liability than bare mutual promises.

A good example of the former tendency can be found in the increasing stress on the legal doctrine of 'mitigation of damages', whereby the innocent party to a breach of contract cannot recover damages for a loss which he has, or even could have, avoided by taking reasonable steps following the breach. In *Lazenby Garages* v. *Wright*,[10] for instance, the defendant contracted to buy a second-hand car from the plaintiffs, who were car dealers. Before the car was delivered or the price paid, the defendant refused to go through with the transaction, and the dealers resold the car to another customer at the same price. The Court held that the dealers could not claim damages as they had suffered no 'loss'. It will be seen that a decision of this kind, although it does not in terms deny the 'binding' nature of the contract, or of the defendant's promise, does in effect remove one of the chief legal consequences of holding a contract to be binding, viz. that it is enforceable by an award of damages. It is, therefore, possible that decisions of this character indicate increasing doubts about the desirability of holding such contracts to be binding, while they remain wholly unperformed and unrelied upon; and this in turn may suggest increasing doubts about whether such contracts (or promises) are even morally binding.

Even where contracts are created as a result of a clear agreement, a clear exchange of promises, there is a trend towards treating the consensual aspects of the arrangements as of less importance when once performance has begun, benefits have been rendered to one side, or acts of justifiable and detrimental reliance have begun on the other. To take one simple example, the 'small print', which is so commonly seen in written consumer transactions, is nowadays usually regarded as something which must give way before the consumer's actual expectations which are nearly always in contradiction to the small print.[11] Yet the consumer will, by his signature on the document, have indicated that he assents to the terms contained in it (the document often says this, even though it may well not be read), so that, in one sense at least, the consumer's expectations are allowed to over-

---

[10] [1976] 1 WLR 459.

[11] Judges formerly resorted to a number of technical devices to arrive at this result, but the process will be much simpler since the enactment of the Unfair Contract Terms Act 1977.

ride the terms to which he has given at least a nominal agreement, or even a nominal promise.[12]

These are no doubt controversial suggestions. Not all lawyers would agree that (even in the limited ways I have argued) judges no longer believe in the sanctity of contract, or in upholding the morally binding nature of promises. Certainly it is true that judges do not say these things very loudly, if at all. It is only through their actual decisions and sometimes in their *obiter dicta*, that one can (as I have attempted to do) draw conclusions about the changing values which influence them. I have argued elsewhere that one of the reasons for this divergence between the theory and the practice of the law is to be found in the history of the subject. Modern contract theory is still largely based on the 'classical contract model', a model which was developed between 1770 and 1870, by which time the ideal of freedom of contract had reached its highest point in the Courts, though it was perhaps already in decline elsewhere. The classical model of contract grew up under the shadow of a number of intellectual movements which stressed the importance of free choice and consent as the origin of legal and moral obligation alike. It is unnecessary here to do more than point to the obvious sources of the legal ideal of freedom of contract—the classical economists, the Benthamite utilitiarians, the radical politicians calling for democracy, and, perhaps more generally, liberalism and all that it stood for.

It is, therefore, a matter of no surprise to find that much contemporary philosophical writing concerning promises appears to be closely related to the classical model of contract theory. In both, one finds the same stress on free choice; in both one finds the promise or contract regarded as the paradigm way of creating obligations merely by declaring one's intention to be bound; in both one finds the same disregard for the distinction between paid-for or relied-upon promises or contracts, on the one hand, and wholly executory promises and contracts, on the other hand; in both one finds the same widespread use of the notion of 'implied' or 'tacit' promises and contracts to explain results otherwise difficult to reconcile with the theory; and in both one finds (I will argue) an apparent or overt belief in the sanctity of promises and contracts which is no longer to be found in the value systems of modern England, at least.

---

[12] And it is only now that judges would agree that such promises or agreements are only 'nominal'. Nineteenth-century judges generally found them real enough.

In this book I propose, therefore, to re-examine the nature and extent of promissory and contractual liability. This re-examination is conducted from the standpoint of a modern contracts lawyer who rejects the classical model of contract as not reflecting contemporary law or legal values. My primary objectives are twofold. First, to see what light is thrown on the moral foundations of the law by examination of the principal philosophical theories concerning promises; and secondly, to see how well these theories themselves stand up to examination in the light both of the law itself and of the empirical data thrown up by any study of the law.

PRELIMINARY NOTE ON TERMINOLOGY

It is well to make clear two points at the outset, as they affect the terminology used throughout this book. The first is that I do not believe that all promises are morally binding; accordingly, I use the term 'promise' without prejudging the question whether the promise creates an obligation. The second is that, where a promise does create an obligation, the reason for that may depend upon whether the promise was explicit or implied. There is thus, in my view, a fundamental distinction between explicit and implied promises, and when I use the word 'promise' without qualification, I normally mean an explicit promise.

Chapter 2

Promising and Natural Law

The notion that a bare promise is, prima facie at least, a binding moral commitment, irrespective of the reason for which it is given, was known to the later Roman lawyers. In modern times it can be traced back at least to the Natural Lawyers of the sixteenth and seventeenth centuries. In the works of Grotius and Pufendorf, for example, one can see legal theory struggling to free itself from the view which survived in the English common law, that promises are only binding if made for some good reason, or consideration. Similar notions had, it seems, been advanced by the French jurist François de Connan (1508-51) who had argued that a promise, by itself, created no 'natural' obligation unless it was relied upon, and so would cause loss if broken, or unless some exchange of considerations, or of promises, was undertaken. These views are remarkably close to those of the English common lawyers, and they seem to have stemmed from the idea that a bare unilateral promise which has not yet been relied upon cannot cause any loss to the promisee. If it is not performed, the promisee is no worse off than he was before; he may have suffered (as we would say) a disappointment of expectation, but nothing else.

In saying that these views were close to those of the early common lawyers, I have not overlooked that, in a formal sense, two distinct questions were being addressed. To the Natural Lawyers,[1] the question was when was a promise morally binding; to the common lawyers, the question was when was a promise legally binding. Since nobody would argue that the answers to these two questions should always be the same, it might be urged that they are quite unrelated questions. But it is precisely the fact that the Natural Lawyers, and the early common lawyers, do seem to have been discussing the same issues which is so interesting. For it is these same questions—the binding legal nature of unrelied-upon promises or contracts—which are being

[1] Natural Law has, of course, a long and complex history. My references to 'Natural Law' and 'the Natural Lawyers' in this Chapter should be understood as references to the rational school represented by Grotius and Pufendorf.

re-opened, or at least re-examined, by common lawyers in modern times; and it is this re-examination which suggests that the time may be ripe for a similar re-examination of the moral issues.

The argument advanced by Connan (which leaves out of account the possiblity that the promise has been paid for by some benefit) appears to treat the obligation to keep a promise as derived from the duty not to cause harm or injury, a derivation also to be found in the very early history of the modern English law of contract. But this approach found no favour with Grotius.[2] Grotius had two principal concerns which greatly coloured his whole approach to the source of promissory obligation. The first was that, in common with other social contractarians, he wished to identify the source of positive law in some kind of agreement by which the people surrendered their individual freedom from restriction in return for a like surrender by others. To Grotius such a surrender could only be based on an agreement, but the problem was to see how such an agreement could be valid. The agreement represented, no doubt, the will of those who made it, or must be taken to have made it, but why was their exercise of will binding on them? Anticipating many later philosophical arguments, Grotius raises the question of how an agreement can be binding unless there has been, or is, some prior rule in existence whereby a person is bound to keep his promises or agreements. The answer to his difficulties he found in Natural Law. There must be a rule of Natural Law that promises and agreements are binding obligations, so that from this rule can be derived the validity of the social contract, which creates the State and makes positive law possible.[3]

Grotius' second main concern was, of course, the implications of any theory of promises and agreements for treaties and contracts made between rulers. Since one of Grotius' main aims was to establish that there was a body of law governing the relationships between rulers, and since the role of treaties was necessarily a large one in this body of law, it was obviously necessary to find some source for the binding obligations created by treaties. This too he found in Natural Law. But further, Connan's views would have led to the conclusion that treaties were not

---

[2] *De Jure Belli ac Pacis,* Book II, Chap. XI.
[3] See generally K. Olivecrona, *Law as Fact,* 2nd edn. (London, 1971), Chap. 1, and 31 *Current Legal Problems* 227 (1978).

binding so long as they had not been partly carried out, a conclusion which Grotius obviously found unacceptable.

The subject received somewhat fuller treatment at the hands
of Grotius' successor, Samuel Pufendorf. He too cites, only to
refute the views of Connan. Most writers, asserts Pufendorf,
agree that promises are 'naturally' binding, and this is true even
if they are without 'cause' or consideration. To deny validity to
gratuitous promises destroys all possibility of kindness and liberality, he argues.[4] This, of course, is quite fallacious. To deny
the binding nature of gratuitous promises does nothing to prevent actual acts of kindness and liberality, nor even to prevent
the making and performance of promises of future acts of kindness and liberality. Pufendorf goes on to argue that although
the probable reliance of a promisee is one of the grounds for
regarding promises as binding, it is 'dangerous' to conclude that
the promise is not binding unless and until it is relied upon. Unfortunately, he is not very explicit as to why he thinks this argument dangerous. True it is, he concedes, that if there is no reliance the promisee will not have been made worse off by the
promise; but the promisor's duty is not limited by his duty not
to injure or harm. He also has a general 'duty of humanity', he
must strive always to further the interests of his fellow men. It
seems thus that it is not possible to derive the duty to keep a
promise solely from the duty not to injure, although on Pufendorf's
reasoning it is still a derivative duty rather than an ultimate one.

Much of this reasoning is, of course, extremely flabby by the
standards of modern philosophy,[5] and it would hardly be worth
serious consideration if it was not for the immense influence
which the Natural Lawyers had, both with lawyers and philosophers; there is, too, a remarkable similarity between their whole
approach, and that of many modern philosophers, notably, but
not exclusively, intuitionists like Sir David Ross. The Natural
Lawyers assumed that one could, by internal reflection, and
the use of reason, deduce from the most meagre premises about
man's 'nature', both that promises were morally binding, and
in addition a great many detailed rules about the precise extent
of this principle. For example, problems about the effect of impossibility, mistake, fraud, and coercion were thought to be

---

[4] *De Jure Naturae et Gentium,* Book III, Chap. V, 11.
[5] The recent book by John Finnis (*Natural Law and Natural Rights,* Oxford, 1980) offers a
modern version of Natural Law which, on the subject of promises, has very little in common
with the theories of Grotius or Pufendorf, see id., pp. 298-308.

deducible by pure reasoning from the principles of Natural Law. The fact that some of these cases (such as that of coercion) raised acute differences of opinion does not seem to have shaken their faith in the procedures which they followed.

Among English writers, the nearest in spirit to Grotius and Pufendorf was perhaps Locke; but on the particular subject or promises it was Hobbes who resembled them more, at least in methodology. There is, however, good ground for thinking that Hobbes was in effect maintaining the views rejected by the Natural Lawyers. In the key passage in *The Leviathan* Hobbes distinguishes between contract, covenant, and promise.[6] Contract, he says, involves a mutual transferring of right; or, as we might say, it involves an exchange of benefit for benefit, so long as it is understood that the mere transfer of a right amounts to a benefit. He proceeds then to deal with the case in which one party to a contract has performed his side, leaving the other to perform in the future. The contract on the part of the latter is called a pact or covenant. Although Hobbes is not fully consistent in his use of these terms, it is surely not without significance that in the one place where he actually attempts to define the term covenant, he clearly limits it to the case of a promise for which the promisor has already received value. There seems no foundation for the general belief that Hobbes's third Law of Nature, *That men perform their Covenants made,* is the equivalent of a general moral obligation to perform all promises. Indeed, after he has dealt with pacts or covenants, Hobbes goes on to the case of the plain promise. A bare promise is to be distinguished from a present act of will, he asserts; for a promise to give something in the future cannot be a present act of will. But, he adds, if there are any other signs of the will to transfer a right besides words, then even a promise to make a bare gift may be binding. He then gives the example of a man who promises a prize to the winner of a race, though at this point Hobbes's reasons become somewhat lame. The promise is binding in this case, he asserts, because if the promisor 'would not have his words so be understood, he should not have let them runne'. The explanation will not do, of course, because it would cover all promises which are clear in their terms, even though Hobbes has just told us that bare gift-promises are not binding. A better explanation, and one which seems to be more consistent with Hobbes's over-all

---

[6] Part I, Chap. 14.

position, is that the winner of the race is entitled to the prize because he has acted in reliance on the promise; perhaps it is not stretching things to equate this case with the common lawyer's detrimental reliance case. Taking the passage as a whole, Hobbes thus seems to be saying that an intimation of intention is binding either if it involves a present 'act of the will', or if it invites some act of reliance or if it is part of a mutual contract in which obligations are exchanged, or if it is part of a bargain in which one person has already performed his side. This was roughly the doctrine which the English common law was in process of evolving in Hobbes's day.

The Natural Lawyers seem to have had a more direct influence on Scots lawyers and writers than they did on the English, perhaps owing to the traditional nature of legal education and literature in the two countries. In England there was, until Blackstone's day, no serious university study of English law, and no writings of a general or institutional nature which encouraged any sort of philosophical or speculative jurisprudence. But in Scotland such a tradition did exist, and the influence of the Natural Lawyers is to be found quite plainly in the works, for example, of Lord Stair, Lord Kames, and, to a lesser extent perhaps, Frances Hutcheson. In Stair's *Institutions of the Laws of Scotland* (first published in 1681) we find[7] a full statement of the classic 'will theory' of contractual obligations. Stair distinguishes between 'obediential obligations' which arise from the will of God, and 'conventional obligations' which arise from the will of man in those areas in which he is left free by God. Conventional obligations arise from 'acts of the will'. There are, he asserts, many different kinds of acts of will, not all of which are irrevocable in their consequences. One may state one's own desire or resolution to act in a certain manner, and that is an act of the will, but not a binding one. But an act of the will which 'conferreth or stateth a power of exaction in another, and thereby becomes engaged to that other to perform' creates a binding obligation.

Henry Home, Lord Kames, was, like Stair, a Scots judge. In his *Essays on the Principles of Morality and Natural Religion*[8] he included a lengthy essay on the Law of Nature in which he criticized the views of his fellow countryman, David Hume. Hume, of course, had argued that there was no such thing as Natural Law,

----

[7] In Book 1.X. 1 ff.
[8] Edinburgh, 1751.

or natural rights relating to property and promises, on the ground that these were essentially artificial concepts which arose from human conventions, and could not possibly antedate the establishment of human societies and laws. In reply, Lord Kames objected that human intercourse and co-operation were 'natural' to men. Man is 'framed' for social living, so that mutual trust and confidence are a natural result of man's nature. Hence the principles of veracity and fidelity—the duty to tell the truth and keep promises—arise from this natural trust and confidence. 'Veracity and fidelity would be of no significance were men not disposed to have faith and to rely upon what is said to them, whether in the way of evidence or engagement. Faith and trust, on the other hand, would be very hurtful principles were mankind void of veracity and fidelity: for upon that supposition the world would be overrun with fraud and deceit.'[9]

It is, of course, evident enough that much of this controversy centred on ambiguities in the words 'nature' and 'natural', so it is not very surprising to find that Frances Hutcheson, Professor of Philosophy at Glasgow during the first half of the eighteenth century, was able to combine Hume's utilitarian approach with the natural law arguments of Stair and Kames. In two works on moral philosophy[10] he argued that speech is a means of communicating our sentiments, desires, and purposes to others, and for the right use of this faculty of speech, we have a 'sublime sense implanted, naturally strengthened by our keen desires of knowledge, by which we naturally approve veracity, sincerity and fidelity; and hate falsehood, dissimulation and deceit'.[11] He goes on to marry the natural law with a consequentialist approach to promises, arguing that the 'sacred obligation of faith in contracts appears, not only from our immediate sense of its beauty, and of the deformity of the contrary, but from the mischiefs which must ensue upon violating it'.[12]

Now it is worth pausing to observe that the seventeenth-century Natural Lawyers, and their followers in Scotland, appear to have been the originators of the legal tradition of attributing all the consequences of a contract to the will, or intention, of those who

---

[9] p. 114. It is scarcely necessary to point out that this does not really explain why unrelied-upon promises should be binding.

[10] *A Short Introduction to Moral Philosophy* (Glasgow, 1747) and *A System of Moral Philosophy* (London, 1755).

[11] *A Short Introduction to Moral Philosophy*, p. 177.

[12] Ibid., p. 178.

made it. This general approach did not reach its full fruition in England until the nineteenth century, when other factors probably combined with these traditional theories to produce an extreme version of 'will theory' in the classical model of contract. But although, from today's perspective, the classical model of contract may seem to have greatly exaggerated the role and the importance of the autonomy of contracting parties in the creation of contractual obligations, there were, from the beginning, many limitations on this autonomy. Neither Grotius nor Pufendorf, for example, ever doubted that obligations cannot be created by purely internal 'acts of the will'. An external manifestation of the intention is always needed.[13] Nor is there any hint in Grotius or Pufendorf of the old Canon Law doctrine that the obligation which would otherwise attach to an external manifestation can be avoided by some secret reservation of the speaker. This idea had been rejected in the English common law from a very early date.[14] In the nineteenth century, there were attempts by some judges to introduce a more subjectivist form of contractual obligation in certain types of case, but these attempts were generally scotched.[15]

It is no cause for surprise that practical and pragmatic lawyers should be inclined to dismiss subjectivist theories of liability, and concentrate exclusively on external behaviour and speech as grounds for liability. Nor perhaps is it even a matter for surprise that lawyers do not ever seem to have asked themselves whether the external behaviour and speech upon which they focused in contractual matters was in itself the justification of the obligation, or whether it was merely to be regarded as (conclusive) evidence of the intention of the parties, that intention being, in the last analysis, the real justification of the obligation. But what perhaps is surprising is that English common lawyers, even in the nineteenth century, adopted an extreme form of objectivism in the law, while, at the same time, they were developing the classical model of contract with its emphasis on free choice and consent. Thus the will or intention of the parties was placed in the centre of the law, while the intention was judged or 'ascertained' by the most objective of methods. The result was that (for example)

---

[13] *De Jure Bellum et Pacis* II. XI. IV and II. XI. XI; Pufendorf, *De Jure Naturae et Gentium*, III. VI. 16.

[14] See A. W. B. Simpson, 'Innovation in Nineteenth Century Contract Law', 91 *Law Q. Rev.* 247, 264 (1975).

[15] See my *Freedom of Contract*, pp. 407-8.

even in cases where convincing proof could be adduced of mistake or misunderstanding a contracting party was normally held to be bound; he was, moreover, bound not simply to make good any loss caused by reliance upon his apparent intentions, but bound to perform the contract (or pay damages to the full value of his performance) as reasonably interpreted by the other party, or a judge.

The difference between these two remedies is of great importance, and it is therefore worth adding a word of explanation. Where a person is simply bound to make good an actual loss suffered by the other, the former will only be liable to the extent that the complainant has actually relied upon the promise, or the contract. In legal parlance, the remedy would be an entitlement to 'reliance damages', for example, to money actually expended in reliance on the contract. But to hold the promisor bound to perform the contract, or to pay damages reflecting the full value of his performance, protects the other party to a much greater degree, in legal parlance, to the extent of his 'expectation losses'. In particular, this protects the other party in two respects in which 'reliance damages' do not. First, he is protected even where he has not relied at all, for example, where the mistake, or misunderstanding, is corrected even before the promisee has done anything in reliance. And secondly, the claimant's entitlement is materially greater, for he is now entitled to have his full expectations protected, even where these are much greater than any loss he may have suffered through reliance. Suppose, for instance, that a person enters into a contract to purchase some machinery to be manufactured for him by the seller, as a result of some mistake. If the buyer is wholly 'bound' to the contract, then he will either have to take and pay for the goods, or pay for the manufacturer's anticipated profit on the contract. But if the manufacturer is only entitled to 'reliance damages', he will not have any remedy at all unless he has acted on the contract (e.g. by ordering material, or commencing performance), and even then he will only be entitled to damages representing the money he has thrown away. The difference, of course, may be very substantial indeed.

Now the point being made here is that English classical contract law largely overlooked the possibility—clearly recognized by Grotius—of recognizing a lower form of obligation or liability, which protects one party against actual loss caused by his reliance upon the other. Although Grotius recognized the possibility of a limited liability of this kind, he did, of course, confine it to marginal or special cases such as those involving mistake or impossibility. To go beyond this would have gone close to accepting the theories of Connan[16] which (as we have seen) Grotius begins by rejecting. However, in modern law, particularly in America, thee are signs of a resurgence of the idea that, in some situations, the law should confine its protection to making good any reliance-losses. Indeed, it has been argued that the case for doing this is very strong in almost all contractual situations outside the straightforward commercial contract.[17] This obviously represents a major attack on the very notion that, in the law at least, a contract consisting of mutual promises should prima facie create an obligation to perform in full. I shall return to this fundamental question later.

The ideas of the Natural Lawyers, and the various 'will theorists' who followed them closely, plainly give rise to many difficulties when examined from a modern standpoint. Many of these were pointed out by David Hume in his *Treatise on Human Nature*.[18] For a start, the notion of an act of the will is quite fictitious.[19] We may desire to do something, or resolve to do something, but a desire does not arise from the will (if there is such a thing), and anyhow is not dependent on our choice. And though we may, of course, decide or resolve to do something by an internal mental process which could be called an act of the will, the Natural Lawyers (and, indeed, most other philosophers) are clear that a mere resolution differs in principle from a promise. One may resolve to do something while yet retaining complete moral freedom to change one's mind. If a promise is created by an act of the will, therefore, it must be some act by which we intend to obligate ourselves. The very nature of such an act is, to most people, something of a mystery; and, in any event, all this totally fails to explain *how* the will can obligate itself. For what the will decides upon today, the will may (it seems) decide against tomorrow—which is only to say that human beings are free agents, and that there is no purely internal

---

[16] Though not quite. There is a difference between making good any losses resulting from reliance, and compensating for the full value of the expectations generated once reliance is proved.

[17] Fuller and Perdue, 'The Reliance Interest in Contract Damages', 46 *Yale Law Journal* 52, 373 (1936).

[18] *Treatise*, III. iii. 5.

[19] See also H. L. A. Hart, 'Acts of Will and Responsibility', in *Punishment and Responsibility* (Oxford, 1973).

or subjective way in which they can surrender this freedom. To 'feign' an act of the will—as Hume says we do—and then conclude that we are 'bound' is obviously fallacious—a 'remarkable piece of self deception' it has been said.[20] A man may *think* he ought to fulfil a promise, but his thinking that he has an obligation cannot actually *be* the (sole) source of the obligation; if it was', only honest men would be bound by promises.

Few writers would today be prepared to defend the proposition that only a sincere promise creates a moral obligation,[21] so any theory of promissory liability must explain why a person can bind himself by a promise when he has no intention of carrying it out. Lawyers—from the earliest times—have never had any doubt that, if the other conditions of liability are present, such a promise can create an obligation, but they are not very explicit as to why this should be so. The seventeenth-century Natural Lawyers (as I have remarked) said very little about this problem. It would, no doubt, be possible to argue that the liability of the dishonest promisor is justified in a distinct way from that of the honest promisor. His liability, it may be urged, does not rest upon his intention to perform or to obligate himself (which *ex hypothesi* does not exist) but on the fact that he has deceived the promisee, and thereby caused him loss. But the difficulty with that argument is that the liability might then be less extensive than that of the honest promisor. An obligation to make good a loss caused by the reliance of the promisee upon the promise is (as we have seen) usually lower than the obligation actually to fulfil the promise. Certainly this distinction is well recognized in the law where a party guilty of deceit may indeed be held liable for any loss caused to a party deceived, though this liability is usually thought to arise in the law of tort, or delict, and not in the law of contract. But a person who makes a dishonest promise is not in law subjected only to the liability of a fraudulent person, but also to that of an ordinary promisor. He is—if the other conditions of liability are present—liable to perform his promise or make good any expectations thereby generated, in exactly the same way as the sincere promisor. It is difficult to see why this legal result should not be reflected in morality also.

An alternative argument might be founded on the legal concept of 'estoppel'; it might be argued, that is, that the insincere prom-

---

[20] A. I. Melden, 'On Promising', LXV *Mind* 49 (1956).

[21] Though J. R. Searle allows for the possibility, see 'What is a Speech Act?', in *The Philosophy of Language*, ed. Searle (Oxford, 1971), p. 39, pp. 50-1.

isor should not be permitted to take advantage of his own wrong, and should not therefore be entitled to deny that he intended to obligate himself to perform the promise. He is, therefore, as between himself and the promisee, in the same position as if he *were* under a duty to perform the promise. Nothing that has so far been said would make this an untenable position, and it may be that, at the end of the day, it is purely a verbal point whether an insincere promise is to be called a promise, próvided that it is accepted that it carries precisely the same legal and moral consequences as a sincere promise.

In modern times, a more fundamental critique of the 'will theory' approach to these problems has been made by Professor Hart.[22] Both in law and, no doubt, in morals, it is widely recognized that there are valid defences to a claim based on a contract or a promise; and these defences—such as lack of age, fraud, coercion, and the like—may be grouped together as factors which all involve some degree of impaired assent, or will. As we shall see, this was precisely what the Natural Lawyers tended to do. But, Hart argues, it does not follow from this—unless the most careful qualifications are made—that one can say that, on the positive side, consent must be full and free in order to give validity to a contract or promise. No doubt this sort of generalization can be made 'as a compendious reference to the defences with which claims in contract may be weakened or met'. But it is fallacious to infer from this 'that there are certain psychological elements required by the law as necessary conditions of contract, and that the defences are merely admitted as negative evidence of these'. In fact, as Hart goes on to argue, defences such as fraud, or undue influence, are not normally treated in law as mere evidence of absence of will, or consent; they are treated as *criteria* of non-liability. If the doctrines or rules of law are satisfied, then a defence is made out; if they are not satisfied, the defence fails, and liability ensues—there is no subsequent stage at which other evidence of lack of a full and free consent may be adduced. And as Hart points out, lawyers generally pay little attention to broad generalizations such as those

---

[22] 'The Ascription of Responsibility and Rights', *Proc. Arist. Soc. Suppt.* (1949-50) 171. Hart later admitted the justice of criticisms of this article (see the Preface to his *Punishment and Responsibility*), but these criticisms seem to have been directed to another aspect of the article. For a searching criticism of the notion of defeasibility, see Baker, 'Defeasibility and Meaning', in *Law, Morality, and Society*, ed. Hacker and Raz (Oxford, 1977).

requiring a full and true consent to be given to found contractual liability. It is in the generalizations of jurists that these wide pronouncements are more likely to be found—and it may be added, that even there, they are somewhat less fashionable today than they used to be.

Another difficulty which faces the traditional Natural Law theory of promises concerns the fact that it is widely agreed that some external act is necessary before a promise becomes binding, either in a legal or in a moral context. If the obligation to keep a promise really arises from some act of the will which somehow thereby obligates itself, it would seem to follow that even before this act of will is communicated to another, indeed, even if it is never communicated at all, it is morally binding. Of course, it could be argued that an act of will is a necessary but not a sufficient condition for the creation of a moral obligation; and that something like communication is necessary to consummate the creation of the obligation. Logically speaking, no doubt, this is a possible argument; but the two requirements—an act of will and a communication—seem to go oddly together. The theory that promises arise from acts of the will is based on the idea that a person is bound to do something because he has willed that obligation upon himself by an internal mental act, an act of will. It is not easy to marry this idea with a further need for communication. Presumably if this is an additional requirement, then a communication which goes astray prevents an obligation from coming into existence. It might be argued that in this event there is indeed no promise at all, because a promise requires that it be communicated—the very idea of an uncommunicated promise being perhaps meaningless. But although this may be plausible in the case of oral promises, it is less plausible with written promises; it seems easier to admit that a written promise is indeed a promise, but that it may not become binding if it is not communicated.

At any rate, few would be prepared to defend the position that an uncommunicated act of the will can create an obligation. That seems a very extravagant position to adopt, even as a matter of morality; certainly one would be hard pressed to find many people who would in fact behave as though this were morally the case. So far as the law is concerned, the position is quite clear. Indeed, the law requires more than an external act by the promisor—it generally requires also that the promise be communicated to the promisee, and further, that it be accepted by some open act by the promisee. An uncommunicated promise is something which lawyers would find difficult to regard as a possible source of liability at all. Is the position different in morals?

The legal requirement of acceptance is perhaps more important, though this was a controversial point among the Natural Lawyers. Because most legal contracts are bilateral arrangements, it makes good sense to modern lawyers that a promise should not generally be binding until it has been accepted by the other party. But what amounts to an acceptance? There is certainly no simple way of telling by the light of nature whether (for instance) one can 'accept' an offer without giving a counter-promise in return. Nor indeed is there any simple way of saying whether a purported acceptance of an offer is to be treated as itself amounting to a promise even where it is not on the face of it promissory at all. The legal answers to all these questions are today fairly clear. First, offers are themselves treated as promises, though they are only binding on acceptance; second, an acceptance must take the form of performance of the act requested, or of a counter-promise; thirdly, a purported acceptance will be treated as amounting to a counter-promise.

The most interesting aspect of these legal rules for present purposes is probably that which declares that an offeree cannot accept an offer (whatever the intention of the offeror may have been) except, either by rendering the performance requested by the offeror, or by promising to do so. There seems no doubt that when these rules were first laid down it was because the judges thought they were *just*. Any other rule would have opened the door to the possibility of a contract in which one party was bound, while the other remained free. Even where that was the intention of the promisor, this was perceived by some judges as simply unfair. Thus, in one of the early decisions on this topic, Best CJ said, 'It is not just that one party should be bound when the other is not.'[23] Legal rules and decisions of this kind may be thought to show that, to lawyers at least, the idea of reciprocity is an important element in determining whether a promise is morally binding. But they may also show a great deal more, because it is arguable that it is the law which interprets many acceptances of offers as themselves amounting to promises, when in fact the offeree may have meant to make no promise at all. Thus the law may have decided that, for policy reasons, a 'deal'

[23] *Routledge* v. *Grant* (1828) 3 C & P 269, 172 ER 415.

or an agreement should be treated as involving a commitment, or obligation, as soon as it is agreed; perhaps changing of mind is regarded as something to be discouraged by the law. Once this decision is made, it is easy to interpret acceptances, and even offers, as amounting to promises, even where there was no clear intention that they should be so treated. But, on the other hand, this policy has also been limited by the desire to maintain reciprocity, so that if an offeror does clearly intend to promise (subject only to acceptance) the law demands that the acceptance should itself be promissory.

PROMISES WHICH ARE NOT BINDING

This problem about acceptances can probably be reduced to a much broader problem which obviously was a source of trouble to Natural Law theories. If a promise is in some sense 'naturally' binding just because it has been made, what explanation can be given of the fact that—as everyone accepts—there are some circumstances in which a promise is not binding. Cases of incapacity (as a modern lawyer would call them) involving promises by children, cases of fraud or coercion, of supervening illegality or impossibility, and some cases of mistake, or misunderstanding, all raise circumstances where it would be very generally agreed that the promise is not binding. The Natural Lawyers broadly answered this problem by arguing that if an apparent promise is in truth not binding, it must be because of some deficiency in the 'act of will' which is supposed to have created it, or because the promise was by implication conditional. The cases of persons with undeveloped or 'defective' wills such as children and the mentally deranged were readily disposed of by these means, though it was sometimes necessary (as it became in law) to concede that there might be a liability to pay for necessary benefits actually supplied to persons in these classes. But cases of coercion, fraud, and mistake raised somewhat more difficulty.

Coercion, in particular, raised highly controversial questions. If a person promised something under threat of violence from some robber, was the promise binding? Does the promisor 'really' consent to make such a promise? Aristotle had said that a man on board a vessel who throws his goods overboard in a storm does so perfectly willingly, given the circumstances, and his arguments were reproduced by Hobbes. Grotius felt that a promise extracted by illegal threats was binding but that the promisee was under a duty to release the promisor. This seemed excessively complicated to Pufendorf, who settled for the simpler view that such promises were not binding at all. Locke concurred, and it was this view which ultimately passed into English law. But to this day, English lawyers use the language of will theory in dealing with cases of coercion. A person must show that his will was 'overborne' by overwhelming pressure in order to treat a contract as not binding on these grounds, though there are other legal doctrines which operate in some cases of less overwhelming pressure. Unfortunately the use of will theory in this way raises many obvious difficulties which English lawyers have simply ignored. For it is evident that some forms of pressure are regarded as more legitimate than others; some are, indeed, sanctioned by the State, or the very judicial process itself. It is a common part of the judicial process for persons to give undertakings of various kinds to judges, for example, to be of good behaviour, or to refrain from breaking a contract. Undertakings, or promises, of this kind may well be entered into under threat of imprisonment or other severe sanction, yet they are oviously not thereby invalidated. Indeed, it is not irrelevant that such undertakings are often given in the form of 'bonds' or that a person may be required to agree to a 'binding-over order', forms of words which all indicate that 'binding' commitments are the result of such undertakings. Clearly, if promises of this nature are to be treated as creating binding obligations, the conventional will-theory explanation of the effect of unlawful coercion or duress will not do.

Another similar case, which worried Grotius a good deal, was that of a peace treaty entered into to end a war between two States. If the vanquished State can plead that the treaty was made under duress and that its promises do not bind for that reason, this would evidently make a large hole in the law of treaties which Grotius was concerned to create.

Similar problems arose with cases of fraud, mistake, and the like. The Natural Lawyers explained these as cases in which the promise is not binding on the ground that the promise is in truth conditional. A promise given in response to an untrue story, for instance, is made conditionally on the truth of the story. If the story is untrue, the promise is not binding, not because the promisor is in any sense released from his 'natural' obligation, but because the promise does not apply in the circumstances. This argument (which surfaced again in the works of Ross in the twentieth century) is very familiar to English lawyers. The notion of 'implying' conditions in a contract which operate in the event of mistake, or supervening events of certain kinds, has been extensively used, particularly since the early nineteenth century. By the twentieth century, doubts began increasingly to be voiced as to the nature of these implications, though in the inter-war period (at the same time that Ross was using the argument in philosophical works) the traditional arguments continued to be vigorously reasserted. Judges, it was said, had no absolving power.[24] Promises and contracts were binding unless, on their 'true construction' they were not intended to operate in the circumstances which had occurred. However, it is now a familiar story among academic lawyers (at least) that the technique of 'implying' conditions of this nature in contracts is often a fictitious device for giving effect to the judicial sense of justice. No doubt, some of these implications are genuine enough; but many others are not, simply because what has occurred is something which the parties have never contemplated. It seems very probable that the traditional legal argument (which is still often adhered to) was influenced both by the Natural Lawyers and also by the intellectual theories of the early nineteenth century which stressed the importance of freedom of contract, and the minimal role of the Judge and the State.

Cases of fraud have, however, not generally been treated by English lawyers in the same way. The fact that a promise obtained by fraud is not binding on the promisor—or at least that he is entitled to repudiate it—has never been justified on the ground that it is an implied condition of the promise that the prior statements made to the promisor are true. Although English lawyers have not clearly enunciated any particular theory on this question, it is possible that they would justify the law by arguing that the fraudulent party has no 'right' to enforce the other's promise; that, in other words, he is undeserving of the fruits of the promise. In effect, the avoidance of liability on a fraudulently induced contract is a penal process.

It is worth concluding this chapter by stressing two points. The first is that there is one profound difference between the views of the Natural Lawyers on these issues and those of the modern English Lawyer. To the Natural Lawyer, the fact that a promise was 'naturally' binding was a matter of fundamental principle. His whole approach led him to see things in black-

---

[24] Lord Loreburn in *F. A. Tamplin SS Co. Ltd.* v. *Anglo-Mexican Petroleum Co.* [1916] 2 AC 397, 404.

and-white terms, and to attempt to draw clear lines between closely related phenomena. The modern common lawyer is a pragmatist who cares little for rigid principles:[25] all principles are subject to exceptions, and whether a case falls within a principle or an exception is often conceded to be a matter of degree and judgment. For example, a promise is binding despite many types of supervening events which may make its performance more onerous; but, on the other hand, some supervening events would render it so different from what was contemplated that the lawyer simply feels it would be unjust to compel performance, and he places the case on the other side of the line. He has the greatest difficulty in saying where the line is to be found, and generally avoids trying to draw it if he can. He prefers to judge each case on its own merits, placing some on one side of the line, and others, on the other side, as they arise. The result is that the line ceases to be sharp, and becomes a blurred grey area between different types of case. To the Natural Lawyer there is an absolutely crucial distinction between a promise and a mere statement of intention. Only if the promisor intends to be bound, intends to commit himself, does the necessary act of will take place. To the modern common lawyer, however, the distinction between a promise and a statement of intention is likely to be a much more blurred line. The lawyer is likely to say that the distinction does not rest upon what the promisor intends, but upon what reasonable persons would understand him to intend. That is, evidently, a matter on which differences of opinion are likely, so that this vital distinction becomes blurred into a grey area on a continuous spectrum. I will return later to the particular question of promises and statements of intention, but it is necessary to say here that if the common lawyer is right in regarding many of these distinctions as ones of degree, then it becomes impossible (as Sidgwick recognized[26]) to settle such questions by an appeal to intuition.

The second concluding point to be made about the Natural Lawyers is that they seem to have originated, or anyhow propagated a mode of thought which is still widely influential among philosophers (to judge from much modern literature) and which has had an equally wide influence among lawyers, though that is now declining. This mode of thought centres on the belief

---

[25] Atiyah, *From Principles to Pragmatism* (Oxford, 1978).
[26] *Methods*, pp. 304-11.

that it is possible to deduce the nature of some abstract concept like a 'promise' merely by internal reflection and use of reason, and then to draw practical conclusions from this reflection. Thus, to take a simple illustration, the question whether it is 'possible' for a person to promise the impossible, is often treated in this fashion. No doubt, in some cases, there are hidden premisses which, if they were spelt out, might make the reasoning more deductive, and less intuitive. Thus, it is probable that the Natural Lawyers accepted as a premiss the moral idea that 'ought' implies 'can', so that it is easy to deduce that an apparent promise which promises the impossible is not a binding promise and hence not 'really' a promise at all.

In much modern philosophical literature, a very similar approach seems to be adopted in attempting to answer many fringe or marginal questions about the concept of promising, such as whether a statement of fact 'can be' a promise, or whether a person 'can' promise that someone else will do something. It is not at all obvious what sort of exercise philosophers think they are engaged upon when they ask questions of this character. Most of them would (presumably) deny that they are engaged solely upon an enquiry into the 'correct' meaning of the term 'promise' as evidenced by contemporary usage. And it is plain enough that these questions do not profess to be concerned with empirical issues as to the actual behaviour of people in the matter of making or keeping promises. It must, therefore, be presumed that questions of this nature are intended to be analytic and to derive, in some sense, from the 'inherent nature' of the very concept of promising. But, if neither linguistic nor empirical inquiry is the object of the exercise, the 'inherent nature' of the concept of promising would appear to be discoverable only by the sort of intuitive reflection used by the Natural Lawyers.

Now this kind of reasoning used to be very common among lawyers, and it is by no means dead even today. An example well known to academic lawyers relates to the treatment of the possibility of a contract to do the impossible in a leading textbook on the law of contract.[27] For several editions this book continued to proclaim that such a contract must be void because the 'parties have merely beaten the air. They have attempted the impossible ... The agreement can be nothing but a phantom since there is nothing upon which it can fasten ... The most

---

[27] Cheshire and Fifoot, *Law of Contract*.

dazzling display of virtuosity will not avail to pour wine [out of] an empty bottle.'[28] The problem with this approach was that it seemed increasingly out of touch with the law. People do sometimes make at least ostensible contracts to do things which are impossible, usually as a result of fraud or mistake; but it does not in the least follow that the law *must* recognize such contracts and promises to be devoid of legal effect, and, indeed, there are many signs that the law does not do so.[29]

Reasoning of this kind among lawyers is not now regarded as intellectually respectable. Although it may be perfectly respectable for philosophers to deny that one can refer to the non-existent, there is no need for lawyers to conclude that the law must therefore deny all legal efficacy to a contract which purports to refer to the non-existent. American Legal Realism is generally credited with having demonstrated that concepts used by lawyers have no 'natural' meaning or delimitation. If the law uses the concept of 'promise' then what is a promise is a matter for legal definition, and lawyers are not bound to follow any non-legal definition, still less are they bound to draw legal conclusions from doubtful and fringe cases to which non-legal usage of the concept may give no clear answer. Now this, in turn, should not be pressed too far. If the law in practice uses concepts which also have a popular usage (like promise), then it is likely that lawyers will feel drawn to maintain some links with the popular usage.[30] Moreover, if they fail to do so, and choose to give their concept some wholly original definition and usage of their own, then what they do is unlikely to have any further interest for moral philosophers. It is precisely because the law does not usually cut itself off wholly from popular usage, and popular ideas of morality, that the lawyer's conception of what is just ought to be of some interest to the philosopher. But, this being admitted, it remains true that one cannot draw from a concept, even though it is in current use, necessary legal conclusions unless one has first put the premisses into the concept. Nor can one draw any conclusions from the concept itself without regard to the way in which people in fact use the concept, both linguistically and

---

[28] See e.g. 6th edn., p.192 (London, 1964). These remarks were finally deleted in the 9th edn. (London, 1976) when responsibility for the book passed to a new editor.

[29] Some examples are given, *post*, p.155.

[30] See A. W. B. Simpson, 'The Analysis of Legal Concepts', 80 *Law Q. Rev.* 535 (1964).

behaviourally. And since the Law Reports contain an unrivalled collection of evidence about how people do use the concept of promising both linguistically and behaviourally, the lawyer's experience ought to be of interest to the philosopher.

Chapter 3

Promising and Utilitarianism

The arrival on the scene of modern utilitarian theories in the eighteenth century enabled a new and much more prosaic explanation to be given of the nature of promissory and contractual obligation. The leading utilitarian accounts of this subject are to be found in the works of Hume, Adam Smith, Paley, John Austin, John Stuart Mill, and, rather later, Henry Sidgwick. Of these, Hume's account remains in many respects the fullest and the most convincing, though he has little to say about the law, or the relationship between morality and the law in this particular area. Adam Smith (as we now know from the recent publication of his lectures on jurisprudence) and Paley were both particularly interested in the relationship between promises and the law of contract.

There are, of course, many varieties of utilitarianism. Apart from the distinction between 'rule utilitarianism' and 'act utilitarianism', to which reference is made later, the precise nature of the utility which is to be maximized is, to some degree, a matter of taste. Bentham himself, of course, wrote as though utility was a form of pleasure; later philosophers have recoiled somewhat from the idea that an optimal world is one which maximizes pleasures, but some of them have been willing to replace pleasures with human well-being, or simply 'good', whatever that may stand for. It is not necessary for me to get involved in these subtleties, and I propose to discuss the utilitarian approach to promising without reference to the precise nature of the utility which it is supposed to maximize.

Utilitarianism had, and retains, many features which made it, and to some, still make it, a fundamentally attractive philosophy. It enables an account to be given of moral questions entirely in terms of social and human needs, desires, and satisfactions. It eliminates the need for a religious basis to ethics. It tends to make moral questions resolvable, at least in principle, by empirical methods. It introduces 'a common currency of moral thought' which enables the utility of individuals to be compared by the moral philosopher, and so to sweep aside the problems in making 'interpersonal comparisons of utility' which have bedevilled much modern economic theory.[1] Moreoever, utilitarianism has been one of the most practically successful philosophies in human history. Since the early nineteenth century, utilitarianism—in a broad sense—has gradually supplanted religion in the minds of a great number of people in Western societies as the source of all moral ideals. The good of human beings has, in a broad and general sense, become the touchstone by which moral issues are decided. Nevertheless, among philosophers themselves, utilitarianism has lost many of its attractions in the twentieth century. This is not the place for any extensive inquiry into the reasons for this, but it is relevant to note that one of the strongest arguments generally adduced against utilitarianism in almost any form, is that there are certain values which override even the desirability of increasing human well-being—in particular the demands of justice. And one of the most frequently adduced examples of these demands which is widely thought to be incompatible with utilitarian theory, is the case of promising. To many philosophers, it is manifest that justice requires promises to be kept even where the result is, on balance, to do less good than could be done by breaking the promise. Any contribution which can be made to reconciling the utilitarian position with the problems raised by promises may, therefore, be of some general interest.

A Utilitarian Account of Promising

A utilitarian account of promising might start (as Hume's did) with the fact that a human being has only a very limited capacity to improve his lot in the world when he acts entirely on his own. It is only by exchanging his surplus goods, and the products of his labour, with others, and by thus joining with them in co-operative activities that man has been able to create the wealth which satisfies the wants of the human race. No single person acting on his own could begin to make one-thousandth of the goods which he uses in his daily life—the food he eats, the house he lives in, the car or train in which he travels to work, are all the result of co-operation by an unimaginable number of people. So it is easy to agree that anything which encourages or facilitates

---

[1] B. Williams, *Morality* (Harmondsworth, 1973), p. 99. But not everyone would agree that these problems can be so easily disposed of. For an alternative method of doing so, see *post*, p.132.

human co-operation is, other things being equal, of great utility. Unfortunately the possibilities of human co-operation are hindered by lack of trust. Co-operation frequently involves that one person renders some assistance to another, in anticipation of some future service being rendered to him. But if the first does not trust the other to reciprocate when the time comes, the manifestly desirable result may not ensue. Promising is one way of helping to overcome this lack of trust. By making a promise, the promisor is able to persuade the promisee that he is to be trusted; the possibility of both moral and, if needed, legal sanctions behind the promise, gives the promisee the assurance that he needs. He can now render his own service in the first instance, in return for the other's promise. The promise stands as a sort of pledge that he in his turn will receive the other's performance.

Utilitarianism has always been concerned with the general social good, rather than with that of individuals; but it is important to appreciate—as Hume stressed—that in most cases self-interest renders it desirable that one should be able to bind oneself by giving a promise, and even that one should be threatened with sanctions to compel compliance. In the modern credit economy it should be evident enough how true this is. A person who could not bind himself with a promise could not obtain credit except from one who is willing to trust him without the protection of a promise. It is, of course, enlightened, or long-term self-interest, and not short-term self-interest, that renders it desirable for a person to be able to bind himself by promising; and, still more obviously, it is enlightened self-interest which generally dictates that he should perform his promise in due course. For the temptation of immediate short-term gratification may incline a person to neglect performance of his promises, but he does this at peril of losing his reputation for trustworthiness and hence of being unable to obtain credit in the future. Again, the reality of all this is easily enough observed in the modern world with its system of credit references and 'blacklists' of bad credit risks. Unfortunately, not everyone is strong-minded enough, or perhaps intelligent enough, to act in accordance with the precepts of enlightened self-interest; accordingly, it is necessary to have some system of sanctions to encourage due observance of promises. These sanctions are provided by the moral and legal system. The notion that promises are 'binding' is an artificial contrivance created and kept alive by those who mould society's moral system. It is inculcated and propagated by education and example, and, to some degree, by the legal sanctions which themselves lie behind the moral ones.

Of course self-interest does not explain all cases. It does not, for instance, explain why wholly benevolent or gratuitous promises should be binding (if they are) except in the trivial sense that the promisor must be assumed to get sufficient satisfaction out of making such promises; nor does self-interest cover the case of the person who finds that performance of a promise may on some particular occasion cost him more than the value of any benefits he is likely to obtain in the future from maintaining his credit. The classical utilitarians said little about these possibilities, but it is fairly evident that they would have regarded these cases as falling within the general principle that promises should be binding, on the ground that even here there would be an over-all gain to social utility. This is probably clear enough in the second of these cases, but it is a good deal more doubtful in the first.

When we attempt to explain more precisely how it is that promises assist in human co-operation, the utilitarian broadly offers two answers. First, it is said, promises generate reliance, confidence, trust; and secondly, they give rise to expectations. These two are rarely disentangled in the literature, and in the writings of some of the classical utilitarians they are often run together as though there were no difference between them.[2] Sidgwick alone points out that there is a difference between the protection of expectations and the protection of actual conduct proceeding in reliance on a promise.[3] The disappointment of any expectations is, he says, *pro tanto* an evil, and the duty to keep a promise is 'commonly conceived as independent of any injury that might be done to the promisee by breaking it'; but he goes on to say that if the promisee has acted in reliance upon the promise, any breach of it would be a much more serious affair. Surprisingly, very little is said by the classical utilitarians about the possibility of a promisor having received value for his promise; it is, after all, one of the commonest occurrences for a promise to be given in order to obtain something, and once the promisor has obtained the thing sought, the case in justice for compelling him to keep his promise would seem a great deal stronger than

[2] For example, Mill, *Utilitarianism,* Chap. 5; Paley, *Principles,* Book III, Part I, Chap. V.

[3] *Methods,* p. 443.

if the promisee's claim is based on a pure expectation. The case is briefly discussed by Mill who, in effect, argues that a person who fails to return good for good— benefit for benefit, as a lawyer might say—disappoints the expectations of the other party. Thus Mill subsumes the benefit justification under the expectation justification, on the face of it a rather curious procedure. It is, however, interesting to note that a similar subsumption was at work in the law in and around the very time when Mill was writing. I have argued elsewhere[4] that, during the course of the first sixty or seventy years of the nineteenth century, promissory liability came to be seen by lawyers as having a coherent over-all justification arising out of the expectations generated; and that one consequence of this shift in legal thinking was that, even where benefits were secured as a result of a promise, the legal liability consequent thereon came to be seen as promise-based. The distinction between a claim based on an exchange of unperformed promises and a claim based on a promise for which value had already been given became of less importance during this period. I have argued that this change in the law was largely due to ideological changes—growing acceptance of the ideology that legal liabilities should be based only on voluntary acts of free choice. The fact that a person had made a promise was a good ground for imposing legal liabilities on him; the fact that he had received a benefit from someone else, was not.

Now, as we have seen in Chapter 1, the three grounds upon which a promise may be held binding in law (that is, cases in which there is a 'consideration' for the promise) are first, where the promisor has received some benefit for his promise; secondly, where the promisee has acted to his detriment on the promise; and thirdly, where the promisee has given his own promise in exchange for the promisor's promise—where, that is, there are mutual promises. In this third case, the promises are binding even prior to any act of performance, any rendering of benefits, any detrimental reliance. It seems clear that these legal grounds for the enforcement of contracts are closely related to the utilitarian grounds for holding promises to be morally obligatory. This is not, of course, to suggest that these legal principles can be derived from utilitarian theory, because (as mentioned in Chapter 1) they long antedate modern utilitarian philosophies, going back at least to the sixteenth century. But it is of course

---

[4] *Freedom of Contract*, pp. 479-80.

possible to argue that both the legal doctrine of consideration and the grounds upon which utilitarians have traditionally regarded promises as morally binding, derive from a common source—that source being, in effect, the sense of justice created by a property-owning society in which a high value was placed on co-operative activity.

BENEFITS

I propose then to look rather more closely at the utilitarian arguments about expectations and reliance as grounds for the rule that promises should be kept. But a few words first need to be said about promises for which some benefit has already been paid. As I have said, this figures very little in the literature, despite its great practical importance. X, let us say, borrows £100 from Y, promising to repay it next month. What is the moral basis for saying that X ought to keep his promise? It seems amazing that anybody could doubt that the actual receipt of the money by X is the most important ground on which he ought to keep his promise. Yet this fact is, both in philosophical and in legal literature, regarded as of little moment.[5] In both cases, the basis of the liability is generally said to be the promise. In law, the receipt of the money is a 'consideration' which makes the promise legally binding, but, as I have said, the doctrine of consideration is now widely thought by lawyers to be a historical anachronism, a mere technicality with no moral basis. And even the utilitarian philosophers would (it seems) have said that X is bound to repay the money because of the expectation he has given to Y. That argument would, of course, apply with the same force, no more and no less, where X promises to give Y a present of £100; yet it is hard to believe that the moral obligation has the same weight in the two cases. Sidgwick would have said that indeed it does not, because the promise has been acted upon in the former case, in that the loan has actually been advanced by Y in reliance on the promise to repay.

This last point may well explain why so little is heard of the benefit argument, either in moral discourse, or in the doctrine of consideration in the law. In the great majority of cases in which some benefit has been rendered, this has been done in reliance

---

[5] The same is generally true of economists, who almost invariably assume that it is desirable to enforce all exchange contracts, but for a radical libertarian view that contracts should only be enforced when already paid for, see Murray N. Rothbard, *Man, Economy and State* (Los Angeles, 1962, 1970), vol. I, pp. 152-4.

on the promise; thus the element of reliance is usually present wherever the element of benefit is present. But the converse is not true. There are many cases in which a person acts to his detriment in reliance on a promise in such a way that no benefit is rendered to the other party. Hence it seems that the idea that detrimental reliance is a more important factor has grown up in the law; indeed, for many years now it has been customary to regard the benefit element of the doctrine of consideration as of little practical importance. Here too, then, we see a close parallel between the thinking of moralists and the thinking of lawyers.

However, the law also shows us that cases do occasionally occur in which a promisor receives some benefit, but the promisee has not rendered the benefit in reliance on the promise. At least three such cases can be identified. First, the promise may be given in gratitude for previously rendered benefits; secondly, the promise may be given in return for a service which is rendered by the promisee in ignorance of the promise; and thirdly, the promisee may render a benefit sought by the promise, but it may be difficult to show that the promisee acted in reliance on the promise because he may have intended to (or been otherwise bound to) render the benefit even absent the promise. It is interesting to note that in every one of these cases legal difficulties have arisen with the doctrine of consideration. This may well reflect some unease at the idea that the elements of benefit and promise together—without the element of detrimental reliance— should suffice to create a legal obligation. On the other hand, the trend in modern law is undoubtedly towards recognizing that a liability does arise in these cases. That trend may indicate that a greater importance is being attached to the element of benefit today than was the case a hundred years ago.

It is right to add also that benefits can be rendered even without any element of promise at all, and yet may still create some legal obligation on the recipient to restore or make good the value of the benefit—a legal liability by way of restitution, as modern lawyers would call it. For benefits can be rendered by mistake, or even by accident; and they can also be rendered in pursuance of arrangements which resemble ordinary contracts, but which fail to qualify as such because of the absence of a valid promise or consent—for example, where there is coercion, or lack of contractual capacity, such as may arise with lunatics, etc. So if the rendering of benefits in cases of this nature gives rise to some obligation on the part of the recipient, it would seem odd if—were a promise subjoined to the circumstances—the nature of the liability should change.

RELIANCE

The second factor, which is much more heavily stressed by utilitarians, and also by lawyers, is the element of reliance. Few would today deny that, in a broad and general sort of way, the fact that promises tend to be relied upon, that they positively invite reliance, is one of the chief grounds for the rule that promises should be kept, and that contracts should be legally enforceable. Action in reliance on a promise can, if the promise is not fulfilled, cause significant trouble, and often serious pecuniary loss, to the promisee. Indeed reliance upon another—even without any explicit promise—is an everyday occurrence of our society, and to let down a person who has relied may be productive of great inconvenience or even worse. A person who, while driving a motor vehicle, signals that he is going to turn right and then in fact turns left may cause serious bodily injury or even death to a following driver who has relied upon the signal. A traffic signal is not normally thought of as a promise, but the point does at least illustrate the obvious importance of reliance as a source of rights.

Now there is a still broader sense in which acts of reliance may lead to inconvenience or loss, for reliance does not have to be invited by a promise or in any other way to produce this result. One man may rely upon another to behave in accustomed ways, all unknown to the second. I may set my watch by the time of my neighbour's departure for work every morning because he is so punctual. If he knows nothing of this practice of mine, he obviously comes under no duty as a result of it. But suppose he does know, though he has not invited me to act in reliance on him, may he not come under some obligation? If, for example, he is sick one day, and intends not to go to work, but knows that I will adjust my own conduct expecting him to leave for work at the accustomed hour, is he not under a duty to warn me of his change of plans? Now whether it is felt that the neighbour ought to be under some obligation in such a case depends largely on one's ideological starting-point. On the one hand, it may be argued that I ought to be encouraged to rely upon myself, and not upon my neighbour; I ought to get a more accurate clock myself; or find other ways of keeping time. What right have I to impose obligations on my neighbour which he has neither invited, nor been paid for?[6] On the other hand, it may be said that human co-operation ought to be encouraged, and that a man is not sole judge of what duties he owes to his fellow men. If others come to rely upon him, whether or not he has sought that reliance, or been paid for it, he must accept some responsibility for the consequences; just as, when he relies in his turn upon others, he is entitled to some protection.

Thus, just as in the case of benefits, promises are not always conjoined to cases of reliance-based liability. And also, as in the case of benefits, the trend over the past hundred years has been away from the ideology of self-reliance, and towards a greater recognition that reliance *per se* may be a source of obligations, even without a promise.

The main problem which has been encountered in treating reliance as a justification for promissory liability might seem less serious if it were borne in mind that reliance even without a promise can create obligations. This problem concerns the difficulty of explaining why a person is entitled to rely upon a promise until it is first established that the promise is binding. To some there has seemed a logical impasse here.[7] A promise is only binding if it is relied upon, but until the promisee is assured that it is binding, he may be unwilling to rely upon it. If it is the binding nature of a promise which induces a promisee to rely upon it, how is it possible to *derive* the binding quality of a promise from the fact that it is relied upon? A very similar conundrum has long been a source of puzzlement to common lawyers. I have previously explained that in the law a promise is generally only legally binding if there is some consideration for it, and a consideration is normally defined as consisting of some benefit to the promisor or some detrimental reliance by the promisee. But it is also axiomatic among lawyers that a contract may be validly made by an exchange of promises, even prior to the passing of any benefit or the performance of any act of reliance. The promises are themselves regarded as consideration for each other. The question then arises, how is it possible for a promise to be regarded as an act of detrimental reliance (or a benefit) until it is first decided whether it is binding or not? To treat mutual promises as consideration for each other appears to

---

[6] It is not surprising to find this view espoused by F. A. Hayek; see his *Law, Liberty and Legislation* (London, 1976), Vol. II, pp. 94-6, 120 ff.

[7] For example, G. J. Warnock, *The Object of Morality* (London, 1971), pp. 99-100.

assume the validity of the promises, which is of course the very question at issue when it is asked whether executory promises can constitute good consideration. The puzzle has been of no practical importance to lawyers, but it has been a source of discussion among academics for many years. It was once referred to as a 'secret paradox of the common law', but I have myself argued that the explanation is largely historical, viz. that mutual executory promises were not originally regarded as creating obligations in the same way that they are in modern law. Only where actual benefits, or actual reliance, occurred, were obligations originally created: the recognition that bare mutual promises could create obligations prior to acts of reliance or the rendering of benefits was a much later development, which only reached its culmination in the nineteenth century.[8]

So far as the philosophical difficulty is concerned, an answer to it has been offered by Professor MacCormick.[9] A promisee does not rely on the fact that a promise creates a binding obligation; he relies on the speaker's intention to do what he has promised to do. If a promisor intends, or thinks it probable that the promisee will so rely, and if he in fact does so, he will suffer harm unless the promise is performed. The promisor will thus have caused harm to the promisee, will have made his position worse, as a result of, first making, and then breaking, the promise. Even if the promise was not known to be binding, for example, in a society which does not recognize binding promises, people will sometimes rely upon statements of intention (or various other kinds of statements), and through such reliance, they will suffer loss. Therefore, MacCormick argues, there is no logical impasse. Of course, once a society exists in which promises are normally conceived of as binding, then this will strengthen the tendency for people to rely upon them, and, at the same time, the greater degree of reliance will strengthen the moral principle that promises should be kept. We thus get a virtuous circle in which promises and actual reliance reinforce each other.

This is, perhaps, one of the strongest statements of the case for regarding reliance as (at least) one basis of promissory obligation, but it is none the less open to objections. MacCormick's case rests in the end upon the argument that the promisor is guilty of causing harm to another who relies upon his promise, and that

---

[8] *Freedom of Contract,* pp. 194-205, 208-12, 687-8.

[9] 'Voluntary Obligations and Normative Powers', *Proc. Arist. Soc. Suppt.* (1972) 59.

it is this which makes the promise binding. Now MacCormick, as himself a lawyer, is quick to appreciate that if his argument stopped there, a promise would not bind unless and until it was actually relied upon. There would then be an awkward hiatus between the making of the promise and the time when the promisee relies upon it, during which the status of the promise would presumably be in some doubt. MacCormick rejects this possibility. Actual reliance is not necessary to make the promise binding; it is the probability of reliance which does that. The fact of actual reliance only goes to the seriousness of the breach; a lawyer would say that that was a matter which went to the damages, but not the existence of the obligation. Now it does not seem to me that the probability of reliance can so easily be equated with the fact of reliance. Suppose that, shortly after making the promise, and prior to any act of reliance, the promisor changes his mind, and informs the promisee that he withdraws his promise. It is clear that if there has in fact been no reliance, there is no actual loss; the promisee suffers a disappointment of his expectations but no more. If such a promise is to be held binding it must surely be on the ground that the disappointment of his expectations is itself sufficient to give the promisee some right to complain.

The distinction between the probability of reliance and the fact of reliance is somewhat blurred by the possibility of a sort of negative reliance, what an economist would call an opportunity cost. *B* promises to dig *A*'s vegetable patch before 1 April, and in consequence, *A* makes no other arrangements to have the patch dug, or to dig it himself. *B* breaks his promise, and come 1 April, *A* has an undug patch. It is too late for him to have it dug now. *A* has relied upon *B* by *doing nothing*. In this sort of case, strictly speaking, we need to know whether, had it not been for *B*'s promise, *A* would in fact have been able to have the patch dug by another, or would have been able to do it himself. Unless we know this, we do not know whether his reliance has made things any worse. Indeed, it is difficult to know whether one can properly say that *A* has actually *relied* on the promise, unless we know these additional facts. Now proof of these facts may be a matter of great difficulty. For a start, we can only arrive at probabilities, not certainties. Since *A* has not in fact tried to find someone else to do the work, we cannot be certain that if he had tried, he would have succeeded. We can only decide this question according to the probabilities. For another thing, it is often hard to say when reliance of this sort begins and ends.

The difficulties of attempting to prove whether this sort of reliance has occurred and, if so, whether it has made the promisee's position worse, are thus great. And even where reliance can be more easily proved after the event before a Court, the promisor will frequently not know, at the time when performance is due, whether the promisee has relied upon his promise. A utilitarian may therefore argue that it is desirable to encourage the performance of promises on the ground that they *might* have been relied upon, and not to insist upon proof of actual reliance, still less, actual detrimental reliance. But it is not at all obvious why this should remain the case if it is actually shown by positive proof (or admission) that there has been no reliance, or no detrimental reliance. Suppose in the above example, *A* admits that even if *B* had made no promise, he would not have done anything about his vegetable patch, is it evident that he has a grievance should *B* fail to perform?

MacCormick himself suggests that reliance must be induced by the speaker either intentionally, or at least with the knowledge of its probability, if the speaker is to be treated as having made a promise. It is, however, not clear that these limitations are always defensible. As we have already noticed, the mere knowledge that one person is relying on another may sometimes suffice, if one adopts a paternalist ideology, to justify imposing obligations on the party relied upon. That is not likely always to be the case, by any means. In the law, sometimes it is necessary to prove that reliance has been knowingly induced; sometimes it suffices that it has been carelessly induced; sometimes it is sufficient to show that it could have been foreseen that reliance was probable; and so on. If reliance is treated as the basis of the obligation, it is not easy to defend the argument that the reliance must always be knowingly induced.

These arguments parallel much that is going on in the law. Especially where promises are implied rather than explicit, and where there is no element of bargain or mutual exchange involved, there is a tendency through legal doctrines like 'estoppel' to protect those who have relied upon others, but only after actual reliance is proved. Doctrines like estoppel do not protect a promisee prior to any action in reliance, merely because a promise was given. They do not thus protect bare expectations as is done by wholly executory contracts. Of course, it might seem, as these relatively new developments take place in the law, that they all represent an increase in legal protection, rather than a decline; but this is not necessarily true. There probably are some estoppel cases in which—fifty or a hundred years ago—the Courts might have 'implied' mutual promises, and found some full contract to exist; in that case they would have protected the bare expectations of the innocent party should the other have defaulted prior to any reliance. In cases like this, it may be that there has actually been a decline in the protection accorded by the law to a promisee. This has certainly happened in America, although in England the question is probably more controversial. If the law is reflecting changes in moral values, these developments may cause one to ask whether, and why, promises should indeed be binding prior to any reliance.

Before leaving the reliance case, one further excursus into the law needs to be made. One of the most puzzling features of the law of contract is that—even in cases where the ground of the obligation seems to be reliance—once the liability is established, the law often provides for compensation to be measured by the full extent of the promisee's expectations. If the promise is not performed, the promisor will have to pay the full monetary value of the promise even though the promisee may only have incurred expenses well below that value in reliance on the promise. This may well suggest that, to the lawyer at least, the ultimate justification for regarding promises as binding is the expectations they create, and not the fact that they may cause harm through reliance. But this view has been controverted in a celebrated article by Fuller and Perdue in 1936.[10] It is here argued that this conclusion is not justified for two reasons. First, that if we attend to actual legal results (and are not mesmerized by the reasoning displayed therein) we shall find many cases in which, in practice, Courts refuse expectation damages, i.e. refuse to protect the expectations of the promisee by giving him as compensation the full monetary equivalent of the promise. Instead, they award 'reliance' damages, i.e. damages representing the harm actually caused by the breach of the promise. It is found that Courts tend, in particular, to adopt this approach where the contract departs for one reason or another from the standard commercial bilateral exchange agreement. An example of this sort of decision is *Lazenby Garages* v. *Wright*, which was discussed on p. 6. And secondly,

---

[10] 'The Reliance Interest in Contract Damages', 46 *Yale Law J.* 52, 373.

Fuller and Perdue argue that even where the full value of the promisee's expectation is protected this does not itself demonstrate that the promise is regarded as binding *because* of the expectations thereby generated, rather than because acts of reliance have taken place. An alternative explanation is that the harm caused by actions of reliance operates as a sort of trigger, which brings into play the full panoply of contractual remedies. And these remedies may have penal, as well as compensatory, purposes. The award of expectation rather than reliance damages may thus be justified, not so much because the promisee's expectations are felt deserving of protection in full, but because it is desired to punish the promisor for breaking his promise. This in turn may have the (wholly utilitarian) purpose of discouraging breach of promise by other promisors. At this point, however, the argument runs into some difficulty, because it is necessary to explain *why* it should be desired to discourage breach of a promise which is still wholly executory, and unrelied upon, if the one thing that the law is really concerned to do is to prevent harm caused by reliance on promises which are then broken. Why is it not sufficient for the law to discourage breach of relied-upon promises? This difficulty will have a familiar appearance for the philosopher, because it is the same objection which is urged against the rule utilitarian in a variety of contexts. As far as I am aware, it has not been answered in this context, though that does not mean that there may not be an answer to it. I will return to this again later. At this stage I only wish to make the point that although the law in theory tends to regard contract damages as being the full monetary value of the promise, it does not necessarily follow that the underlying rationale of the law is that the promisee's expectations deserve protection. The law may still be primarily concerned with the protection of the person who has relied upon a promise.

EXPECTATIONS

As I have said, many utilitarians have tended to muddle the expectation and the reliance justification for the rule that promises must be kept. Reliance may be the stronger justification where there has in fact been reliance. Yet, as I have also said, reliance cannot always be proven, and indeed can in some cases be disproved. Moreover, it is generally assumed that there is no hiatus between the communication (or anyhow the acceptance) of the promise and the moment at which the promisee relies upon it.

It is assumed to become binding forthwith, so that (for instance) the promisor can no longer resile. And, indeed, in law (provided that there is a return promise) this is so. Even where it is quite evident that there has been no reliance, and nothing in the way of a benefit rendered to the promisor, mutually exchanged promises are binding as soon as there has been acceptance: no withdrawal is thereafter permitted.

In cases of this kind the utilitarian must be prepared to argue that it is the expectation alone which deserves protection and which justifies us in regarding the promise as morally and legally binding. Many of the classical utilitarians, including Bentham and Adam Smith, as well as Mill and Sidgwick, say this in terms. What is the case for it? One starts, perhaps, with the fact that an expectation is similar to, and in some sense perhaps even a species of reliance. It is, in effect, a form of psychological reliance. To disappoint expectations is to 'let the promisee down', to dash his hopes, and many people would say that it actually makes the promisee worse off than he would have been if no promise had been given. I do not think this is self-evidently true; it is an emprical question whether a disappointed promisee feels worse off than he would have felt if there had never been a promise. And a utilitarian would be entitled to argue that the pleasurable anticipation of the promise being performed must itself be brought into the scales against this subsequent disappointment. I do not know of any means of discovering whether most disappointed promisees feel worse off than they would have been if there had never been a promise, and if so, whether that is in a sufficient degree offset by the pleasures of anticipation while they lasted.

If the utilitarian case rested upon demonstration of these facts it would seem that the case is, and must remain, not proven. But the utilitarian may argue that this does not matter. He may say that what concerns him is the position once the promise has been given and the expectations aroused. From that moment on, he may say, there will be an undoubted evil if the expectation is disappointed. It is the fact that people do derive expectations from promises, and the fact that they will be disappointed if promises are not kept, that justifies the creation of the obligation. Thus expectations, like actions in reliance, deserve protection merely because they are in fact intentionally created by promises.

Now it can hardly be denied that this is not a very weighty ground for treating promises as binding. If no benefit has been rendered to the promisor and the promisee has not relied on the promise, it would seem that the utilitarian would have to treat the duty to keep a promise as of relatively little significance, and a duty that could easily be outweighed by countervailing considerations. Some modern utilitarians have indeed taken this view, arguing that the duty to keep promises has too often been invested with a sanctity or even sanctimoniousness not justified by the desirability of protecting expectations.[11] It may be that, historically, the great weight attached to the importance of protecting expectations by early utilitarians (for example Hume and Bentham) was due to their tendency to treat rights of property as essentially based on expectations. But the expectations of a promisee when unsupported by other elements are not in themselves either as important or as powerful as property-right expectations. In very many situations, the practical implications of protecting promissory expectations pure and simple are extremely limited. It is only in the relatively unusual case where the promisor expresses his desire to resile prior to any acts of reliance by the promisee, and prior to his receipt of any benefit, that it is necessary to fall back on the case for protecting expectations.[12] And in such cases, the expectations will not usually have been entertained for any great length of time, and *ex hypothesi* will not have been acted upon. There is, therefore, no need to be alarmed at the utilitarian's emphasis on the need to prevent the disappointment of expectations as the basis of promissory obligations. As we shall see later, in law the protection of pure expectations is, indeed, circumscribed in all manner of ways. In particular, the law draws an important line between gratuitous and unrelied-upon promises on the one hand, and an exchange of promises on the other. The former are not generally protected at all. Most lawyers see this as a conflict with moral principles; and the utilitarian justification for promising, insofar as it rests upon expectations, must support this criticism of the law. I shall, however, suggest that this is an over-simplification, and that there are significant distinctions between the mutual exchange of promises and the single unrelied-upon promise.

---

[11] For example, Pall Ardal, 'And That's a Promise', 18 *Phil. Q.* 225, 234-5 (1968). See further on this, *post*, p.139.

[12] That is not to say that once reliance occurs, expectations cease to matter. They may remain important, both legally and morally.

The Strength of the Utilitarian Case

The utilitarian approach to promising has many attractive features, and much of it is supported by the law. It starts from the supposition that moral principles are designed to improve human well-being in some way; the utilitarian never has to defend himself against the charge which may be levelled against adherents of other philosophical schools, that they advocate conformity to an abstract principle even though it may lead to avoidable human suffering.[13] The utilitarian approach also helps to explain many of the limits which are generally agreed to exist (and which the law often recognizes) on the principle that promises must be kept.

For example, we may start with the need for communication and acceptance of promises. Plainly, an uncommunicated promise will not be acted upon, nor will it lead to any expectations, so there is no utilitarian justification for holding such a promise to be binding at all. Acceptance is not a logical prerequisite to reliance or the creation of expectations, but, as John Austin pointed out, it performs the useful function of informing the promisor that the promisee does indeed have an expectation and that he may thereafter be expected to act upon it.[14]

Next, the utilitarian case is important in that it enables us to recognize promises of differing weights for the simple reason that the consequences of promises are likely to differ. Less consequentialist theories of promising are perhaps less easily reconcilable with the idea that promissory obligations can vary in weight. If you ought to perform a promise simply because of its nature (for example) as an obligation-creating act, then you ought to do it; but it is not easy to see how there can be degrees of 'oughtness', as it were.[15]

But the utilitarian case justifies us quite generally in distinguishing between more and less serious promises according to the extent of the expectations and reliance that they generate. This is particularly important in that it enables the utilitarian

---

[13] J. J. C. Smart, *Utilitarianism, For and Against* (Cambridge, 1973), p. 6.
[14] *Province of Jurisprudence Determined,* 2nd edn. (London, 1861), pp. 298-300. Cf. the account given by R. Samek, 'Performative Utterances and the Concept of Contract', 43 *Aust. J. of Phil.* 196 (1965).
[15] Thus J. Finnis, *Natural Law and Natural Rights,* pp. 309-10, argues that even in law, there are no degrees of legal obligation: this is quite unacceptable to a legal realist for it overlooks the fact that obligations carry different penalties of varying weights, see further, *post,* p. 141.

to give some rational explanation of the fact that—as everyone agrees—the duty to keep a promise may be negatived by certain types of supervening event. For the utilitarian, the question always is, what is likely to do the most good, or lead to the greatest happiness, or pleasure, etc. (depending upon the particular brand of utilitarianism selected)? In many cases the question may be answered by a straightforward attempt to balance the utilities of keeping and breaking the promise. Moralists tend to think in simple terms of a person who (for instance) having given an engagement to act for a friend in some capacity then finds that his son has fallen dangerously ill. In legal cases, which are usually a good deal more complex than this, lawyers have a doctrine of 'frustration' which enables them to declare a contract discharged where it is rendered totally impossible, or where it is overwhelmed by supervening events. This doctrine may not, at first sight, appear to have much in common with utilitarian methods, because the doctrine rarely involves a simple balancing of utilities. On the other hand, the doctrine does have a great deal to do with risk allocation, and some of the grounds on which risks are allocated are highly utilitarian in character. For example, contracting parties are normally saddled with risks which they could have foreseen and guarded against. So the refusal to allow a contract to be frustrated because of the occurrence of risks of this character can be said to be based on utilitarian-type considerations—parties should be encouraged to anticipate and guard against risks.

Then again, utilitarianism offers what is, at least in principle, a relatively straightforward way of dealing with many of the problems arising from defences such as mistake, misunderstanding, fraud, and coercion. Once the notion that a promise is somehow created by an act of the will is eliminated, it becomes apparent that utility is likely to be maximized by permitting people to rely upon external manifestations of assent rather than expecting them to discover what someone actually intended by his words or conduct. Human co-operation, which (as we saw earlier) it is one of the main functions of promising to further, is likely, according to utilitarian theory, to be advanced by encouraging people to avoid misleading others by careless speech or conduct; and it is also likely to be furthered by permitting people to enter into transactions on the basis that others will be held bound by a reasonable interpretation of their conduct. No doubt this does not solve all problems: for example, it leaves open the question whether a promise is to be interpreted in the sense reasonably understood by the promisee, or reasonably interpreted by an independent judge.[16] But some attempt could be made to solve even this problem along utilitarian lines.

Similarly, the problem of coercion, which has (as we saw earlier) long been a controversial question, could be dealt with along utilitarian lines. For example, Paley, showing a greater sophistication than he is generally credited with, discusses the case of the promise to a highwayman to leave a purse for him at an appointed place.[17] This, he says, may have good immediate consequences, for the highwayman may be induced thereby to spare the victim's life; but it has long-term evil consequences, since it does nothing to deter highwaymen. The difficulty, says Paley, is to balance one against the other and discover which preponderates. The problem still exists. If a modern Government promises safe conduct to a party of hijackers in return for freeing a plane-load of passengers, is this promise 'binding' on the Government? The legal answer to this is emphatic and unambiguous. Lawyers seem to have answered Paley's question by assuming that the long-term evil consequences of enforcing such promises will always outweigh the short-term good. But it is possible that another consideration has entered into the legal dimension which does not trouble the utilitarian philosopher. Courts of Justice need to be above suspicion. For them to be seen to be giving hijackers a legal right to sue for their booty may shake confidence in the justice of the whole legal system. Still, it does seem odd if a moral code is to be somehow less sensitive or scrupulous about sullying its hands by condoning deals with hijackers, blackmailers, and the like. No doubt the utilitarian must accept that, in the end, he will be willing to regard promises to hijackers etc. as binding if he thinks more good will come of them. But he could, of course, invoke the sort of arguments which the Courts seem to have adopted here, if *sub silentio*. He could, that is, take account of the general belief that it is undesirable for Governments to do deals with violent criminals as a fact which must enter into his calculations.

Another relatively straightforward result of adopting the utilitarian case is that it becomes easy to decide what, in principle, actually amounts to a promise. Nobody would today deny that

[16] This was for long a controversial issue. See Paley, *Principles*, Book III, Part I, Chap. V; *Smith* v. *Hughes* (1867) LR 6 QB 597; *Rose* v. *Pim* [1953] 2 QB 450.

[17] *Principles*, Book III, Part I, Chap. V.

a person can make a promise without using the words, 'I promise'; yet, it is very widely denied that a mere declaration of
one's intention to behave in a certain way amounts to a promise.
Such a declaration, it is usually argued, reserves to the declarer
full freedom of action. But in practice it is often difficult to draw
any very clear line. To the utilitarian, the answer, at least in
principle, is simple. Everything depends upon whether the
speaker, or writer (or even actor, for words are not needed),
has excited expectations in another.[18] But the lawyer would
want to make certain reservations to this, because in practice
one often has to act at one's peril, even where one does, in fact,
rely upon expectations generated by others. A man goes to the
railway station to catch the advertised 9.22. When he gets there
he finds it has been cancelled. Is the railway guilty of a breach
of promise? A mid-nineteenth-century Court said Yes,[19] but a
lawyer would be very surprised if any modern Court answered the
question in the same way. I propose to postpone any further
discussion of this point because any study of the law shows that
the whole question of what *is* a promise anyhow (and especially
what is an implied promise) is a much more complex question
than has hitherto been generally supposed.

The Case against the Utilitarian Account of Promising

Since the beginning of the twentieth century a considerable case
has been built up by anti-utilitarian writers, and much of their
ammunition has been directed quite specifically at the utilitarian
account of promising. I propose in this section to examine the
main points which have been made in this debate.

(1) Could Promising Exist in a Wholly Utilitarian World?

The argument has been advanced by D. H. Hodgson[20] that it
would be impossible to conceive of anybody making a binding
promise in a wholly utilitarian world, in a world, that is, in
which everybody always acted in such a way as to produce the
maximum possible good (or happiness, or whatever). This is,
indeed, part of a general case against utilitarianism, but I am only
concerned with the implications of the argument for promising.

---

[18] See, e.g., Paley, *Principles,* Book III, Part I, Chap. V, and Adam Smith, *Lectures
on Jurisprudence,* p. 87.

[19] *Denton* v. *Great Northern Rly.* (1856) 5 E & B 860.

[20] *Consequences of Utilitarianism* (Oxford, 1967).

The argument basically is a variant of the general argument, previously discussed, that to base the binding force of promises on the likelihood of reliance, leads to a logical impasse. If, argues Hodgson, the promisee knows that the promisor is a utilitarian who always acts in accordance with his principles, then the promisee will not rely on the promise being performed. For he will know that, where it would be best to break the promise, the promisor will indeed break it. Further, the promisor will know that the promisee will not rely on the promise, which will also eliminate the need for him to keep the promise. Then again, the promisee will, in turn, know that the promisor will know that the promisee will not rely on the promise. Thus we get an infinite regress; promises are not even made, and trust itself becomes impossible. Perhaps, indeed, all communication among humans would cease.

There are many answers to this improbable picture. In the first place, even if the argument were valid, it would not necessarily weaken the case for utilitarianism. In our actual world, promises are a useful device for reconciling conflicts of interest and enabling much co-operative activity to take place. It is immaterial that in a different world peopled by different people— unselfish people, always motivated to act in the social interest rather than their own—promises would not work.

But, in the second place, it may well be argued that, if people were in fact all utilitarians who always acted for the common good, promises would not work only to the extent that they would not be necessary. It would be unnecessary for a person to bind himself in advance to co-operate with others, because he would do this even in the absence of his promise. As the utopian Godwin wrote many years ago, in anticipation of this same kind of objection, 'it will be a sufficient answer in the majority of instances to say that [the affairs of the world] will be carried on by rational and intelligent beings acting as if they were rational and intelligent.'[21] And in modern times the same point has been made by (among others) Mackie and Singer, both of whom point out that if everybody always acted for the common good, there would be no motive for fraud or deceit, and statements of intention would, therefore, be reliable, and in fact relied upon much as

---

[21] *Enquiry Concerning Political Justice* (first published, 1793; Pelican edn., Harmondsworth, 1977), p. 222.

promises are today.[22] If it is argued that this only demonstrates that declarations of intention would survive in the wholly utilitarian world, and that these are not promises, two replies can be given. First, in this unreal utilitarian world, declarations of intention (coupled with a recommendation to the hearer to count upon the declaration) would operate just as promises do now; and secondly, this (even today) may, in fact, be precisely what a promise really is. I discuss the relationship between declarations of intent and promises at a later point.[23]

It is, perhaps, worth noticing that in small communities where the members do largely act for the common good, rather than in their own interests (most strikingly in a united and affectionate family), promises do tend to be superseded. In such a community, members rarely find any need to bind themselves to each other by promises; but this does not preclude co-operation. Similarly, in commercial and other institutions, co-operation on common aims may be secured without promises or contracts, by administrative and other hierarchical procedures.

(2) Promises and Declarations of Intention

As I have said, I wish to discuss this controversial question at a later point. But it needs to be said here that one of the standard criticisms of the utilitarian account of promising is that it blurs the distinction between a promise and a mere statement of intent. If promises are binding—as the utilitarian would have it—because of the expectations they generate, and the acts of reliance to which they lead, then how is one to distinguish between a promise and (say) a firm resolve, or declaration that one intends to act in a certain way? Yet, it may be urged that it is evident that these two are not the same. A person who states that he intends to act in a particular manner may, quite rationally, provoke the response, 'But do you promise?', and that question would be meaningless if the statement of intent could itself amount to a promise.[24]

Again, if it is reliance and expectations which make promises binding, it would have to be admitted that the question whether

---

[22] J. L. Mackie, 'The Disutility of Act-Utilitarianism', 23 *Phil. Q.* 289 (1973); J. L. Mackie, *Ethics: Inventing Right and Wrong* (Harmondsworth, 1977), p. 114; P. Singer, 'Is Act-Utilitarianism Self-Defeating?', 81 *Phil. Rev.* 94 (1972).

[23] See *post*, p. 165 ff.

[24] For example, H. A. Prichard, 'The Obligation to Keep a Promise', in his *Moral Obligation* (Oxford, 1949), pp. 168, 169-70; G. R. Grice, *The Grounds of Moral Judgment* (Cambridge, 1967), pp. 48-51. Many other writers have taken this point.

a particular utterance was a binding promise would often be incapable of a precise answer. As a lawyer would say, it would become a question of degree. Promises and statements of intent would both be on the same spectrum, and if there is any line to be drawn between them it can only be done in rather an arbitrary fashion.[25] But to many philosophers this is unacceptable. There is, on this view, something unique about promises. They are not on the same spectrum as statements of intent. They actually create obligations in a way in which statements of intent do not.

I do not think it can be doubted that these views are irreconcilable with the utilitarian account of promising. But, for my part, I cannot see that there is much substance in the anti-utilitarian case on this point. In practice it is true that statements of intent and promises are frequently difficult to distinguish from one another. As every lawyer knows, the line between them does tend to merge into a grey area. Nor is it absurd or meaningless to ask a person whether he is making a promise when he has stated his intention even in some positive fashion. Whether a person whose utterances lead another to have expectations, or to act on them, is under a moral obligation as a result, is often a complex and difficult question. Nobody is likely to dispute that in most circumstances, at least, it will be relevant to this inquiry to know whether the expectations or reliance were reasonable, or justified. And any attempt to answer that question must surely pay some regard to the terms of an explicit promise. Thus when a person makes an utterance which another thinks may justify him in entertaining expectations, or taking certain action, a request for an explicit promise is an attempt to minimize the area of doubt and potential controversy. I shall argue later that this is, indeed, one of the principal functions of a promise, and that it is a mistake to think of the main function of a promise as that of creating a liability.

[25] It may be argued that this is itself contrary to principles of utility, since it makes it difficult to determine whether an utterance creates an obligation or not. The answer to that is that the difficulty arises out of circumstances, and not from the analysis. No matter how clear a conceptual distinction is recognized between promises and statements of intent, the practical difficulties involved in distinguishing between them in a particular case would remain.

(3) People do not Feel Obliged to Keep Promises for Utilitarian Reasons

The argument has occasionally been put (for example, by Sir David Ross[26]) that a person does not keep a promise for utilitarian reasons, for example, because he thinks that this is the best way to maximize the common good, or the happiness of the human race. Indeed, perhaps most people keep promises without thinking about the consequences at all. Certainly it is true that a person who keeps a promise without even thinking about the consequences, merely because of a sense of duty, because he feels bound to keep it, is likely to be regarded as a more 'moral' man than one who keeps it after due calculation of the consequences in promoting human welfare. I do not think that many philosophers would take this objection very seriously today. Motives for action raise psychological rather than philosophical issues. A person may feel bound to act in certain ways because of his moral training; and moral training is often designed to inculcate habits of behaviour which are unquestioning. Indeed, moral training is often so powerful that it overshoots the mark. Many people, for example, find great difficulty in telling 'white lies' even where there is every social justification for them. This does not prove that it is wrong to tell such a lie; it may merely demonstrate how hard it is to act in unaccustomed ways. In the same way it may sometimes be the case that the moral feelings which people have about the duty to keep a promise are stronger than the utilitarian case for promise-keeping would justify. Indeed, one may still *feel* one should keep a promise even where there is no real utilitarian case for it at all, as where, for instance, much more good could be done by breaking it than by keeping it. But feelings of this kind may be no more than residual nagging doubts arising from irrational sentimentalism or a confused intellect.[27] They do not seem to raise any serious objection to the utilitarian case.

(4) Are Expectations a Necessary Condition of there Being a Promise?

As we have seen, the utilitarian account of promising rests ultimately on the expectations which promises generate. I have also stressed the possibilities of payment and of action in reliance

---

[26] *The Right and the Good* (Oxford, 1930), p. 9.
[27] See e.g. Pickard-Cambridge, 'Two Problems about Duty', LXI *Mind* 145, 171 (1932).

as factors which add greatly to the weight of a promise. But it is clear that, to the utilitarian, reliance and payment must be secondary factors, and are certainly not necessary conditions of the existence of a binding promise. On the other hand, for the utilitarian, it does seem at first sight a necessary condition of the existence of a binding promise that it generates some expectations.

A requirement that a promise should create expectations helps to explain why a promise in which the promisee has no legitimate interest would not normally be regarded as creating an obligation, indeed, might not be regarded as a genuine promise at all. For instance, if a rejected suitor were to promise that he would never marry anyone else, a utilitarian would readily argue that no legitimate, or perhaps any, expectation is created by this promise, and that it therefore creates no obligation at all. (Such promises were not legally binding even in the days when promises to marry did prima facie constitute a binding contract.) An anti-utilitarian would either have to regard such a promise as binding, or offer some other explanation of why it should not be binding.[28]

But the argument that expectations are a necessary condition for the creation of a binding promise has caused a good deal of difficulty. One common anti-utilitarian argument is to adduce counter-examples where the existence of a promise seems undeniable and yet where no expectations are generated. Now it should first be made clear that the utilitarian case does not treat the voluntary excitement of expectations in another as a sufficient condition for the existence of a promise. No doubt, intentionally to create such expectations, and *a fortiori,* to recommend expressly that the hearer should rely on the expectations, is a common enough way of making a promise. But if the words of the speaker clearly negative his promissory intention, then there is no reason why the utilitarian should not be perfectly free to deny the existence of a promise.[29] I have already given the example of the railway timetable which raises expectations, and is likely to be relied upon by would-be travellers. Yet the railway authorities always guard themselves against the supposition that they are guaranteeing that the trains will run according to timetable; and even in the absence of such a caveat, few people today would think

---

[28] See, e.g. J. R. Searle, 'What is a Speech Act?', in *The Philosophy of Language,* at pp. 48-9.

[29] Subject, however, to the possibility that the speaker is unreasonably trying to have things both ways, see below, p. 168.

that they were making any promises. Counter-examples, which are designed to show that a person can raise expectations and even invite the hearer to rely upon him without making a promise, appear to me, therefore, to be misconceived,[30] and certainly no rebuttal of the utilitarian case.

However, counter-examples have also been adduced of what are alleged to be promises even though no expectations exist, and these remain to be considered. The first such example is that of the vow. A person who makes a vow to himself, or (perhaps) to his God, is said to have made a promise which binds him, even in the absence of a promisee and hence of any expectations or reliance on the part of a promisee.[31] The case of the religious vow must be put on one side. Obviously the introduction of a God changes the rules of all moral debate; the present discussion is a secular one, and does not profess to examine the nature of promissory obligations on the supposition of the existence of a God. There remains the case of the vow to oneself. Does this create any obligation? No doubt a person may feel a sense of obligation when he makes a vow, and if it is publicized in some way, it may serve a useful purpose. But if it is publicized, it may be acceptable to a utilitarian as a species of promise which does create some expectations even though no individual person can claim that the vow was made to him. A secret vow, unknown to anybody except the party himself, however, cannot be treated as creating any obligation, consistently with the utilitarian account of promising; at any rate, it cannot rank as a promise. It is surely very odd to regard a secret vow to oneself as creating an obligation of any kind. If it does, the obligation is one without a corresponding right, and it is, furthermore, an obligation which can be violated without risk of legal, moral, or social censure. Again, if a vow is regarded as creating a moral obligation, it would seem that promises which are intended for another should then become morally binding without the need for communication or acceptance; but we have seen that in law, and, in the view of most philosophers, in morality also, this is not acceptable. It is unnecessary to labour the point. Vows are a very special case, and if any obligation does attach to them, it is for different reasons. I do not think this counter-example seriously dents the utilitarian explanation of promising.

---

[30] See, e.g., J. Raz, 'Voluntary Obligations and Normative Powers—II', *Proc. Arist. Soc. Suppt.* 59, 99 (1972).
[31] Ibid., p. 97.

A second counter-example that has sometimes been put, is the case of the promise which is simply not believed in by the promisee. Several types of case deserve discussion here. One case that has been put is that of the alcoholic who has promised to stop drinking so often that nobody believes his promises any more. Yet (it is argued),[32] if he renews his words, he must still be taken to be promising. Indeed, he may not even expect to be believed, for he might say, 'I know you won't believe me, but I promise etc.' Several possible answers might be made to this counter-example. First, it presupposes perhaps too readily that the promisee has absolutely no expectations from what has been said. Can one be sure that there is absolutely no glimmer of hope in the mind of the promisee that perhaps this time, just possibly, things might be different? Can the promisor himself be sure of this? And if so, what is the point of his remarks? But perhaps the counter-example requires us to take this as the hypothesis. Very well then. So be it. If the promisee has absolutely *no* expectation that the promise will be performed, the promisee will suffer no disappointment of expectations from its breach, and will have no ground to feel aggrieved; no ground, that is, from the mere fact of the 'promise'. But alcoholism is generally regarded as socially undesirable anyhow. A person who is an alcoholic, it would readily be said by a utilitarian, has anyhow a duty to stop or try to control his alcoholism. The 'promise' adds nothing to this duty, except perhaps to identify one particular person as having the right to feel aggrieved—and we have seen that this particular 'promise' does not justify the 'promisee' in feeling aggrieved.

However, it may be conceded that it is possible that on these or similar facts the promisor *may* find that he is slightly addition- ally motivated by the promise to do something which he ought to do anyhow, but which he may be too weak to do without the benefit of this additional factor. Anyone who believed this would have a utilitarian reason for wishing to persuade the promisor that his promise does create some sort of obligation. To that extent it may be recognized that there may, in rare cases of this nature, be a utilitarian ground for maintaining that promises are binding even though nobody expects them to be performed. It must of course be said that the combination of suppositions is in the highest degree implausible; for we are invited to imagine

---

[32] See, e.g. David H. Jones, 'Making and Keeping Promises', 76 *Ethics* 287 (1965-6); M. H. Robins, 'The Primacy of Promising', LXXXV *Mind,* 321, 328 (1976).

a person who has broken his promise so often in the past that nobody else retains even a glimmer of hope that he may perform on the umpteenth occasion, and yet the promisor himself is supposed to feel a sufficient sense of obligation to influence his own conduct.

Surprisingly, the law on this point of unbelieved promises is somewhat obscure. It is, I think, clear enough that the law would reject any 'action in reliance' as relevant if the promisee did not believe that the promise would be performed. For it would be said that one cannot truly act in reliance upon a promise if one does not believe it will be performed; the promisee will be held to have acted at his own risk, on his judgment. Any consequent loss will have been *caused* by his own actions. There is no doubt that this is the law where false statements are made, as opposed to promises respecting the future. But in the case of promises respecting the future the difficulty is that the promisee may well be relying upon his legal remedies (and have expectations therefrom) even if he does not believe the promise will be performed without the aid of legal sanctions. The point is illustrated by two old and not unamusing cases from the English law reports. In *James* v. *Morgan*[33] in 1665, the plaintiff sold a horse to the defendant, the price to be fixed as follows: the defendant was to pay a barley-corn for the first nail in the horse's shoes, doubling that for the second, and so on for every further nail. There being 32 nails in the horse's shoes, the defendant eventually discovered what he had promised, and defaulted; when sued he claimed that the total quantity of barley required would have been some 500 quarters. It seems pretty clear that the plaintiff did not really expect the defendant to perform his promise, and that he had tricked him into the contract; but at the same time, the plaintiff may well have expected the law to uphold his right to the monetary equivalent of 500 quarters of barley. In fact the judge took a fairly robust view of the law, directing the jury to award the plaintiff the value of the horse as damages (some £8), which they did. The second case was very similar. In *Thornborrow* v. *Whitacre*[34] in 1705 the plaintiff gave the defendant 2*s*.6*d*. and promised an additional £4.17*s*.6*d*. on performance by the defendant of the following obligation, viz. to deliver 2 grains of rye the next Monday, doubling this amount the follow-

---

[33] 1 Lev. 111, 83 ER 323.
[34] Lord. Ray. 1164, 92 ER 270.

ing Monday, and so on for 'every other Monday' for a year.[35] The defendant pleaded that there was not sufficient rye in the whole world to perform this obligation, but the Court seemed against him at first, perhaps because the defendant had actually received some value—if only 2s. 6d.—from the plaintiff already. Eventually the defendant offered to repay the 2s. 6d., and costs, and the plaintiff accepted this offer, so the case did not go to judgment.

In both these cases, it seems clear enough that the promisee did not expect performance of the promise, except with the aid of the law. In effect (unless, which is just possible, they were bets), these were cases of substantially impossible promises, extracted by trickery, in order that some profitable claim for damages could later be made. Given the element of trickery in these cases, it does not seem to me probable that a modern Court would uphold promises of this kind as valid contracts. It is true that there is no overt recognition in the legal books that a promise, which the promisee does not believe is going to be performed, is for that reason not binding. In practice, it would be rare (in the absence of trickery or fraud) for a promisee to have absolutely *no* belief that the promise will be performed. If a promisee was really in that state of mind, it is obviously unlikely that he would be willing to make any sort of a contract, and, if he did, it would presumably be because he was relying on his legal right to damages, not to the performance of the contract.[36] But there are cases where one or more clauses in the contract may raise this issue, while other clauses are perfectly normal.

In particular, the question is raised by 'penalty' clauses. It not infrequently happens that contracts provide for what is to happen in the event of a breach by the parties, or by one of them. Such provisions may be perfectly simple attempts to avoid future disputes, and to quantify the probable amount of any loss. That is unobjectionable. But sometimes clauses of this kind are not designed to quantify the amount of the probable loss, but are designed to terrorize, or frighten, the party into performance. For example, a contract may provide that the promisor is to

---

[35] There was some controversy as to the meaning of the expression 'every other Monday'. The Court wanted to interpret this to mean 'every alternate Monday', which would have made performance more possible.

[36] Thus it has been suggested that a man can validly contract that it shall rain tomorrow: clearly the promisee here would be relying on his legal rights alone (in the present state of technology).

pay £5 on a certain event, but if he fails to do so, he must then pay £500. Now a clause of that kind is called a penalty clause by lawyers, and for several hundred years it has been the law that such promises cannot be enforced. The standard justification for the law here is that it is unfair and unconscionable to enforce clauses which are designed to act *in terrorem*. It could be argued that this is simply a way of saying that these penalty clauses do not really give rise to expectations, and that there is therefore no reason why they should be treated as binding.[37] No doubt the lawyer, like the philosopher, has difficulty with cases of this nature. Even if the general utilitarian case for maintaining the sanctity of promises is accepted, doubts and difficulties are going to arise in marginal cases of this nature. As I have said, the moral feelings resulting from moral training may overshoot the mark and persuade us that certain utterances are promises because they look like promises, even though their utilitarian justification is absent; similarly, the lawyer may feel he is somehow making a concession to sentiment in refusing to enforce penalty clauses, that he is permitting a binding promise to be broken, rather than denying that the clause really has the characteristics of a proper promise. Moral feelings of this kind, and the parallel phenomenon of legal reasoning based on such feelings, may tell us more about the psychology of the mind than about the nature of promises.

Still, the utilitarian may have difficulty in holding to the extreme position that the creation of expectations is a necessary condition for the existence of a binding promise. For a start, a promisee may well have doubts about the promisor's capacity or willingness to perform the promise; and these doubts may, on balance, amount to a belief that the promise is not likely to be performed. If the plumber promises to call in order to repair a broken pipe, it would be odd to say that this is not a binding promise because one's experience of plumbers' promises leads one to believe that, on balance, he probably will not come when he promised. At most the utilitarian could perhaps insist that a state of active disbelief, as opposed to a state of doubt, is incompatible with the expectations needed to have a promise.

But this last example is in truth an illustration of a wider problem. Once the institution of promising does exist, so that promises do actually come to be treated as creating moral obli-

---

[37] In effect this is argued by Professor Macneil, 'Power of Contract and Agreed Damages', 47 *Cornell L. Q.* 495 (1962).

gations, it may sometimes happen that the institution is used for the deliberate purpose of creating (or trying to create) obligations even where expectations are absent. And where this happens the promisee may accept the promise in reliance on his belief that he has the right to have the promise performed even where he believes that it will not be performed. Similarly, as the cases cited above illustrate, it may happen that a person enters into a legal contract relying on his (supposed) right to have the contract enforced, even though he believes that the promise will not be performed—until the law's sanctions are applied. These cases may all, in a sense, be thought to result from the fact that moral and legal rules may (as previously suggested) overshoot the mark. Moreoever, there may be a utilitarian case for permitting them to do so. Once the utilitarian has accepted this position it would seem that he must abandon the view that the creation of expectations is a necessary condition for the existence of a promise. But he need only abandon it to a very limited extent. Promises of this character are parasitic on the general institution of promising; and the utilitarian may insist that the general institution rests on the desirability of protecting expectations. It would be possible to have an institution of promising which did insist that expectations exist before a promise is recognized, though such an institution would not be optimal, given the above arguments. But it would certainly not be possible to have an institution of promising which only recognized these parasitic promises.

A third type of counter-example which has been much discussed in the literature is illustrated by the so-called 'desert-island promises', or 'deathbed promises'. We are invited to believe that two persons are alone on a desert island, and that one of them, who is dying, extracts a promise from the other that, on his safe return to civilization, he will dispose of some valuables then and there handed over to the promisor. Or the scene may simply be placed at the promisee's deathbed where a similar promise is made, but is not heard or recorded by anyone other than the promisee. In effect we have a perfectly ordinary promise except that the promisee dies shortly after it is made, and that nobody knows anything about it except the promisor himself. We are then asked to assume that the promisor could do far more good by using the money in some other way than by giving effect to the promisee's wishes. The promisee, in one extreme version of the case, is an eccentric who has asked that the money be donated to the Society for the Propagation of Cacti and Other Succulents. The anti-utilitarian regards the promise in such circumstances as plainly binding, despite the fact that nobody's expectations will be disappointed if the promise is broken.

Before attempting to meet this counter-example, it is necessary to disentangle two distinct elements involved in it. The first concerns the possibility of the promisee's death; and the second concerns the element of secrecy. If the promisee dies before the promise is performed, then nobody will suffer a disappointment of expectations if the promise is not performed. Up to a point this may be true; and the rights of the promisee's heirs to demand performance of the promise may well be thought to depend on other obligations rather than those deriving from the binding force of promises. If a debtor borrows money from a creditor, and the creditor dies before the money is repaid, the right of his heirs to demand that the money be repaid may well stem from ideas about property entitlements, rather than from the law of contracts, or the moral force of promises. The heirs may have known nothing of the debt when the creditor died, so they may have had no expectations.

But it is, anyhow, wrong to assume that the death of a promisee is a good ground for arguing that, on utilitarian principles, the promise need no longer be performed. The mere fact that dying persons do sometimes ask those near to them for a promise to do something after their death (as well, of course, as the custom of making wills) indicates that many people, while still alive, are concerned as to what may happen after their death. If they knew that promises made to them in such circumstances would not be binding, it is evident that some distress would be caused to them by this fact. And although, once the promisee is dead, he of course will feel no further distress, other promisees may receive less comfort from deathbed promises than they would so long as it is generally believed that they will be acted upon. There is, therefore, a simple utilitarian case for maintaining the binding force of such promises, so long at least as the facts are publicly known.

But the main thrust of this counter-example is that the facts are to be assumed to be known only to the promisee. This aspect of the case has, in truth, nothing to do with circumstances under which the promise was made. We can put aside the desert island and the deathbed scene as irrelevant to the problem. Their only function is to act as plausible explanations of how it is that the only person who knows about the promise is the promisor himself; but this condition may be satisfied in many circumstances not involving such facts as these. Wherever a promisee dies, or perhaps becomes insane or senile, or simply forgets about the promise, it may happen that the only person knowing about it is the promisor himself.[38] What justification can the utilitarian put forward for regarding the promise so made as still binding? One answer is to point to the fact that the promisor's own tendency to adhere to promises may be weakened if he breaks a promise in such circumstances; and to stress that one can never be quite certain that the secret will not be discovered by others, thereby weakening the general confidence in maintaining the sanctity of promises. But, as has been pointed out,[39] these attempts at evading the problem are useless, because the 'relentless desert-islander' will break them down, by adding stipulations to the terms of the problem which simply rule them out. It is always possible to construct a problem in which absolute secrecy is a certain part of the case. In these circumstances, one answer is simply to shrug one's shoulders, in effect, and admit that moral language is not designed to deal with such freak situations.[40] A more heroic answer is to deny that the promise is still binding. Taking the example of the desert-island promise to give a hoard of gold to the Jockey Club, J. J. C. Smart roundly denies that he would be doing wrong if he gave it instead to the local hospital which badly needed an X-ray machine. 'Could anybody deny that I had done rightly without being open to the charge of heartlessness?', he asks.[41] But to most philosophers this is simply unacceptable. The desert-island promise is generally regarded as manifestly binding, no matter what the circumstances.[42] One person at least will always know of the promise, namely the promisor himself. Somehow, it seems offensive to conclude that he will only be bound by the promise if he feels bound by it. Moreover, it must be pointed out that if the utilitarian is prepared to break a secret promise whenever he thinks

---

[38] Hence, there is no real refuge in the argument offered by Narveson, *Morality and Utility* (Baltimore, 1967), pp. 196-7, that deathbed promises and the like are made under emotional stress and so not binding.

[39] By Nowell-Smith, *Ethics* (Oxford, 1957), p. 210.

[40] Ibid., pp. 210-11.

[41] *Utilitarianism, For and Against,* p. 62.

[42] See for two out of many expressions of this viewpoint, Melden, 'Two Comments on Utilitarianism', 60 *Phil. Rev.* 508, 527 (1951); D. W. Hamlyn, 'The Obligation to Keep a Promise', *Proc. Arist. Soc.* 179, 181, (1961-2).

more good can come from breaking than performing it, he must be committed to many forms of conduct which most people reckon more heinous than promise-breaking. What about fraud, non-payment of debts, tax evasion, or even theft? Suppose, for instance, that *A* has lent money to *B*, and dies before the money is repaid. Nobody except *B* knows of the debt. *A*'s heir is a dissipated drunkard who is sure to waste the money on drink. Would the utilitarian feel so cheerful about not repaying the money (or giving it to a charity) as he would about breaking a promise? And indeed, how can he stop short of justifying even plain theft if he is quite certain that he can avoid discovery? Why should not the utilitarian take to playing Robin Hood so long as he can maintain absolute secrecy all round?

There is no doubt that we have a difficult problem on our hands. But the utilitarian may still present some sort of case along the following lines. He may, first, stress that the 'relentless desert-islander' is having to impose a number of stipulations which make the problem a highly improbable one. For one thing, *absolute* secrecy is surely hardly ever attainable. There will always be doubt; someone may know, or may find out; written evidence may exist; the promisor may himself—in a different frame of mind—feel the urge to confess. Secondly, it is highly dangerous to allow a promisor to decide when he will break a promise. It is tempting to think that one's own case is always sufficiently exceptional to justify departing from the ordinary rule. But the utilitarian knows that impartiality in one's own case is not normally to be expected of human beings. However honourable a person may be, unconscious motivations may tempt him into giving himself the benefit of the doubt. The law is most rigorous in its insistence that under no circumstances shall a man be judge in his own cause, and not without good reason. Thirdly, one may argue that, even if moral principles (like the law) sometimes overshoot the mark, it is in general likely to prove better if the principle is observed than if individuals are permitted the right to decide not to observe them. That, however, raises an issue of a more complex character, which I will look at when I turn to deal with the question of rule utilitarianism.

And finally the utilitarian may argue that in those relatively rare cases where all the stipulations are met as to secrecy, etc., it is futile to expect morality to give an answer to the problem. To pursue the method of inquiry adopted in this book, we may look to the law by way of analogy. We will then find that the problem as constructed by the traditional, or anyhow, the 'relent-less' desert-islander is a logically impossible problem. The law and the legal process are designed to deal with problems whose facts are known and can be proved before a Court of Law. They do not profess to deal with a problem arising from facts which are known only to one person, and which are firmly locked in his brain. No doubt in theory legal rules may appear to govern facts of cases whether these are known or secret, but this is only because lawyers tend to speak of 'facts' as though they were the same thing as 'provable and known facts'. This is normally a reasonable equation to make; but, where it breaks down, the law has no answer to the problem because the problem arises from circumstances which ensure, *ex hypothesi,* that the law will never be called upon to solve it. Does this analogy hold good for the moral dimension also? A case can be made for saying that it does. There is something paradoxical in asking what would the position be in the case of a promise which is not known to anybody but the promisor; if this is indeed the case, there can be nothing to discuss. To discuss it presupposes that one is already in possession of the facts, which *ex hypothesi* one cannot be. But, in the last resort, the validity of this analogy depends upon one's perception of what morality *is*, and what moral rules are *for*. If one thinks of moral rules as having a similar purpose to legal rules, then the analogy seems to stand up. I shall look at this question in Chapter 5, below.

(5) The Logical Impasse

As we have seen, the utilitarian account of promising places most of its weight on the expectations created by promises and on the fact that people rely upon them, and would suffer harm as a result of so relying, if promises were not kept. We must now face up to the critic who argues that this is all circular.[43] If it is true that promises create expectations, it is also true that one reason why they create expectations is because promisees expect promisors to keep their promises. And if it is true that people rely upon promises, one reason why they rely is because of the principle that promises ought to be kept. If there were no such principle, what would justify the promisee in relying on the promise? There appears thus to be something of a logical

---

[43] Many writers have made this point. See e.g. Prichard, op. cit., p. 171; Warnock, op. cit., pp. 98-100; M. H. Robins, op. cit., pp. 324-6; Hodgson, op. cit., pp. 39-45.

impasse. *If* a promise is regarded as creating an obligation, and as therefore creating a reason for performance, then it becomes natural for the promisee to expect performance and even to rely upon it; but (it is argued) this is only true if we first make the assumption that the promise is binding. How do we get into this situation in the first place?

I referred above to MacCormick's argument that in the end it is the *fact* (or, anyhow, the likelihood) of knowingly induced reliance actually causing harm to the promisee which justifies us in holding the promise to be binding. On this view, what the promisee relies upon is not the binding quality of the promise, but some assertion-content in the promise itself. The question whether a promise does have such a content is in itself a controversial one which I will return to later; at this point I will assume that promises do contain such propositions, implicit or explicit. Generally, the proposition is that the promisor intends to do something; MacCormick's argument is that the promisee acts upon the belief that the promisor will do as he says, and if the promise is broken, the result is that the promisee will actually suffer harm. Similarly, of course, it could be argued that expectations derive from the fact that the promisee expects the promise to be performed; this does not necessarily, and certainly does not exclusively, derive from the fact that the promise is binding. It may arise from the mere fact that the promisor has said he intends to do something.[44] But, in the end, this argument seems to fail, or at least it fails as it has hitherto been put, though it may yet be open to some utilitarian rescue operation.

The case as put by MacCormick and others seems to fail because it places too much weight on the mere fact of (knowingly induced) reliance, or the mere fact that expectations are (intentionally) roused; a weight which these facts cannot by themselves bear. Even if we take the strongest case of reliance, it is a fallacy to say that the promisee will suffer harm as a result of the breaking of the promise. He may indeed suffer harm through relying on the promisee, but the harm would not occur but for the promisee's own voluntary action. What entitles us to lay this harm to the door of the promisor? What entitles the promisee to claim that the harm was attributable to the breach of promise? This is not a factual statement: it is an ascription of moral responsibility. The only way of salvaging the argument would seem

[44] MacCormick, op. cit.; Narveson, 'Promising, Expecting and Utility', *Can. J. Phil.* 1, 207 (1971); F. S. McNeilly, 'Promises De-Moralized', 81 *Phil. Rev.* 63 (1971).

to be to assume the validity of some prior principle of obligation, for example, that a person who intentionally induces another to act in a certain way must be held responsible for the consequences if the other does so, and suffers harm. But even this salvage operation will not really work. In the first place, nobody limits the relevance of reliance to cases where it is intentionally induced; MacCormick, for instance, admits that a person must be taken to have promised where he states his intention in such a way that he knows (or ought to know?) that it is probable that the addressee will act on the statement. Once on this slope some limitations are needed before we can say, 'This is a promise', or 'This creates an obligation'. For it may be quite reasonable to suppose that the addressee will rely on the statement of intent, and yet equally reasonable to say that he does so at his own risk.

Even where the speaker actually intends the addressee to act in reliance on the statement of his intentions, there remains a problem unless we presuppose some prior principle of obligation of considerable width. Indeed, the principle we would have to presuppose is, on any view, impossibly wide. There can be no principle of obligation which says, simply and starkly, that if I intentionally induce you to behave in a way which causes you harm, I am responsible. Such a principle would make a surgeon answerable to a patient who accepts his advice to have an operation, and suffers a catastrophic reaction to the anaesthetic. Here too, it must be recognized that actions may be intentionally induced, and yet there may be good reasons for saying that the agent acts at his own risk.

There is no escape from the fact that a value-judgment is involved in saying that harm is attributable even to the breach of an express promise, as is clearly enough perceived by imagining a society in which commercial or even social morality is less developed than it is in modern England. In such a society, it may be cogently argued that a person who relies on a promise acts at his own peril, since he is a fool to trust to the promisor. Indeed, there is no need to imagine this society, because something close to this situation actually prevailed in England prior to the late eighteenth century.[45] It is, both in law, and in commercial affairs, a common refrain of writers and judges in the

---

[45] See on this K. Llewellyn, 'What Price Contract?', 40 *Yale Law J.* 704, 708-10 (1931): 'The beginning is in a society in which bargains and promises are as rare as are some hundred other matters of our present daily life ... In such conditions reliance on promises and even on bargains is in natural consequence unusual, unreasonable, an individual risk of the relier.'

seventeenth and early eighteenth centuries that a person who relies upon another frequently does so at his own risk; 'of his own head', through his 'own folly'. Sir Josiah Child, the famous merchant, writing in 1693, refers to the maxim *caveat emptor* and says that, among merchants, it is well known that no man can be cheated except it be with his own consent.[46]

What tends to conceal this is that, in the modern world, so many promises are so readily and naturally relied upon, that we take it as a matter of course that the reliance is the natural result of the promise; we think that any harm flowing from breach has therefore been 'caused' by (in the sense of being attributable to) the promise, almost intuitively, without even perceiving that a value-judgment is involved. But where implied rather than explicit promises are in question, it can much more readily be seen what is involved in this process of reasoning. To the utilitarian, it must be remembered, expectations and reliance are the very heart and essence of promises; so much so, that any act which voluntarily creates an expectation or leads to some act of reliance may sometimes have to be treated as the equivalent of an express promise.[47] But it is surely clear that one cannot justify imposing an obligation on a person from the bare facts that (1) he acted in such a way as to lead another to rely upon him, and (2) the other did so act in reliance on the first. Something is missing here, something which tells us whether the second person was *justified* in acting in the way he did, and *justified* in regarding the result as the responsiblity of the first party. In societies such as ours there is a huge amount of interdependence, of knowingly induced reliance, of intentionally aroused expectations; much of this reliance and many of these expectations must be disappointed, if only (but not only) because conflicting reliance and expectations are induced.

Take a simple example. An auctioneer advertises that he intends to sell a named property by auction at a specified time and place. He does this with the manifest intention of persuading members of the public to attend and bid at the auction. Evidently some people will make arrangements to be present, and may even spend money in having the property examined, applying for mortgages, etc. Undoubtedly it would be discourteous of the auctioneer to cancel the auction *without notice* (though,

---

[46] *A Discourse Upon Trade* (1693), p. 111.
[47] Paley, op. cit., says this quite explicitly.

of course, even if he did give notice that would not guarantee that everybody who read the original announcement would hear of the new one); but the question at issue is whether the auctioneer can cancel the auction at all? Has he, in effect, promised to hold the auction? Members of the public, it may be said, have had their expectations intentionally roused by the auctioneer; and they are entitled to have those expectations honoured. Surely it is evident that there is a gap in this reasoning, for the auctioneer may have his expectations too—he may, for instance, expect to be free to continue to seek a private sale prior to the holding of the auction. If the auctioneer has the right—the entitlement—to cancel the auction, then the expectations held by the public ought to allow for that fact; if they do not allow for it, their expectations are too high. They should have discounted their expectations, and they are not entitled to undiscounted expectations. This initial question of entitlement is, in this instance, settled by the law in favour of the auctioneer, and there seem evident reasons for this. First, there is an absence of reciprocity: is it fair that the auctioneer should be bound while others are not? Second, there is a considerable disparity in interest: the auctioneer may stand to lose a significant amount if he cannot sell privately while the losses of the individual members of the public will be small. Precisely for these reasons it is in fact customary, in advertising auctions to reserve the seller's right to sell privately prior to the auction, but this is not strictly necessary in law. The precise solution to this particular case is of no general importance; but what is of general importance is to appreciate that somebody must decide which of two sets of conflicting expectations is more *justified*.

In the law—and perhaps outside the law too—the process of implication of a promise is often the *result* of deciding that some act of reliance is or is not justified. On matters of this kind values may change over the years. If a person buys some manufactured article it is, today, taken for granted that the buyer is entitled to a sound commodity, and there is an implied promise to this effect in the contract, but that is because modern lawyers think the buyer is justified in relying upon the seller. In the eighteenth century no such implication was normally made, because lawyers thought buyers were not justified in relying upon sellers—on the contrary they thought buyers ought to look after their own interests.

It may be less easy to accept that this is also true of express promises. Certainly an express promise does seem prima facie to carry on its face its own justification for the promisee's expectations or reliance. But this is not always true; there are exceptional cases where, for one reason or another, it is accepted, morally or legally, or both, that even an express promise should not be binding. For example, there are cases of fraud, coercion and imposition, and the like. And there are also less obvious cases like (for example) those provisions of the Consumer Credit Act 1974 which enable a person to resile from a hire-purchase transaction obtained from him by a door-to-door salesman, if he acts within four days. If we ask whether the hire-purchase company has any expectations as a result of the contract obtained by its salesman, we must recognize that if if does, its expectations are in some sense not 'justified'. The company is not *entitled* to these expectations.

It is, therefore, clear that the mere fact of expectations and of reliance (however intentionally induced) cannot alone create the grounds upon which promises are held to be obligatory. Something else is needed before this conclusion can be reached. The extra element, it is suggested, is compliance with some socially accepted values which determine when expectations and/or reliance are sufficiently justifiable to be given some measure of protection. These social values are needed to enable us to determine entitlements just as much as they are needed for similar purposes in order to support the recognition of property rights. Just as the State must make some initial allocation of property entitlements in order to support a system of property law, the moral code, if it is to recognize moral obligations concerning property rights, must make a similar allocation of entitlements. Equally the law of contracts and the moral code governing promises must make analogous allocations. It must be decided *when* one person is sufficiently entitled to entertain expectations, and to act upon them, so as to hold another responsible if those expectations, or conduct in reliance, are subsequently disappointed.

If it is now asked what are the social values which determine these questions of entitlement, and how they are allocated, the answer must be—so far as the legal allocation is concerned—'Look at the Law of Contract'. That is what the Law of Contract is all about. It is, of course, less easy to give a comprehensive answer to the question of moral entitlements. But even a moral code must surely start with the law of contract, just as moral wrongs relating to theft must start with the law of property. No doubt there will be differences between law and morality; but it would be a strange moral code which did not coincide with a large part of the law of contract in making these decisions. I will return again to this idea later; here, as I am only discussing the utilitarian case, it is enough to say that these socially determined criteria may be of a strictly utilitarian character, but of course they need not be. A legal or moral system which wants, for example, to 'take rights seriously' could adopt criteria for determining when expectations should be protected which are not strictly utilitarian. It does therefore seem that the utilitarian case, so far as it rests on the need to protect reliance and expectations, is significantly incomplete.

(6) Does Utilitarianism Make Promises Irrelevant?

I turn now to consider what is often thought to be the most serious objection to the utilitarian account of promising. If a person is always morally obliged to do what will produce the most good anyhow, then, it is objected, promises cease to have any purpose. If the thing promised is something which the promisor ought to do, even apart from the promise, then the promise adds nothing; and if he promises to do something which is not, all things considered, the best thing to do, then he ought to break his promise. Thus the promise appears to be irrelevant. Whatever the situation, the promisor is still bound simply to do what, all things considered, is best.[48] This view was, indeed, largely adopted by Godwin, who argued that a promise is either to do something which ought to be done anyway, or to do something which ought not to be done anyway: in either case the promise cannot add anything to the previous situation.[49] He went on to reject the possibility that there might be cases where, absent the promise, the situation is morally indifferent, but he gave no convincing reason for this last point. On any view it might be thought that there will often be cases where, at least on the facts known to the promisor, such a situation of moral indifference will exist. And in such a case, there seems no reason why the promise should not tip the balance, as it were. However, this is a minor point. The major question is whether the utilitarian can explain why a promise should add something to a situation which is not

[48] For two examples (though the point is made by many others) see Hodgson, op. cit., p.40, and Warnock, op. cit., p. 33.
[49] *Enquiry Concerning Political Justice*, Book III, Chap. III.

otherwise morally indifferent. The answer can be divided into three.

(a) Promises to Do What the Promisor Ought to Do Anyhow

It should first be noted that promises of this kind are probably much more common in practice than is often thought, perhaps by lawyers as much as philosophers. One of the commonest uses of the promise is in fact to reinforce, in some sense, an existing obligation. People promise to tell the truth, they promise to pay their debts, they promise to recompense those to whom they are morally obliged, they promise to make good any harm or injury they may have done. And so on. Cases of this nature ought to raise just as much difficulty for the anti-utilitarian as for the utilitarian. If the promisor is already under an obligation, what purpose does it serve, on any theory of promising, for him to reiterate the obligation by promising? The answer, of course, is that in practice a wide variety of very useful purposes is served by making such promises. For example, a promise to do what you are already obliged to do shows that the promisor *acknowledges* that he is under the obligation in question. It is one thing to say the obligation exists; quite another to say that the promisor admits that it exists. Moreover, the promise may also give clarity and precision to a merely vague and indefinite pre-existing obligation. So also the utilitarian can again pray in aid his arguments about expectations. Insofar as expectations do justify us in holding a promise to create an obligation, there is no reason why we should disregard expectations which arise out of promises to do something the promisor was, in some sense, already obliged to do.

(b) Does Utilitarianism Require a Promise to be Broken Whenever it is Best on the Whole?

The utilitarian must concede that a promise ought not to be kept where more good can be done by breaking it than by keeping it. He will want to make many important qualifications and add a number of caveats to this concession (which I shall deal with shortly), but in the end he must stand by it. The anti-utilitarian then mounts a double-barrelled attack against the utilitarian. First, he objects that the felicific calculus simply fails to pay due regard to the identity of the parties concerned. It is, he argues, vitally important that the person who will get the good which the promisor will do by breaking the promise is not the person entitled to it. And the second objection is the more general one that the very notion of a promise simply rules out the possibility that one can break it because more good will be done by doing so. I will take these objections in turn.

(i) *The Identity of the Beneficiary.* The anti-utilitarian objects that the promisee is entitled to the performance of the promise: it seems impossible to suppose, because the promisor could do ten times as much good to a third party than he can do by keeping his promise, that this in any way absolves him of the duty to keep the promise. What concern is it to the promisee that more good can be done to anyone else by breaking the promise?[50] Thus the felicific calculus of the utilitarian seems to be concerned with maximizing human welfare in some form or another (whether we take it as good, happiness, or anything similar) but appears indifferent to its distribution. Justice, says the anti-utilitarian, demands that the benefits of the performance of a promise go to the promisee. The distribution of the good, or welfare or whatever, which the utilitarian wants to maximize, is as important as the total quantity.

The utilitarian may, of course, answer that this overlooks the expectations, and perhaps actions in reliance which the promisee has performed. Since it is only he, and nobody else, who has the expectations and acts in reliance, it is only he who is entitled to performance. But the anti-utilitarian can meet this by simply raising the stakes, as it were.[51] The good which the promisor may be able to render to some third party may, in quantity, outweigh all possible good which would be done to the promisee, even after due allowance has been made for his disappointed expectations and actions in reliance. Now if this is, indeed, the case, it may be possible for the promisor and the third party to compensate the promisee for his disappointed expectations out of the extra good which will be created by breaking the promise; in fact, it should be possible to compensate him sufficiently to induce him to release the promisor from his promise. There is no doubt that, where commercial or other contractual arrangements are in question, this is both theoretically possible and quite practicable. Indeed, it probably actually happens quite a lot.

[50] The point is made by many writers, see e.g. Ross, *The Right and the Good*, pp. 22, 34-5; Grice, op. cit., p. 61; Warnock, *The Object of Morality*, p. 30.
[51] Ross, op. cit., pp. 37-9.

Suppose, to take a concrete example, *A* has a machine which he wants to sell. The value of the machine to *B*, a prospective buyer, is, let us say, £10,000; he contracts to buy the machine for (say) £8,000. He expects, by using the machine in some fashion, to make a profit of £2,000. That, therefore, is the value of his expectations. We may disregard any reliance expenditure, because it would be double counting to take that into consideration as well as the value of the expectation. Suppose now that *C* discovers that the machine is for sale, and thinks that he can put it to some novel and ingenious use which will be much more profitable than the use which *B* has in mind. *C* therefore thinks the machine is worth £20,000 to him, and would be prepared to buy it from *A* for any sum not exceeding £17,000. Now it seems evident that more good will be done if *A* breaks his contract to sell the machine to *B*, and sells it instead to *C*. Furthermore, there is no reason why *B* should not recognize that fact, and allow himself to be bought out. *A* can sell the machine to *C* for £17,000, and pay *B* £2,000 for his lost expectations. The consequence is that *A, B,* and *C* are all better off than they would have been if *A* had sold the machine to *B* at the original figure.[52] It would, therefore, be perfectly possible and, indeed, likely that *B* would agree to release *A* from his contract in return for £2,000 compensation for his disappointed expectations. Indeed, in the law, it would make no difference if *B* were not so amenable, for *A* could break his contract with *B*, sell the machine to *C*, and simply await an action for breach of contract by *B*. In such an action, the damages would be fixed at £2,000 for *B*'s lost expectations; so the result is, once again, that all parties are better off.

The legal solution to this problem thus appears to be a highly utilitarian one; but it is wrong to think of this as merely a 'legal' solution. The solution is one that all parties can voluntarily arrive at so long as the benefit from breaking the contract is greater than from keeping it.

It may be objected that the result is still in some sense unfair and morally wrong. Why should not *A* be required to deliver the machine to *B* under the original contract, leaving *B* to resell to *C* and so make the extra profit derivable from that sale? This objection may be sound but it does not weaken the point of the example, which is designed to show that if more good will come

---

[52] Even *B* is better off because, although he only receives the same sum by way of compensation for his lost expectations, he receives a certainty in lieu of an expectation.

from breaking a promise than from keeping it, it is probable that the promisee can be adequately compensated for the breach out of the extra good. If, in fact, it is not the case that more good will come from breaking the promise than from keeping it, the example ceases to be relevant.

But there are still difficulties. Sometimes it seems clear that one can do more good by breaking a promise than by keeping it, and yet there is no possibility of compensating the promisee out of this extra good. Suppose *A* promises to dine with a friend, and subsequently an opportunity arises for him to do much more good (say, appear at a charity concert) on the same night; in such a case, if *A* breaks his promise to his friend, there is no possibility of the friend being compensated for out of the greater good which can be done by *A* at the charity concert. Yet the utilitarian case seems to require the special rights of the friend as a promisee to be outweighed by the greater good which can be done by breaking the promise. Now it is evident that breach of the promise in this situation involves some redistribution of 'good'. *A*'s friend must lose his expectations on the one side; the beneficiaries of the charity concert will gain on the other side. Is it desirable that this redistribution should be made?

One answer to questions of this sort may be to invoke the 'negative utilitarian' argument that the avoidance of harm has a higher priority than the positive doing of good, especially where the harm done would be irrevocable, but the good may yet be done on another occasion. Recognition of such a principle, which obviously has much to be said for it on utilitarian grounds, could solve a lot of cases of this kind. But it does not seem to meet them all. For the failure to do the good on this occasion may be just as irrevocable as the harm, and then one has nothing utilitarian about the argument, but is compelled to fall back on the principle that it is somehow 'worse' to do harm than not to do good.

But a more general argument may perhaps be mounted along the following lines. The problem is essentially one of redistribution of good. Proposed redistributions of good raise very difficult issues. It is possible that, at any given moment, more good could be done in the world by taking some 'good' from one person and giving it to another. Indeed, our political and fiscal system is carrying out a great deal of redistribution all the time for precisely these reasons. But there is no easy answer to the question, how much redistribution will increase the amount of good in the world? The utilitarian may object to the practice of dreaming up counter-examples in which it seems 'clear' that more good can be done by breaking a promise than by keeping it. For what seems clear to one person will seem violently controversial to another. Of course if we can assume that virtually everyone, *including the promisee himself,* would agree that more good would be done by breaking the promise, then perhaps, indeed, it is right to break the promise. But if, as is more likely to be the case, the promisor knows full well that there are likely to be serious arguments about which is the 'best' thing to do, then the utilitarian would be entitled to claim that more good is likely to be done in the long run by sticking to the rules.

(ii) *Breaking a Promise Because it Does More Good.* The more general objection to the utilitarian case on promising lays much stress on the idea that a promise somehow precludes a *general* defence of 'greater good', as it were. No doubt most philosophers would concede that, in extreme cases, the duty to keep a promise may be overridden by the possibility of doing some much greater good. Few would deny that a person would be morally justified in breaking a lunch engagement in order to rescue a child from drowning. But the argument is that the very idea of a promise— the whole purpose of a promise—is to exclude arguments based on a mere balance of convenience, or even of good. A promisor does not, it is forcefully argued, mean by his promise, 'I promise but ... before I keep the promise I shall review the situation and then determine whether or not the effects would be better if I break it; and if so, I'll break it'.[53] Those who press this argument could also add that if it is a mere expectation which is the utilitarian ground for holding the promise binding, then it would be natural to suppose that something relatively trifling could outweigh the duty to keep the promise. And yet the duty to keep a promise is generally conceived (at any rate by many philosophers) to be of a particularly sacrosanct character.

The utilitarian answer to this objection is a complex one, and, in the end, perhaps incomplete. But nevertheless, much can be said against the objection. There are, first, a number of standard points which have frequently been made by utilitarians. For example, stress is laid on the fact that it is often doubtful

---

[53] D. Lyons, *Forms and Limits of Utilitarianism* (Oxford, 1965), pp. 187-8; see too J. Rawls, 'Two Concepts of Rules'. 64 *Phil. Rev.* 1, 15-17 (1955).

where the most good will be done, and the promisor is not an impartial judge because he may be tempted to break rather than keep his promise. And stress will also be laid on the fact that the ill consequences of breaking a promise may not stop with the particular promise in question. The example of the promisor may be all-important to others, and even to himself; his own habits of promise-keeping may be weakened by breaking this promise. And so on. Some of these objections may have been overstated by utilitarians; but others have not been given the importance they deserve. In particular, it seems to be generally assumed both by utilitarians and their opponents, that the utilitarian must accept his own right to decide when more good will be done by breaking a promise than by keeping it;[54] of course the utilitarian then stresses that because of the possibility of bias, conscious or unconscious, he must be chary of making this decision.[55] But—to pray in aid the legal analogy again—it seems unnecessary to suppose that the promisor is entitled to make this decision at all. To a lawyer, it would be absurd even to contemplate a rule which said the promisor is entitled to break his promise whenever he thinks (even bona fide, and after due and careful reflection) that more good will be done by breaking than by keeping it. But there would be nothing absurd about a rule which said that the promisor is entitled to break his promise if some independent third party, such as a judge, decides, after full consideration, that more good is likely to be done by breaking the promise than by keeping it. Indeed, not only would there be nothing absurd about such a rule, but something quite close to this rule does exist in the laws of most countries.

It is not, indeed, put quite so baldly as to say that a promise should be broken when that will do more good than harm; but it is a part of the law of most civilized States that a contract which is contrary to public policy is void and unenforceable. And this does not mean anything very different from the proposition that if the contract does more harm than good, it should not be enforceable. This is very far from destroying the whole law of contracts for a number of reasons. First, because what judges think often differs from what promisors think. Secondly, because the fact of the promise (or contract) is one of the facts to be reckoned with; and the fact that a decision against the promise

---

[54] Thus Lyons (op. cit., at pp. 187-8) and Rawls (op. cit., at pp. 3, 14 and 19) both clearly make this assumption.
[55] See e.g. Pickard-Cambridge, XLI *Mind* (1932) 145, 156-7.

will prima facie be a wrong is to enter into the scales and be weighed against the wrong that enforcing this particular promise will do. It is thus a mistake to suppose that the promise somehow becomes irrelevant if it is decided that, in the end, breaking it is better than keeping it. This decision is only made after due weight has been given to the promise and the expectations thereby generated and so on. Every judge who is asked to declare a promise void on the ground that it conflicts with public policy starts from the position that prima facie it is in accord with public policy that promises should be kept.[56] Consequently, there is, in practice, a substantial bias towards upholding contracts, and a strong disinclination towards holding them to be contrary to public policy. Lawyers are well aware of how very difficult and controversial it often is to decide whether keeping or breaking a promise will do more harm than good. And for that reason they are inclined, as Lord Atkin said in a famous case, to give the contract the benefit of the doubt.[57]

A similar situation occurs where, as happens in various legal cases, Courts are empowered to make broadly equitable decisions in accordance with what seems fair and reasonable. In cases of this nature, the question sometimes arises whether a promise must be enforced irrespective of what might otherwise seem fair and reasonable; and the answer is clearly No. This does not mean (as has sometimes been urged by counsel)[58] that to do this involves the Court in simply disregarding the promise and deciding what would be just and reasonable as though no promise had ever been given. The promise is one of the facts of the situation, but it is not a conclusive fact. A simple example is provided by *Dean* v. *Dean*[59] which concerned a dispute between a husband and wife, who were in process of being divorced, as to the appropriate financial provision to be made for the wife. The parties were both advised by lawyers, and after prolonged negotiations, a bargain was made, from which the wife afterwards sought to resile. Strictly, the bargain, or contract, was not legally binding on the parties, for the Court has an unfettered discretion to order maintenance, and it could have overridden the bargain on the ground (for example) that it provided for manifestly inadequate

---

[56] A very well-known pronouncement to this effect can be found in *Printing and Numerical Co.* v. *Sampson* (1875) L.R. 19 Eq. 462.

[57] *Fender* v. *Mildmay* [1938] AC 1, 13.

[58] For example, in *Ebrahimi* v. *Westbourne Galleries* [1972] 2 All ER 492.

[59] [1978] 3 All ER 758.

maintenance. Indeed, the Court has a statutory duty 'to have regard to all the circumstances of the case'; this is a common legal formula which differs little from the utilitarian notion that the Court should do 'what is best on the whole'.[60] In fact, in this instance, the judge treated the agreement as prima-facie evidence of the reasonableness of the maintenance to be provided under it, and although he examined the circumstances of the case to see if that prima-facie reasonableness was rebutted, in the end he upheld the bargain.

It is worth adding a word about the historical background to the law in this sort of situation. In the period of classical contract law—say the mid-nineteenth century, when freedom of contract was the dominant ideology of the times—it was widely believed that contracts provided the mechanism whereby private and public interests were brought into harmony. Many of the classical utilitarians and the classical economists shared the belief that contracts (and promises) represented the free choice of the parties, and that the enforcement of contracts and promises was a method of ensuring that there was always a harmony between private and public interests.[61] At its most optimistic, this ideology led (very nearly) to the view that breaking a promise could never be best on the whole, because it could *never* create more good than keeping it. A century and a half of experience has convinced most lawyers (and economists) that this is a travesty of the truth, and that there are many circumstances in which it would be better on the whole if promises were broken. But the question of what is best on the whole is still inordinately difficult. Many philosophers write as though it is easy to identify what is best on the whole, and that promises would be greatly weakened if they could be departed from whenever it is best on the whole. But this is quite untrue. There are so many circumstances in which it is in practice impossible to be sure what is best on the whole that rules like the rule that promises should be kept, become almost conclusive over a wide spectrum of activity.

In stating that it is often inordinately difficult to determine what is best on the whole, I may have understated the problem. It is arguable that this is not merely difficult in practice, but impossible in principle. What is good for some causes harm to others, and vice versa. Therefore there is not even a theoretically

---

[60] Subject of course to the fact that the judge is limited to dealing with the particular parties and issues before him.

[61] See e.g. E. Halevy, *The Growth of Philosophic Radicalism* (reprinted, London, 1972).

optimum decision or action which can be said to be best on the whole. Given a majoritarian principle, one can, of course, deduce when the balance of good outweighs the harm; but even this requires us to take account of inter-personal comparisons of utility. Alternatively, it may be argued that one can in principle discover what is best on the whole by invoking the economists' Pareto principle, that a change which benefits some sufficiently to compensate those who lose, is better on the whole than the *status quo*. But so many qualifications need to be made to the Pareto principle that it cannot seriously be claimed even in principle to give an answer to the problem of whether it is best on the whole that a particular promise should be broken. To those who do accept the principle, what becomes all important is the nature of the decision-making procedure and the identity of the decision-maker. It thus becomes all the more necessary that the decision to break a promise on the ground that it is best on the whole should not rest with the promisor, but with some impartial third person.

I turn now to say something about the argument from example. The utilitarian is accused of placing too much weight on the possible effects, by way of example, of a single breach of a promise. Even if it becomes publicly known (and we have seen that there are problems about secrecy, also), it is improbable that a single breach of a promise is likely to have any cataclysmic consequences. The utilitarian may, in reply, point out that there are indeed some situations in which a single breach of promise may have a very dramatic effect. For example, breach of a promise enshrined in an international treaty (say the treaty against proliferation of nuclear weapons) could rapidly, even immediately, lead to the treaty being denounced by other parties to it, with possibly calamitous results for the entire human race. And, even in less cosmic circumstances, single breaches of promise may have rapid chain reactions. For example, breach of a promise by a bank to honour its financial obligations could lead to a rapid loss of credit; breach by a single member of a cartel, or monopoly group, could lead to the collapse of the cartel arrangements (and not all cartels are bad). Moreover, even though chain reactions may not occur, there can certainly be a loss of confidence in a limited sphere, which would itself be a serious consequence of breaking a promise. For example, failure by a trade union to honour a 'no strike clause' may lead the employer to place no further reliance on such a clause in his negotiations with the union; this may itself cause loss, even to the union itself. Even a failure by a consumer to pay his hire-purchase debts may be recorded in credit references, and affect his ability to obtain future credit.

But it is obvious that it is the chain reaction which is the more dangerous possibility; and it is unwise to assume that minor breaches of promise here or there involve no risk of a total collapse of confidence, or of credit. The risk is no doubt a very small one in most circumstances, but the consequences of such a break-down would be so very great that it is undesirable to take such risks unless the gain manifestly outweighs the dangers. It is much easier to trigger off a collapse of confidence than it is to re-create it, and although a collapse of confidence is usually thought to affect only currency and financial dealings, there is no reason to doubt that if it were serious enough, it would extend to many other types of contracts and promises.

Nevertheless, even when all due allowances are made for these arguments, it must be admitted that there do seem to be significant numbers of cases in which it would be easy to demonstrate that a single breach of promise would create more good than harm; and yet the utilitarian cannot concede that the promise should be broken because there are many others in like case. A widow defaults on her mortgage; she has several children; the mortgagee already has more money than he needs.[62] Taken in isolation, it seems evident that more good than harm would follow from allowing the widow to break her promise. But if all defaulting widows were allowed to escape the consequences of promise-breaking, widows would soon be unable to get mortgages, and so more harm than good would ensue. This brings us to the distinction between rule utilitarianism and act utilitarianism.

Promises and Rule Utilitarianism

I referred earlier to the possibility that legal and moral rules may sometimes overshoot the mark, as it were, that is, they may sometimes apply (or appear to apply) to circumstances where, all things considered, it would be best if they did not. As a matter of empirical fact, it is almost certain that legal and moral rules do sometimes induce behaviour which is not likely to lead to

---

[62] See Wasserstrom, *The Judicial Decision* (Stanford, London, 1961), pp. 141-2.

the most good on the whole. Is it possible to justify this result on utilitarian grounds?

The rule utilitarian takes the position that it is not usually possible or desirable (on utilitarian grounds) to weigh up the probable consequences of every single act which we are called upon to perform. What the utilitarian should do is to adopt general rules of conduct of a utilitarian character. These rules will be adopted because it is found that on balance, and in general, adherence to them does more good than adherence to any other relevant rule. When called upon to make a decision as to a particular action, the utilitarian is then absolved from the necessity of deciding what is likely to be best on the whole: he should simply comply with the rule. The example of promising comes once again readily to hand.[63] The rule utilitarian argues that there is no need, nor is it desirable, for a promisor to inquire into the likely consequences of performing or breaking his promise: it is enough for him to ensure that his promise falls under the general rule (which of course might contain exceptions) that promises should be kept. The rule itself must be adopted on utilitarian grounds; but the individual act need not be.

The rule utilitarian is able to point to many utilitarian reasons for adopting this distinction. For example, people frequently have no time to weigh up all the likely consequences of an action; they may be biased in making decisions which favour themselves; it is often difficult to weigh up the consequences of a single act; and so on. But many difficulties remain. The generalization problem is as intractable as ever. For it is not enough to show that if everybody broke their promises under the same circumstances, it must therefore be wrong for one person to do so. One person might break his promise without causing others to do the same. No doubt, each breach of promise may have some slight effect by way of example upon others, and no doubt (as we have seen) there are some particular cases where breach even of a single promise could have chain-reaction results. But in very many cases, it would be extravagant to attribute the likelihood of such results to a single breach of a promise. So the breach of that promise, taken by itself, might do more good than harm, yet neither lawyer, nor philosopher (nor even the

[63] Especially in J. Rawls's influential paper, 'Two Concepts of Rules', 64 *Phil. Rev.* 1 (1955).

common man), would accept that it thereby becomes right to break that promise.[64]

Some utilitarians therefore reject the new version of utilitarianism. For these act utilitarians, rules are, indeed, important, but only as prima-facie guides to conduct. They accept the obvious utilitarian case for having rules of behaviour which are generally likely to maximize human welfare, happiness, or good. But they insist that these moral rules must be treated as rules of thumb only. J. J. C. Smart, for example, asks rhetorically whether it is not monstrous to suppose that 'if we *have* worked out the consequences [of breaking a rule] and if we have perfect faith in the impartiality of our calculations, and if we *know* that in this instance to break [the rule] will have better results than to keep it, we should nevertheless obey the rule?' This, he goes on, is to erect the rule into a sort of idol, and to be guilty of 'rule-worship', a form of superstition.[65] The utilitarian who adopts this position is, on this view, in danger of abandoning his utilitarian convictions in favour of the deontological view that the duty to observe a rule may be binding, irrespective of its consequences.

But rule utilitarianism has also been roughly handled by those who are not utilitarians at all. In particular, the sustained critique of David Lyons has been found by many philosophers to be unanswerable.[66] Lyons in effect argues that rule utilitarianism and act utilitarianism are, in the end, indistinguishable. If it can be demonstrated that, in a particular situation, breaking a rule produces better results than keeping it, the rule utilitarian must logically agree that optimal results would only be attained by a sub-rule or exception to the main rule which leads to a different result. For, if this demonstration is sound, it must be true of all other identical cases; and it then follows that it will be better on the whole to have such a sub-rule (or exception) than to maintain the rule unqualified. But what is true of one sub-rule must, in the end, be true of all special situations. No matter how special, the rule utilitarian must concede that a rule to cover that special situation will, in the end, produce more good than a lack of

---

[64] See e.g. M. Singer, 'Generalization in Ethics', *Mind,* LXIV 361 (1955) and his book of the same title (London, 1963); D. Ross, *Foundations of Ethics* (Oxford, 1939), Chap. V; D. Lyons, op. cit., *passim.*

[65] 'Extreme and Restricted Utilitarianism', 6 *Phil. Q.* 344 (1956), pp. 348-9.

[66] *Forms and Limits of Utilitarianism;* see too R. Wasserstrom, *The Judicial Decision,* for a very similar argument in the legal context.

such a rule. We thus find that rules will have to be broken down into further and smaller sub-rules and sub-sub rules, until, in the end, we reach the position of having to have a special rule for every case. At that stage, of course, rule utilitarianism and act utilitarianism merge. Rules thus disappear from the scene, and we are back to the necessity of judging each case on its merits.

A similar, though much simpler, point is made by Warnock, who argues that moral rules cannot really be reasons for actions at all. Moral rules encapsulate reasons for action, but (unlike legal rules) have no inherent validity of their own.[67] A rule cannot alter the moral character of an act; an act is not morally wrong *because* it infringes a moral rule. Indeed, Warnock rejects the idea that there is any such thing as a moral *rule* at all; there are only reasons for acting in particular circumstances, so that in the end the actor must 'examine the full concrete merits of each individual case'.[68]

A number of possible answers to these objections have already been touched upon earlier, but more needs to be said about them here. It must once again be said that these arguments gloss over far too readily the problems arising from doubt and uncertainty about what is likely to produce the most good. But what now needs to be stressed is that there is often greater uncertainty in the particular than in the aggregate. It is often arguable whether the results of breaking a particular promise would produce more harm than good; but there can be *no* argument that breaking all promises (or even, all promises of a certain class) would do infinitely more harm than good. This is why the process of individualization of rules into sub-rules and sub-sub rules will, in practice, usually stop a long way short of the individual case. It is perfectly plausible to argue that an unqualified rule that *all* promises be kept will produce less good than a rule that all promises should be kept, with certain limited exceptions. And it would not be difficult to make a list of the main classes of cases which would justifiably be placed in the exceptional category—the law, after all, has to do this. But it is not in the least plausible to argue that the process of creating exceptions, and exceptions to exceptions, will go on until we reach each individual case; for long before we reach that stage we shall have reached the limits of our knowledge of what is likely to

---

[67] Op. cit., Chap. 5.
[68] Ibid., p. 67.

produce the most good. And when we get there, it is not only wasteful to attempt to go further; it is likely to lead to worse results.

The act utilitarian who thinks, following Lyons, that he can always break down classes of cases until he has only single cases to deal with, may, in practice, be more liable to go wrong in the aggregate. It is, over many spheres of behaviour, much easier to predict aggregate consequences than individual consequences. Divorce statistics can tell us with reasonable accuracy how many divorces there are likely to be over the next few years; but would anybody who tried to calculate the number by examining every individual case be more likely to produce an accurate figure? If the price of coffee goes up by 20p per pound, economists can predict with some accuracy what will happen to total coffee consumption; but any attempt to predict the behaviour of individual consumers and then sum the total is hardly likely to be more accurate. Similarly, the attempt to decide what will do the most good by looking at all the individual circumstances of a case may, in the end, be less likely to lead to the best results than sticking to rules. It is ignorance, not knowledge, that leads to the need for rules.[69]

But having said all this, it must be admitted that even in the law, which one might assume to be in much greater need of rules than any moral system, there are today many signs of a tendency to break down rules into smaller and smaller subclasses; until, in the end, we arrive at the result that many decisions turn upon the discretion of the judge to do what he thinks just and equitable in all the circumstances of the case. I have written of this tendency elsewhere, and given some reasons for thinking that the process is a dangerous one.[70] I need not pursue it further here.

Another possible escape from these criticisms of the rule-utilitarian position may be found in a suggestion made (though not for this purpose) by Raz,[71] who introduces the idea of different-order reasons. We take decisions, he argues, for reasons which are not always of the same order. Some reasons are first-order reasons, for example, reasons directly bearing on whether an act is likely to produce certain results; other reasons are second-order reasons, such as, for example, the desirability of observing

---

[69] F. A. Hayek, *Law, Liberty and Legislation*, Vol. II, pp. 20-1.
[70] In my inaugural lecture at Oxford: *From Principles to Pragmatism* (Oxford, 1978).
[71] *Practical Reason and Norms* (London, 1975).

promises, or obeying orders. Second-order reasons are reasons
which bear on the desirability or otherwise of acting for first-
order reasons.[72] When first- and second-order reasons clash, we
do not weigh them up as though they were reasons of the same
kind. One second-order reason may simply rule out of court a
first-order reason. A soldier who is given an order should not
pause to inquire whether it is the best thing to do in all the circumstances (though he may ask himself whether it is a lawful
order); lawfulness apart, he should simply obey. Similarly, a
promise excludes from consideration (anyhow within certain
limits) the question whether the promise should have been made
at all.[73] But that does not mean that second-order reasons like
the desirability of keeping promises are not themselves reasons
for action, nor does it mean that they are just arbitrary or irrational grounds for action. They are real reasons; indeed, they
may be adopted because they produce the best results on the
whole. This sounds helpful at first, but on analysis it may be
found that it does not really offer any help to the rule utilitarian.
For it is clear that there are some occasions on which second-
order reasons are open for review, or re-examination, just because they do not seem to lead to results which commend themselves to first-order reasons. And the real difficulty is to know
when, and under what circumstances, that review is right.

Another argument which has occasionally been relied upon
in favour of rule utilitarianism, but is now generally found to
involve certain unpalatable assumptions, is the argument from
principle. It is desirable that simple principles like promise-
keeping should be adhered to because, once the door is open
to exceptions, people may mistakenly think that their case falls
under one of the exceptions when it does not. It is true, no doubt,
that there are some exceptional cases where it would be best to
break a promise, but it is dangerous to allow people to act on
this truth. It is therefore best to encourage people to keep their
promises in all cases, even though the best results would actually
be reached if they sometimes broke them. It has been objected
that this assumes very remarkable stupidity in men. 'They are
told that the only right conduct is to try to produce the greatest
happiness, and also that they must perform the act called paying
a debt, even when it manifestly does not produce the greatest
happiness, for fear that they should encourage people not to

perform it when it manifestly does.'[74] But not everyone will be so sanguine as to the ability of most people to draw distinctions of this kind; whether it is due to stupidity, or to the inability to be impartial where one's own affairs are in question, or to a combination of the two, is immaterial. The fact of the matter is that in law, and in many activities of life, this assumption is regularly made. Who has not sat on a committee which has rejected an application for some special dispensation on the ground that, however meritorious in itself, it would create a dangerous precedent? What can a decision of this kind mean if it is not that the committee fears that other, less meritorious, cases will be brought forward in future, and the present case used as a precedent, even though the facts are different, even though, as a lawyer would say, they are clearly distinguishable. The committee can hardly mean that if the facts are in all respects identical, they would wish the decision to be different next time, for this would be irrational. Even judges have been known to say that they hope their decision will not be cited as a precedent in future, and here the position must be even clearer; for a judge can hardly mean that if an identical case were to be brought before the Court, the result should be different.

In the moral sphere, however, the argument has been found unpalatable by some because it may have undertones of élitism. The rule utilitarian may, in fact, believe that the masses are incapable of deciding intelligently and impartially when principles of conduct should be adhered to, and when there is a sufficient case for departing from them. But he may be willing to concede that some intellectual élite is capable of making such distinctions. In effect, he may end up by preaching rule utilitarianism as a creed for the masses, while reserving act utilitarianism as the privilege of the intellectual élite. There is, in fact, very little doubt that most of the early classical utilitarians would have taken this position, though they did not perceive the problem as it has been put in modern times, and some of the classical texts are themselves ambiguous.[75] But to modern writers this is a repellent, and perhaps unworkable, because undemocratic, philosophy.[76]

---

[74] Carritt, *Theory of Morals* (Oxford, 1928), p. 39.

[75] The élitist position is plainly stated by John Austin, in *The Province of Jurisprudence Determined,* especially Lecture III. It is also stated, in the context of the right to rebellion, by Hume, *History of England* (Edinburgh, 1792), VII, pp. 148-50.

[76] See e.g. B. Williams in *Morality*, pp. 111-12; G. C. Kerner, 'The Immorality of Utilitarianism', 21 *Phil. Q.* 36 (1971).

Rule utilitarianism thus seems to lead nowhere in the end. At any rate, no version so far put forward resolves all the difficulties which we have reviewed. But extreme act utilitarianism also has formidable problems. Except for the revolutionary or the anarchist, much of the law and the moral system in a modern State is derived from property rights, and the distribution of property at any given moment is something which can only be defended by appealing to the value of the rules of the system as a whole.[77] I have already pointed out that there must, at any given moment, be considerable sums of money which could do much more good if they were redistributed from their present owners to others. Yet even the most extreme left-wing socialist (unless he is also a revolutionary) would presumably be hesitant about the moral right of any person to help himself (or others) to property merely on this ground. And similarly (as I have pointed out), to break a promise on the ground that this will do more harm than good is to redistribute good from the promisee who is entitled to it, to others who are not. If this sort of redistribution is to be permitted, at the sole discretion of the promisor (however well motivated and reflective), why should the promisor not be just as morally entitled to break into the promisee's house and rifle the contents for the benefit of some deserving charity?

We thus seem, for the moment, to have reached the end of the road. In particular, utilitarianism seems to leave us with two unresolved problems. First, the argument that promises are binding because of the expectations and the actions in reliance to which they give rise, seems to be incomplete, as we saw previously. And secondly, neither rule utilitarianism nor act utilitarianism seems able to offer an acceptable explanation of why (or whether) a promise remains binding when it would be best on the whole to break it. It is time now to look at some alternative accounts of the moral basis of promises.

---

[77] The classic statement is in Hume's *Treatise*, Book III, Part II, Sects. 1 and 2.

Chapter 4

Promising and Non-Utilitarian Philosophies

To the utilitarians, the morality, or rightness, of conduct is determined by its consequences, or, sometimes, by its likely or probable consequences. And morality therefore becomes, in the end, an empirical question. But there have been other traditional philosophical ideas about ethics, many of which long antedate modern utilitarianism. There is, for instance, the Cartesian tradition, which is fundamentally anti-empirical, and which tries to deduce moral duties from internal reflection: we have already seen some specimens of this tradition in the discussion of Natural Law in Chapter 2. And there is the Kantian tradition which treats duty as the irreducible idea at the base of all moral principles. The highest morality is the act performed from a Sense of Duty, and it is compliance with duty, not utility, which determines the rightness of an act. In more modern times, a variety of other ethical theories have been widely debated, some of which have stressed the linguistic aspects of moral language, and the variety of purposes which language may serve. It is, of course, not the purpose of this work to offer any general survey of these ethical theories, but rather to review some of the principle accounts given by these theories of the morality of promises.

Intuitionism

In the decades after the publication of G. E. Moore's *Principia Ethica* in 1901, a new version of intuitionist ethics flourished among English philosophers, particularly in the writings of Sir David Ross. Ross discussed the subject of promises at some length in his two principal works, *The Right and the Good*[1] and *The Foundation of Ethics*.[2] Much of his account was taken up with criticisms of the utilitarian theory of promises which I have already discussed. But Ross also offered his own account, which turns out to resemble the theories of the Natural Lawyers in many

[1] Oxford, 1930.
[2] Oxford, 1939.

respects. To Ross, the essence of right conduct was that it was compliance with duty; and duties were obligations which could only be perceived by internal reflection. They were self-evident, although Ross recognized that the question of what is self-evident to an adult is not necessarily self-evident to a child. One learns moral truths in the same way that one learns mathematical truths:

The general principles of duty are obviously not self-evident from the beginning of our lives. How do they come to be so? The answer is that they come to be self-evident to us just as mathematical axioms do. We find by experience that this couple of matches and that couple of matches make four matches, and that this couple of balls on a wire and that couple make four balls: and by reflection on these and similar discoveries we come to see that it is of the nature of two and two to make four. In a precisely similar way, we see the *prima facie* rightness of an act which would be the fulfilment of a particular promise, and of another which would be the fulfilment of another promise, and when we have reached sufficient maturity to think in general terms, we apprehend *prima facie* rightness to belong to the nature of any fulfilment of promise.[3]

And then again:

To me it seems as self-evident as anything could be, that to make a promise, for instance, is to create a moral claim on us in someone else. Many readers will perhaps say that they do *not* know this to be true. If so, I certainly cannot prove it to them; I can only ask them to reflect again, in the hope that they will ultimately agree that they also know it to be true.[4]

As we have already seen when examining the theories of the Natural Lawyers, this simplistic idea raises many serious objections. For example, is it not clear that—even to the intuitionist— a promise ought to be broken at least if its performance will lead to much greater harm than good? Or if, by breaking it, much greater good may be done? Ross accepted this, but argued that this was not because the morality of the problem was disposed of by balancing the good against the harmful consequences; it was because of a conflict of duties. A person has a prima-facie duty to keep a promise; but he also has prima-facie duties not to injure his neighbours, and even, in some circumstances, to render them aid and succour. Hence, if these duties clash, one of them must overcome the other. Which of them is to give way in these circumstances is not settled by asking which causes the most harm, or good, but by internal reflection.

Then again, the intuitionist, like the Natural Lawyer, must explain why certain defences are traditionally recognized to legal or moral claims based on promises and contracts. Here, too,

---

[3] *The Right and the Good*, pp. 32-3.
[4] Ibid., p. 21 n. 1.

the parallel was maintained, for Ross, like the seventeenth-century Natural Lawyers, argued that the answer to these difficulties was to give a reasonable construction to the promise. Reasonably construed, many promises might not be binding in certain eventualities which were not anticipated or counted on by the promisor.[5] Even the possibility of the promisor being released because of the deceit or fraud of the promisee is explained as resting upon some 'implied condition' in the promise. Reasonably construed, the promise only covers the case where the facts stated by the promisee are true; if they are deliberate frauds, then the promise is not 'intended' to operate.[6] As I have already pointed out, this sort of argument was widely used by English lawyers in many cases of mistake, or supervening impossibility, particularly around the period when Ross was writing. But even in the 1920s some judges expressed considerable scepticism about the nature of these 'implications'. As a Scots judge said in 1922, 'A tiger has escaped from a travelling menagerie. The milk girl fails to deliver the milk. Possibly the milkman may be exonerated from any breach of contract, but, even so, it would seem hardly reasonable to base that exoneration on the ground that "tiger days excepted" must be held as if written into the contract.'[7]

Since that date, many judges have rejected the idea that exonerating circumstances of this nature are in any sense genuine 'implications' of what the parties intended. Too often, the problems which have beset the contract arise precisely because the parties did not foresee the events which have occurred, and they did not, therefore, have any relevant intentions at all. It is true, of course, that a person may use language intended to cover (or exclude) a general class of things without necessarily adverting to each item in the class individually. Wittgenstein gives a well-known example: 'Someone says to me: "shew the children a game". I teach them gaming with a dice, and the other says, "I didn't mean that sort of game".'[8] Nobody would deny that although the speaker did not have a mental image of all the games he thought permissible or impermissible when he gave his instructions, he is entitled to claim that he did not intend to include games of dice. But too often in the law, one finds cases

---

[5] *Foundations of Ethics*, p. 96. The same argument is maintained by Grice, *The Grounds of Moral Judgment*, pp. 52-6.

[6] *Foundations of Ethics*, p. 97; Grice, op. cit., p. 54.

[7] Lord Sands in *James Scott & Sons Ltd.* v. *Del Sel* (1922) SC 592, 597.

[8] *Philosophical Grammar* (Oxford, 1974), p. 119.

in which promises or contracts have been made which clearly must encompass certain eventualities or risks, while other similar eventualities or risks are felt to be just on the other side of the line. For example, a person sells a house which is occupied by a tenant believed to be rent-protected; he is mistaken and the tenant can be turned out at a week's notice, so the house is worth three times as much as the contract price.[9] The contract is held not binding; yet if the house had been burnt down before the sale was completed, the contract would have stood. Is it really possible to argue that the parties 'intended' the promises to be binding in the one eventuality but not in the other?

Or take another example: a small farmer agreed to sell a cow for $80 to a buyer for meat. It was thought that the cow was barren and only fit for slaughter. When the buyer came to collect the cow shortly after, it was found to be with calf, and worth ten times as much.[10] An American Court divided on the result, the majority holding that the contract was not binding, but can it really be said that the parties did not 'intend' the sale to go through in these circumstances?

Although common lawyers have always been very free in using the technique of 'implying terms' in promises or contracts, it would now be widely (though not universally) agreed among lawyers that often this is simply a technical, or 'doctrinal' process designed to give effect to the Court's sense of fairness.

The case of fraud is perhaps even more dubious. As Sidgwick pointed out, a false statement may be only one consideration among many, and it may, moreover, be of any degree of weight.[11] In the law, it has been specifically decided that a fraudulent misstatement will justify refusal to perform a contract even though there were other inducing factors which would probably have led to the contract being made anyway.[12] It is, therefore, not possible to argue that the law regards a promise induced by fraud as not binding because it is intended to be conditional on the truth of the statement; but (as I suggested earlier) this may be because the Courts are willing to penalize a person guilty of fraud.

One of the chief reasons for dissatisfaction with intuitionism—especially perhaps for a lawyer—is that the intuitionist exonerates

---

[9] *Grist* v. *Bailey* [1967] Ch. 532.

[10] *Sherwood* v. *Walker* (1877) 33 NW 919.

[11] *Methods*, p. 306.

[12] *Edgington* v. *Fitzmaurice* (1885) 29 Ch D. 459.

himself from giving any *reasons* for his moral principles. No justification is offered which can be weighed, evaluated, discussed, or tested. To anyone who believes that moral principles, like legal principles, are to do with social behaviour, it is unacceptable to be told that this is the right thing to do without any reason. Either the intuitionist must follow his own intuition, which seems a recipe for anarchy; or he must follow someone else's, which seems a recipe for slavery.

Another obvious weakness of intuitionism is that our intuition is liable to fail us as soon as we move away from the central case to more marginal issues. One of the surprising features of Ross's account is that he makes no mention of the careful and detailed criticism made of similar ideas by Sidgwick some half century earlier. Sidgwick begins by asking what criteria can be used to identify self-evident, or common-sense, moral principles.[13] He suggests four criteria: first, they must be relatively clear and precise; secondly, they must be ascertained by careful reflection; thirdly, they must be mutually consistent; and fourthly, they must be generally or even universally shared. He then goes on to take the example of the duty to keep promises as one which seems to surpass in simplicity, certainty, and definiteness other moral rules, and therefore to be considered as an obvious candidate for the role of 'common sense' principle. But he then goes on to consider many of the problems which arise in marginal cases, for example, the case of promises obtained by fraud or coercion, the effect of a change of circumstance, the problem of misunderstanding, and so on. Cases of this character, he concludes, show that one cannot, in the end, adopt the simple and unqualified principle that 'promises should be kept'. Too many qualifications and reservations need to be made, many of which involve difficult choices, and perhaps decisions on pure matters of degree.

In modern times, the very idea that there could be self-evident moral principles has been regarded as unacceptable. R. M. Hare, for example, suggests that it is not at all clear what it could mean for a moral principle to be self-evident.[14] There is also the obvious difficulty that moral intuitions appear to be culturally determined. Indeed, we know only too well that, socially or anthropologically speaking, moral principles have been extremely diverse among different peoples and at different times. It is too easy to assume

---

[13] Op. cit., Book III, Chap. IV.
[14] *The Language of Morals* (Oxford, 1964), pp. 41-3.

that 'rationality' is a characteristic of one's own age and social milieu.

This last point is worth further notice. In nineteenth-century England, when contractual ideology was at the centre of law, political theory, economics, and much of the Victorian moral code, there was a tendency to assume that this ideology expressed universal and immutable principles. The author of a legal text-book on the law of contract published in 1847 declared in his Preface: 'The law of contracts may justly indeed be said to be a universal law adapted to all times and races, and all places and circumstances, being founded upon those great and fundamental principles of right and wrong deduced from natural reason which are immutable and eternal.'[15] In 1861, Sir Henry Maine, in his famous work, *Ancient Law,* uttered a warning about the historical and anthropological accuracy of sweeping generalizations of this sort. It was, he insisted, an utter misconception to think that a developed law of contract was a basic feature of all societies; on the contrary, most primitive societies paid little attention to the enforcement of contractual rights. Rights and duties in primitive communities were, urged Maine, more often the result of status (and custom) than of contract; the idea that a person could alter his legal relationship with others merely by his free choice is a feature of advanced legal systems.[16]

It is clear that Maine is not drawing any distinction (which would be anachronistic in the sort of early societies he is discussing) between the legal and the moral. 'No trustworthy primitive record can be read without perceiving that the habit of mind which induces us to make good a promise is as yet imperfectly developed, and that acts of flagrant perfidy are often mentioned without blame, and sometimes described with approbation.'[17] In the light of this evidence of the diversity of values between modern and primitive communities (and Maine's basic point remains unchallenged today),[18] it is remarkable how tenacious

---

[15] Addison, *Treatise On Contract* (London, 1847), Preface.

[16] *Ancient Law* (London, 1861), Chap. IX.

[17] *Ancient Law,* 10th edn. (London, 1890), p. 312.

[18] See e.g. A. S. Diamond, *Primitive Law, Past and Present* (London, 1971), p. 386; M. Gluckman, *The Judicial Process Among the Barotse,* 2nd edn. (Manchester, 1967), pp. 28, 30, 200, 440-2 and *The Ideas in Barotse Jurisprudence* (New Haven, 1965), pp. 181 ff. Gluckman found that the Barotse had no understanding of executory contracts although they did have a general moral disapprobation for promise-breaking. When Gluckman suggested that the absence of executory contracts in their legal system represented a serious gap, they altered their law, but in practice this made no difference. For the Barotse apparently had no understanding of the concept of

has been the idea that the duty to keep a promise is somehow 'self-evident' and derivable from pure reason, or internal reflection.

Indeed, developments in Western societies since Maine's day are widely thought by lawyers to demonstrate that belief in the sanctity of contracts and promises has declined a great deal since then. It must be remembered that Maine was writing at a time when it seemed to many that 'advanced' societies moved in a linear progression, and when Herbert Spencer was able to popularize the idea that the advancing tide of freedom of contract would eventually cause all State coercion to wither away. Today, we are all well aware that freedom of choice and freedom of contract have greatly receded from the high tide of Victorian liberalism and *laissez-faire*. But the declining belief in freedom of contract among lawyers (as well as the politicians, who today make most of the law and the public who elect them) does not yet seem to have been matched by a corresponding decline in belief in the sanctity of promises among many philosophers. Certainly, there was no sign of this in the 1930s. To the contemporary lawyer, the writings of Ross bear a curiously faded, old-fashioned appearance today. No doubt many of the lawyers of Ross's own times would have found his views still quite acceptable, but today the right place for these views seems to have been Victorian England.

Subjectivism

Subjectivism—if one can treat it as one phenomenon—involves a radical break with most previous theories of ethics. It begins by rejecting the idea that an ethical statement is a proposition like a factual statement. To say (for example) that 'breaking a promise is wrong' does not state a proposition which can be verified; indeed, in certain extreme versions, it is vigorously argued that this states no proposition at all, and is literally a meaningless statement. For example, A. J. Ayer, in his celebrated book, *Language, Truth and Logic*, insisted that to say 'stealing money is wrong' is 'to produce a sentence which has no factual meaning—that is,

expectation damages; and they thus only enforced promise-breaking when they found a 'loss', i.e. where the promisor had benefited from the transaction, or the promisee had relied to his detriment upon the promise. See also Farnsworth, 'The Past of Promises : An Historical Introduction to Contract', 69 *Columbia Law Rev.* 576 (1965). Cf. Mary Midgley, 'The Game Game', 49 *Philosophy* 231 (1974), who asserts, without citing any sources, that anthropology has shown that promising is an essential feature of all human societies.

expresses no proposition which can be either true or false'.[19]
Ethical judgments, therefore, far from having some 'absolute'
validity which 'is mysteriously independent of ordinary sense-
experience', have in truth no objective validity at all.[20] All moral
judgments are, it seems, value-judgments which are entirely
subjective. They may express the feelings of the speaker, or they
may be designed to persuade or move others to share those feelings, or to behave in certain ways. Thus to say (for instance)
'promises ought to be kept' is only a way of saying 'it makes me
feel unhappy (or insecure, or even sick) if a promise is not kept';
or, alternatively, it might 'mean' 'I think promises ought to be
kept, and I want you to think and act accordingly'.

In the hand of C. L. Stevenson[21] and of J. L. Austin,[22] the idea
that one can *do* things with words, as well as say things, was
developed and refined. It came to be seen that words often have
the purpose of expressing tastes, making decisions, criticizing,
praising, grading, persuading, and so on. Stevenson, in particular, stressed the 'emotive' significance of words, and the
concept of 'emotive language' has now become part of the common currency of speech. To Stevenson, '[t]he emotive meaning
of a word is the power the word acquires, on account of its history
in emotional situations, to evoke or directly express attitudes,
as distinct from describing or designating them.'[23] In modern
usage, the term 'emotive' is often used in a somewhat wider
sense, so as to include, for example, the power derived from the
metaphorical use of language. And of all metaphors, none is
more clearly relevant to this work, than the notion of being
'bound', or of making a 'binding' promise or contract.

In the years that have elapsed since 1936, much of the work
of these philosophers has become accepted as part of the common
stock of ideas of educated people. Few would any longer argue
that to pass a moral judgment is in any sense to make a statement of fact. The distinction between verifiable propositions
and value-judgments is accepted by the common man as well
as by philosophers. Moreover, subjectivism has lost some of
its most extreme characteristics. Few would now insist that
moral judgments are *entirely* subjective, and this has helped to

---

[19] 2nd edn. (London, 1946), p. 107.
[20] Ibid., pp. 108-9.
[21] *Ethics and Language* (New Haven and London, 1944).
[22] *How to do Things with Words* (Oxford, 1962).
[23] Op. cit., p. 33.

eliminate some of the more alarming implications of subjectivism. For it is now widely agreed than when people use moral language, it is normally implicit that they are expressing opinions which are at least likely to be generally shared, even if they do not have universal, or 'absolute' validity. Of course, moral judgments will disagree, but '[it] is precisely a mark of morality that *de gustibus non disputandum* is a maxim which does not apply to it'.[24] Subjective morality, in short, does not have to be entirely subjective. To deny that there is an objective, observable, sense of 'good' does not involve saying that 'good' means no more than 'I like it', or 'I approve of it', or 'You ought to do it'. It can also be used (and generally is used) to mean: 'Most people (under ordinary conditions) like it, or approve it, etc.' Indeed, this is usually implied when one uses ordinary commendatory words. So, to say 'You ought to do this', or 'A promise is binding so you ought to keep it', does not only mean, '*I think* this, but others may think differently'. It usually means, 'Most people, under ordinary circumstances, would think this was something you ought to do',[25] or perhaps, 'An ideal and impartial observer would think this was something you ought to do.'[26]

For the lawyer, the problem is somewhat complicated by the fact that even the most extreme statement of the subjective position has never doubted that some statements of the form 'This is good' may be used in a descriptive sense, in an appropriate context. This is, perhaps, best brought out in that form of subjectivism known as 'prescriptivism' which owes its origins to the work of Professor R. M. Hare.[27] Hare stresses that 'ought' sentences can be of three types. They may be purely descriptive sentences, as when the speaker is explaining the norms or conventions of a society or institution. Or they may be statements of psychological fact, as where a person states that he *feels* he ought to do something. But thirdly, they may be value-judgments, and in particular, moral value-judgments. Statements of the first two types do not 'entail an imperative': a person may say, without self-contradiction, that (according to the prevailing customs) '*X* is the right thing to do', or '*X* ought to be done', and go on to add, 'but I don't advise you to do it'. Similarly, a person may say, 'Somehow I *feel* that is wrong of *A* to do *X*, but I know

---

[24] B. Williams, *Morality,* p. 31.
[25] See generally, P. Nowell-Smith, *Ethics,* especially Chaps. 5 and 6.
[26] See G. Harman, *The Nature of Morality* (New York, 1977), Chap. 4.
[27] In particular, *The Language of Morals.*

that this is irrational and I couldn't honestly advise him against doing it.' On the other hand, a statement of the third type, according to Hare, entails an imperative. It is logically contradictory to say, 'Morally, you ought to do this, but I don't advise you to do it.' Since the primary purpose of moral judgments is 'to prescribe, or advise, or instruct',[28] it is contradictory, to say that, in a particular situation, a person's moral duty is to do something, but then to advise him not to do it. But that is not all. Moral judgments must be 'universalizable'. Once a person assents to a moral judgment, he must (logically) accept the validity of that judgment in all relevantly identical circumstances. So if a person assents to the moral judgment that, in a particular situation, a person ought to behave in a particular way—say, ought to keep a promise—it follows (logically) that he is bound to treat the duty to keep a promise as a moral principle applicable in all relevantly identical circumstances.

Hare readily concedes (as I have said) that 'ought' statements of a purely descriptive character are very commonly made. Moreover, in some circumstances, the prevailing customs, or conventions, are so generally accepted by speakers and listeners that it may be difficult to tell whether an 'ought' statement is descriptive or evaluative. Particularly where speaker and listener are both members of some institutional group, 'ought' propositions may be made which are only descriptive of the institution's conventions or practices. This is, of course, particularly the case where lawyers are concerned. To say, for example, 'This contract is binding' may not carry any implications at all about the feelings or wishes of the speaker, if he is merely describing what the legal system regards as a binding contract.

Another reason why subjectivism is now generally less extreme and alarming than it seemed to threaten at one time, is that it does not necessarily rule out *argument* about values and ethical judgments. It may be true that, at the end of the day, argument may run out, and we may then, as Ayer says, 'resort to mere abuse',[29] but there is a good deal to be said before we reach that stage. It is not only that the facts underlying ethical judgments are themselves frequently the source of controversies which often appear to be purely about values; of course, nobody disputes that, in such circumstances, there is scope for rational

---

[28] Ibid., p. 159.
[29] *Language, Truth and Logic*, 2nd edn., p. 111.

argument. But even where the facts are not in issue, there is some room for argument and rational controversy before combatants descend to Ayer's stage of 'mere abuse'. Value-judgments of a non-ethical nature, such as artistic criticism, are an obvious example of judgments about which much can be said. And it is possible, too, to have experts of a sort, literary and artistic critics, for instance, or even, to take an example from a more extremely subjective sphere, wine-tasters or tea-tasters.

For the lawyer, the admission that argument is possible about value-judgments, even though, in the end, the decision cannot perhaps be settled by such argument, is an important point. One reason why English lawyers (especially judges) often resist the idea that the law requires policy choices to be made, is that they sometimes seem to think this means that cases must be decided according to the personal value system of the judge. They often appear unaware that articulated justification of policy decisions can be made without necessarily falling back on personal value choices.[30] But apart from cases of this character, where the judge's task is to apply law, judges are today often called upon to exercise discretions. Lawyers are now often required to argue cases before a judge in which the arguments are not directed to persuade the judge what the law is, but to persuade him to exercise a discretion in a particular direction. Argument of this nature can often follow traditional legal patterns in some respects (for instance, in the use made of precedent) but in other respects it involves a more open appeal to the sense of fairness and equity.

I have already pointed out that few metaphorical expressions carry a greater emotive power than the notion of the 'binding' contract. Now it is arguable that many legal rules, and still more the manner, and concepts in which they are expressed, are designed to have powerful emotive functions. Take, for example, the rules (to which I adverted in Chapter 1) which require a party complaining of a breach of contract to mitigate his loss, the result of which is often to deprive the promisee of any right to sue for breach of contract at all. Now the lawyer does not hesitate to say that in such a case, the contract is and remains throughout 'binding'; he only qualifies this by adding that if

---

[30] For an attempt to explore this issue in the legal context, see R. S. Summers, 'Two Types of Substantive Reasons: The Core of a Theory of Common-Law Justification', 63 *Cornell Law Rev.* 707 (1978).

there is no 'loss' as a result of the breach, no damages can be awarded.

I have previously pointed out that, to the realist lawyer, there is some unreality in saying that a contract is 'binding' while conceding that it may be broken with impunity. But it is arguable that, in adopting this kind of terminology, and this kind of conceptual apparatus, lawyers have, albeit unconsciously, made use of the emotive force of language. Even where it is shown that no harm will ensue or has ensued from a breach of contract, and where, in consequence, no legal remedy is available, lawyers still prefer to regard the contract as in some sense 'binding', in much the same way that some philosophers regard a moral duty as somehow continuing to subsist, even though it may be overridden in the particular circumstances of a case. To override it is not the same as to eliminate it as a relevant consideration.

In a legal context, the concept of the emotive uses of language is possibly suggestive of an élitist institution where it is desirable that people should be persuaded to observe legal rules as a matter of habit and even intuitively, without always pausing to examine whether it is in the particular circumstances of the case best to do so. But in the moral context, emotive theories only take us part of the way. It may be helpful to appreciate that the concept of a 'binding' promise (if it is not being used in a descriptive sense) is simply expressive of the speaker's desire that the promise be kept; but this does not tell us why (in our sort of society) people commonly have this desire, nor whether it is, in a social or utilitarian sense, a 'good thing' that they have this desire.

An extreme subjectivist might answer that any further inquiry would be either of a psychological or of an empirical nature. To explore the origins of people's moral beliefs (about promises or anything else) is to study the psychology of human beings in various social situations, the effect and nature of moral training, and so forth. With that, this book has nothing to do. But alternatively, it might involve some empirical inquiry into the actual consequences of the moral belief in question, and what consequences would ensue if the belief did not exist, or existed in a modified form. The utilitarian would, of course, concur in thinking that an empirical inquiry of this sort would be useful. Not only would it be useful to know whether an existing moral principle increases the sum of human good, but it would also be useful to know whether even more good might follow from some modification of the principle. At the end of the day, it is no doubt necessary to acknowledge that no answer, even in principle, to these questions is possible, because they all depend upon subjective views as to what, indeed, is good. At that point, the utilitarian and the subjectivist may have to part company. If, for instance, it is the case that promises increases the possibility of cooperation among human beings, but the subjectivist takes the view that the ultimate good has nothing to do with social relations, and depends entirely on a man's internal communion with his soul, then he may reject the idea that promises are a 'good thing'. But in the meantime, some clarification, at least may have been achieved.

Performatives and Promises

The idea that certain words, or formations of words, are used to *do* something rather than to assert something is, of course, derived from the work of J. L. Austin.[31] The use of certain verbs, particularly in the first person singular form, was identified by Austin as having this 'performative' function. Thus, when a person says, for example, 'I applaud', or 'I warn', or 'I reprimand', he actually does these things in the act of saying them. Similarly, to say 'I promise' is not to assert something, but to do something, to place oneself under an obligation. Promising is an act, a 'speech act' whose purpose is to place oneself under an obligation; and if one performs the act correctly the result is to create an obligation.

It is, on this view, a mistake to think that a promise asserts anything. It does not contain any propositions which the promisor is asserting, or stating. It is not a statement which can be subject to verification, and there is, therefore, no question of a promise being true or false. Austin actually invoked the analogy of the law, and suggested that a performative was something like what lawyers referred to as 'operative words'.[32]

---

[31] *How to do Things with Words;* 'Performative Utterances', in *Philosophical Papers* ed. J. O. Urmson and G. J. Warnock (2nd edn., Oxford, 1962). Among Austin's many followers are G. R. Grice, *The Grounds of Moral Judgment*, pp. 41 ff.; H. Jack, 'On the Analysis of Promises', LV *J. of Philosophy* 597 (1958); David Jones, 'Making and Keeping Promises', 76 *Ethics* 287 (1965-6); for J. R. Searle's views, see *post*, p. 101.

[32] *Philosophical Papers* (2nd edn.), pp. 222-3.

But although a performative, or a speech act, does not assert anything, and so cannot be false, it may, according to Austin, somehow misfire, or be 'infelicitous' in a related, though different manner. A performative, in his view, 'misfires' if it doesn't work, if the necessary conditions don't exist for the word to perform the act it is supposed to. But there are also other forms of 'infelicities', as for example, a promise which the promisor does not intend to perform. This is not a 'misfire' because the promise creates the necessary obligation, but it is somehow wrong all the same. So also, a promise to sell something which does not exist may be void for lack of reference, or for ambiguity. One consequence of this theory, which may be of some importance, is to stress that there may be an important distinction between the significance of saying, 'I promise' and saying, 'I promised', or, indeed, 'You promised'. In the first phrase, the verb is used performatively; in the second, it is used descriptively. Similarly, the expression 'your promise' may refer either to an act of promising or to the content or result of a promise.[33] The importance of this lies in the fact that although one may promise by using the performative, 'I promise', it is also possible to promise in many ways which do not involve use of the performative, or, indeed, any words at all. Consequently, there is a descriptive sense to the word 'promise' in 'I promised' while there is none in the performative, 'I promise'. It is possible that those who take the performative, 'I promise' as the paradigm way of creating a promissory obligation, tend in the result to feel that other ways of creating obligations are somehow not truly promissory, even though they would be covered by normal use of 'promise' in a broad descriptive way.

As we have previously seen, the utilitarian basically takes the binding force of promises to come from the expectations and reliance which they generate, and in the attempt to avoid a *petitio principii* (whether successfully or not) he argues that promises do contain or imply assertions. These are nearly always assumed to be assertions about the promisor's future conduct. Thus the utilitarian and the performative theories are fundamentally opposed on this point. The utilitarian says that a promise implies or asserts that the promisor intends to do something; the performative theorist declares that it makes no such assertion, but simply creates an obligation to do the act promised.

---

[33] Forguson, 'Locutionary and Illocutionary Acts', in *Essays on J. L. Austin,* by I. Berlin and others (Oxford, 1973), p. 183.

Of course, some things are generally agreed. Thus, few would deny that it is possible to promise without using the performative, 'I promise'. Nor, again, would it be denied that a person often may declare his intention to do X, *and* promise to do X. Still further, it would be generally agreed that a person may say he intends to do something in such an emphatic manner that, given other appropriate circumstances, his statement amounts to, or includes, a promise. But what does divide the theories sharply is whether a promise can be seen as merely a declaration of intention *plus* something else which creates the obligation. The utilitarian thinks this is the case, and the 'something else' is the element of expectation and reliance; the performative theorist finds it difficult to identify any additional element which creates the obligation.[34]

What is that extra something which creates the obligation? The natural temptation is to say that it is the intention of the speaker to commit himself to an obligation; but once it is conceded that even the dishonest speaker who intends to make no such commitment is bound by a promise, it becomes exceedingly difficult to formulate any other set of conditions which explain what is to count as a promise. It is this, I think, that explains the great difficulty which Searle encountered when he tried to formulate the necessary and sufficient conditions under which an utterance may be said to count as a promise.[35] He did not commit himself to the idea that the speaker must intend to perform the promise; but he nevertheless argued for two other states of mind which he thought necessary: first, that the speaker must intend his utterance to place him under an obligation, and secondly, he must intend that the utterance 'will make him responsible for intending' to do the act promised. These are surely open to grave objection. First, it is hard to see why a person must intend to place himself under an obligation by his utterance, if he has no intention of keeping the promise. The dishonest promisor surely intends neither to perform the promise nor to assume any obligation to do so. What he wants is to persuade the promisee

---

[34] A third alternative is suggested by Hanfling, 'Promises, Games and Institution', *Proc. Arist. Soc.* 13 (1975), namely that the expression 'I promise' derives its additional obligation-creating power, not from being *per se* a performative, but because it is used only in circumstances in which an obligation would arise. In such a case even 'I will' would create an obligation. But this is difficult to sustain because it involves saying that 'I promise' will only create an obligation where 'I will' would do so, surely an extravagant argument.

[35] J. R. Searle, 'What is a Speech Act?', in *The Philosophy of Language*, p. 39.

to think that he means to perform the promise. As for Searle's second condition, one is left boggling at the state of mind of the speaker who is deemed to have the intention to make himself responsible for intending to do what he has said he will do. I confess to a total inability to imagine what this state of mind can be.

It is surely clear that these are desperate attempts to salvage some element of intentionality to the obligation resulting from a promise, and that they simply will not do. An alternative, and perhaps simpler, suggestion is that a promisor need only communicate to the promisee an intention to assume an obligation.[36] In this formulation it is immaterial whether or not the promisor actually has the intention which he communicates, though it leaves open the question whether he must at least intend to communicate an intention to assume an obligation. In law, it is clear that he need not have the intention to do this—he may do it inadvertently, and many moral philosophers would agree with this result. But at any rate, on this view, the one thing necessary, in addition to the actual performance of the speech act, is that the act communicates the intent to assume an obligation, i.e. persuades the listener that the speaker intends to assume an obligation. Put in this way, there is little that a lawyer would need to quarrel with, provided that it is recognized that these are still not sufficient conditions for the creation of an obligation. Moreover, put in this way, the performative theory must still presuppose a great deal; in particular it must presuppose the desirability of permitting individuals to create relationships amongst themselves by merely communicating their intention to assume obligations. The theory thus begins to look increasingly vacuous. A speech act like 'I promise' is now regarded as creating a moral obligation only, (1) if we presuppose the desirability of a moral principle which enables people to bind themselves by obligations in this way, and (2) if the particular circumstances under which the speech act is performed fall into the class of circumstances in which it is desirable that such obligations should be capable of being so created.[37]

The performative theory of promising thus leaves much unexplained. It may illuminate certain verbal forms, but it does not really explain how and why the form 'I promise' actually creates an obligation. Moral obligations normally arise from

---

[36] See e.g. J. Raz, 'Promises and Obligations', in *Law, Morality and Society,* ed. Raz and Hacker (Oxford, 1977), p. 210.

[37] Raz, ibid., concedes both these points.

what people *do*, for example, in rendering benefits to their neighbours (creating obligations of reciprocity) or in harming their
neighbours (creating obligations to compensate).[38] But a performative, though it may be called a speech act, still resembles
words rather than actions, in that it does not *by itself* create physical consequences. And even if it did, it is not the consequences
which create the obligation. The performative theorist is insistent
that the act creates an obligation simply because it is an obligation-creating sort of act. Put in this fashion, it is not obvious
that the theory has much explanatory power. The difficulty,
as H. A. Prichard pointed out long before the theory of performatives was born,[39] is to see how one can create a moral obligation
just by saying that one does so.

Prichard himself toyed rather half-heartedly with a sort of
contractarian explanation. Promises seem only to be binding,
he mused, if one has first promised or agreed to be bound by
one's promises; and yet that is obviously a hopelessly slippery
slope. Moreover, there is the difficulty of trying to deduce an
'ought' from an 'is', if the bare fact of having made the appropriate noises is to be treated as sufficient to give rise to an obligatory 'ought'. And that is widely thought to transgress the
rules of meaning, for one cannot deduce a prescriptive proposition from premises which do not themselves contain any
prescriptive propositions. Thus it is not an analytic truth to
say, 'Promises ought to be kept', and to call the making of a
promise a performative does not, by itself, overcome this hurdle.

PROMISES AND TRUTH-TELLING

Many philosophers have commented on the relationship between
the duty to keep promises and the duty to tell the truth. It is
evident that the two sorts of obligations are similar. To a utilitarian, both arise out of the use of language for communicating
information. Promises and statements of fact both create expectations, and both are liable to be relied upon, and to cause
loss or disappointment if the speaker lets the other party down.
Is it possible to explain one duty in terms of the other? Both
possibilities have been tried. Ross argued that a person 'impliedly
promises to tell the truth, and is therefore guilty of a breach of

[38] To be sure there is nothing immutable about these obligations. In New Zealand,
for instance, an injured person has no (legal) right to sue for personal injuries, this
right having been replaced by rights against the State.
[39] 'The Obligation to Keep a Promise', in *Moral Obligation*.

that promise when he lies'.[40] But to most people this would seem a somewhat extravagant (and unnecessary) implication; and anyhow I have already given my reasons for rejecting Ross's intuitionist explanation of the duty to keep a promise. So there seems no assistance here.

Other writers have sometimes tried the alternative argument, that to break a promise is akin to, if not, in some sense, the same as to lie. This line of argument has been traced back to a work of the 1750s,[41] but it has been more recently put forward by Warnock.[42] Warnock argues that a promise is not a mere performative, but also has a truth value. A promise contains a prediction, but a prediction of a particular kind. Since it refers to the future conduct of the promisor (Warnock assumes), it is a prediction which it is within the power of the promisor to bring about. A promisor, in effect, asserts what the future will bring, and also undertakes to bring it about that the facts will be made to correspond with his promise. Thus the reason why a promisor is bound to keep his promise is essentially the same as the reason why a man ought to tell the truth.

One objection which has been made is that Warnock's theory would lead to the view that a threat might become binding, like a promise; for a threat is equally a prediction about some future state within the power of the promisor.[43] But this objection fails, because (as I shall later illustrate), threats can sometimes be 'binding' anyhow; and insofar as they are not binding, Warnock's theory seems easily enough adjusted to exclude them. But there are other problems. As we shall see later, it is a misconception (though a common one) to think that all promises must relate to the promisor's own future conduct. Promises can relate to facts, and also to the future conduct of third parties. Warnock's theory would render the first sort of promise (that a fact is so) redundant, and the second, impossible. A second objection to Warnock's theory was in fact anticipated by Sidgwick,[44] who pointed out that it would extend to mere statements of intention. If a man is under a duty to see that statements as to the

[40] *Foundations of Ethics*, pp. 112-13; see also Antony Flew, *Thinking about Thinking* (Glasgow, 1975), p. 77, though Flew is perhaps writing metaphorically rather than offering a serious theory; Paley, *Principles*, Book II, Chap. 15.

[41] Richard Price, *Review of the Principal Questions in Morals*, cited by Michael Clark, 'Obligations', *Proc. Arist. Soc.* 53 (1972/3).

[42] *The Object of Morality*, pp. 98 ff.

[43] Michael Clark, op. cit.

[44] *Methods*, pp. 303-4.

future 'square' with the facts when the time comes, then it becomes difficult to see why this does not go for all statements of
intention.

There are dicta here and there in the law which indicate support for Warnock's theory,[45] but on the whole the law does
distinguish between a lie and a breach of promise. It is possible
to promise that a fact is so (and thus make a contract), but in
general the law distinguishes the results of a statement of fact
from a promise. Indeed, rather surprisingly (as Adam Smith
commented),[46] breaking a promise may be seen as more serious
than telling a falsehood, at any rate if it is innocently told; for
breach of contract, no matter how innocent, is usually actionable; whereas telling an untruth is not usually actionable unless
it was deliberate, or at least careless. Moreover, it is (I think)
never possible to sue in law for an untrue statement unless and
until it has been acted upon to the loss of the agent; whereas,
breach of a promise is often actionable, even if the promisee's
only complaint is that his expectations have been disappointed.
Thus the law appears to protect the expectations derived from
a promise more highly than the expectations derived from a bare
statement. A lie is a form of deceit, and the law is concerned
with deceit because it causes harm; but the law is concerned
with breaches of promise even where they cause no harm, other
than the disappointment of expectations. Doubtless, these rules
may be dismissed as technical idiosyncrasies, but they probably
reflect real differences. The fact is that an explicit promise, at
any rate, does differ from an ordinary assertion in that the former
invites reliance and expectations in a way which the latter does
not. Statements are often made in the course of ordinary discourse, and these may in fact be relied upon; but statements
do not, as explicit promises do, plainly invite reliance.

However, at the end of the day, it may not matter a great
deal—certainly not to the utilitarian—whether Warnock's theory
is sound. There is, as I have said, no doubt that the two duties
are closely related, nor that one of the similarities between them
is that they both give rise to expectations and reliance. So it

---

[45] See e.g. Romilly, MR in *Laver* v. *Fielder* (1862) 32 Beav. 1, 12-13, 55 ER. 15:
'[The Court] exercises its jurisdiction for the enforcement of the truth, and makes a
man's acts square with his words, by compelling him to perform what he has undertaken.'
[46] *Lectures on Jurisprudence,* pp. 93-4. Smith also makes the interesting point that a
person who deceives another with an insincere promise, but then decides to perform
it in order, after all, not to let the promisee down, is a more moral man than he
who makes a sincere promise but then breaks it. Ibid., pp. 93-4.

should matter little to the utilitarian whether one derives from the other, or whether they are both independently derived from their utility. But to the performative theorist, it perhaps matters rather more, for he can scarcely derive the general duty to tell the truth from any speech-act analysis. So we return again to the problem posed by the theory of performatives. If an explicit promise is a performative we must still try to explain why and how it creates an obligation.

Promising as a Practice

One possible answer to this question, which has attracted many adherents, derives in modern times from the work of H. L. A. Hart, though it was subsequently developed by John Rawls in the form in which it became best known. In his influential inaugural lecture at Oxford in 1953,[47] Hart argued that words and concepts like 'law' could not be defined in a traditional way by saying: 'law is ...' Concepts like law presuppose a background of fact, of social and institutional facts. Only in the over-all context is it possible to explain what law is. Similarly, it came to be said of promises that one could not define a promise by saying: 'a promise is ...' The concept of a promise can only be explained against the background of various rules and conventions which determine what it is to make a promise.[48] Hart himself then returned to his theme.[49] Before it is possible to conceive of a promise, he argued, there must be some procedures established and generally accepted, whereby the utterance or writing of certain words or expressions is sufficient to create an obligation. Such procedures, he went on, must logically be antecedent to the concept of promising. 'If no such procedures exist, promising would be logically impossible, just as saluting would be logically impossible if there were no accepted conventions specifying the gestures of formal recognition within a military group.' Hence, the obligation to perform a promise derives not from the nature of what is promised, nor even from the expectations and reliance to which it may lead, but from the use of certain procedures which establish and regulate the convention of promise-making. These procedures thus create the opportunity of promising:

---

[47] 'Definition and Theory in Jurisprudence', 70 *Law Q. Rev.* 37 (1954).

[48] A. I. Melden, 'On Promising', LXV *Mind* 49 (1956).

[49] 'Legal and Moral Obligation', in *Essays in Moral Philosophy*, ed. Melden (Seattle and London, 1958), at pp. 101-5.

they confer 'power' on those subject to them to bind themselves by promising.[50] The institution of promising is an example of a power-conferring institution. In this account, much use is made of the analogy of games. Concepts like 'goal' in football, or 'run' in cricket can only be defined against the background of the rules of the game. These rules create the possibility of scoring goals or runs which would not exist without them. One cannot score a goal or a run if there are no appropriate rules recognizing these concepts.

The argument was developed by Rawls in a well-known paper[51] in which he distinguished between two types of rules. There are regulative rules, which regulate existing activities, for example, laws which control the way in which vehicles may be driven, or parked, etc. And there are constitutive rules which create the possibility of a new kind of activity which cannot exist without the rule. Once again, the example of promising came to hand; as in Hart's presentation, it was argued that the practice of promising is actually created by the rules of the practice. Without these rules, promises simply could not, logically, be made at all. Thus, the performative theory, which says that the words 'I promise' actually create the obligation, was now bolstered by the idea that the performative function presupposes a background set of constitutive rules. 'Saying the words, "I promise" will only be promising given the existence of the practice.'[52]

The next stage in the story came with the publication of a paper by J. R. Searle in which he argued that it was, after all, possible, to derive 'ought' from 'is'.[53] Searle's argument was simplicity itself. To utter the words 'I promise to pay you, Smith, five dollars' is a promise (given certain appropriate circumstances). As a promise, it is a performative which amounts to the speaker placing himself under an obligation. That obligation means that the speaker 'ought' to pay Smith five dollars. Thus from the fact of having said certain words, an obligation is created. 'Ought' can indeed be derived from 'is'. This argument aroused widespread interest among philosophers, though it would scarcely have caused a lawyer to bat an eyelid. It is

[50] H. L. A. Hart, *The Concept of Law* (Oxford, 1961), pp. 42-3.
[51] 'Two Concepts of Rules', 64 *Phil. Rev.* 1 (1955).
[52] Ibid., p. 30.
[53] 'How to Derive "Ought" from "Is" ', 73 *Phil. Rev.* 43 (1964), reprinted in *Theories of Ethics,* ed. Foot (Oxford, 1967).

true that to lawyers brought up in the Benthamite tradition, rules of law have been seen as mere predictions that if a person behaves in a specified manner, pleasant or unpleasant things may be done to him. But another, and perhaps stronger, legal tradition has led lawyers to perceive laws as normative statements, of the form 'If the facts are *X*, the legal result ought to be *Y*'. So to a lawyer, the idea that 'ought' can be derived from 'is' is scarcely exciting.

Searle proceeded to follow this paper with another,[54] in which he attempted to state more precisely the conditions under which the utterance of the words 'I promise' would have the performative effect of actually creating the obligation. Among the more interesting of these was the suggestion that an utterance must 'predicate a future act' of the speaker if it is 'to count' as a promise (i.e. one cannot promise a fact, nor that a third person will do something); that an utterance will only be a promise if the hearer would prefer it to be done, than not (this effectively prevents a threat from falling within the concept of a promise); and that the speaker must either intend to do the act or (if he is insincere in his promise) at least intend that the utterance 'will make him responsible for intending to do' the act. The most interesting feature about this latter paper is, in some respects, the fact that Searle seems to resort here to the methodology which I have previously ascribed to the Natural Lawyers and the intuitionists. He makes no empirical inquiries of any kind at all as to how people in fact use the concept of promising; what is normally regarded as 'counting' as a promise and so forth. This methodology, unsatisfactory enough when used by intuitionists and Natural Lawyers, seems quite absurd when used by those who believe promises derive their validity from 'the practice of promising'. For it would seem obvious that the only permissible methodology is to inquire into the practice. What is 'to count' as a promise, how to make a promise, and so forth, must surely be determined by the rules of the practice. Naturally, there would be difficulties in a sociological inquiry of this nature, and some have even argued that there are no identifiable 'rules' of the practice of promising.[55] But this is wrong. The law provides a

---

[54] 'What is a Speech Act?', *supra*, p. 101, n. 35.

[55] Thus Hanfling, op. cit., p. 52, says: 'What, after all are the "rules" of promising? In games and institutions (of the kind favoured for analogy) there is a system of rules, a system which can be said to constitute the activity in question. But in promising there seems to be just one basic rule—to do what one promised.' See also, Lyons, *Forms and Limits of Utilitarianism*, pp. 192-4; Rawls, *A Theory of Justice* (Oxford, 1972), pp. 344-5.

great reservoir of recorded situations in which people have made promises, or done things, or said things, which others allege to amount to promises; and even if the legal solutions to these problems are dismissed (which they should not be since judges are profoundly moved by moral considerations), the facts themselves, and the nature of the disputes which they generate, are a valuable source of data. I shall return to this in Chapter 6.

Searle's papers have given rise to a large response in the literature, but for my purpose it will suffice to concentrate on a number of key points. I propose to discuss three questions. First, I want to look at some aspects of the derivation from 'is' to 'ought'; secondly, the question, why should the rules of 'the practice of promising' bind the promisor?; and thirdly, the question whether in fact the distinction between regulative and constitutive rules is valid.

'OUGHT' AND 'IS'

Searle's derivation of 'ought' from 'is' was rapidly stigmatized as a logical fraud by a number of philosophers, of whom I can take R. M. Hare as representative.[56] A promise only binds the promisor if in making his promise he is somehow acting under, or invoking, the procedures of the practice, or institution of promising. The mere fact that one makes the promise does not entail that one thereby becomes bound, unless one also accepts the rules of the practice. For unless one accepts the rules of the practice or institution, one is not a 'subscribing member' and cannot be *logically* compelled to accept the consequent obligations which ensue from the fact of uttering the relevant words. Of course, as Hare concedes, it may be said that a person who says 'I promise' is regarded as bound by a promise and so obliged to keep it by the social morality of the society in which he lives; but this is to use the concepts of 'binding' and 'being obliged' in the descriptive sense alone. Unless the promisor *accepts* the relevant principle, or practice, he is not morally, because not logically, obliged to keep his promise. If he does accept the principle, or practice, it would then be *illogical,* because self-contradictory, to reject the conclusion that he must keep his promise. Thus it is not, Hare insists, a tautology that promises must be kept. A person may, without contradicting himself, say,

---

[56] 'The Promising Game', 18 *Rev. Internationale de Phil.* 398 (1964), reprinted in *Theories of Ethics,* ed. Foot, p. 115.

'I promise to do X but I ought not to do it', because, for instance, he rejects the whole institution of promising. A person may acknowledge that, within the rules of an institution, certain things 'ought' to be done, but he may reject the institution as a whole, e.g. duelling. Indeed, one could, without rejecting the 'institution' as a whole, simply take the view that it does not cover all the ground. And the legal dimension provides an obvious example. To say that a person is legally bound by his promise does not entail that he ought to perform it morally, unless he has, in some sense, accepted the arbitrament of the law as conclusive.

Searle himself seems to have largely accepted these criticisms; and indeed, his own papers in effect concede that the 'ought' he has deduced from 'is' is not a moral 'ought', but an institutional 'ought'. But much remains to be said, despite these concessions. The first difficulty in Hare's view is why *acceptance* of the institution or practice of promising should make so much difference. This does not look very different from the half-hearted suggestion of Prichard that a person is only bound to keep a promise if he has previously promised to keep his promises. This seems to lead to an infinite regress, for why should he not revoke his prior promise to keep his promises whenever he finds it convenient? Similarly, why should Hare's 'subscribing member' of the institution not decide to cease subscribing to the institution whenever he feels like it? The fact that he has 'accepted' it does not, it would seem, bind him to continue accepting it in the future, any more than if he had promised to do so.[57] It has, however, been argued that this is wrong, and that once one has accepted the institution of promising, one cannot just quit of one's own free will, any more than one can just quit the institution of marriage.[58] The analogy with marriage is mistaken. Marriage as we know it is a legal institution, so the rules of the institution must be found in the law; similarly, with contracting. But promising, as a social, non-legal institution, corresponds with the mere fact of co-habitation, rather than with marriage; and there is no obvious reason why one cannot quit the practice of co-habitation, so why should one not quit the practice of promising? This, indeed, has been accepted by some philosophers who have pursued the analogy of the game

---

[57] J. L. Mackie, *Ethics: Inventing Right and Wrong*, p. 70.
[58] J. Rudinow, 'Quitting the Promising Game', 22 *Phil. Q.* 355 (1972).

to the extent of urging that one can quit the institution at any time, without notice, and without even informing anybody else.[59] This seems quite absurd, as I shall argue later; but what prevents one from quitting the institution of promising is one's membership of the group which makes the rules, and not the fact that one has accepted the institution.

The second difficulty is that of understanding what general moral rules can exist at all, other than institutional rules, if these latter are to be taken to include the positive morality of a given society. If the whole of a society is to be treated as an institution, and its actual moral rules, the positive morality which is generally accepted in that society, are to be treated as creating purely descriptive 'oughts' then it is difficult to understand what other kind of morality there can be at all. Putting aside the possibility of a divinely based morality, the *only* kind of moral rule now seems to be an institutional rule. True, individuals may *accept* certain other rules which thereupon become *logically* binding upon them, but since individuals may accept all kinds of differing rules (many of them perhaps abhorrent to the positive morality of a society), it is not clear why these have the right to be called *moral rules* at all. To the vast majority they may be neither moral nor rules.

The third difficulty with Hare's critique of Searle relates specifically to the example of promising around which so much of the debate has centred. The problem is to understand how a person becomes (or can refuse to become) a 'subscribing member' of the 'institution' of promising. It is not in the least evident what this can actually mean.[60] Does a person subscribe by making and keeping promises? Or by making and breaking them, but having a guilty conscience, and acknowledging that he has done wrong? Or by accepting promises from others, and reproaching them if they break *their* promises? Can one make promises at all, and still not be a subscribing member? And when does all this begin? When a child first learns to say 'I promise' with some vague understanding of what this involves? Or does one— as in law—only become capable of taking out a binding subscription when one becomes 18? In any realistic sense it is difficult to imagine how anybody, unless he is literally a lunatic, could possibly grow to adulthood in a modern society without

[59] E. M. Zemach, 'Ought, Is, and a Game called "Promise"', 21 *Phil. Q.* 61 (1971).
[60] See Midgley, 'The Game Game', 49 *Philosophy* 231 (1974).

having become a subscribing member of the institution of promising.

The fourth, and perhaps most serious, difficulty with Hare's position is that it concentrates exclusively on the state of mind of the agent, and pays too little attention to the social context in which promises are made, and in which moral rules exist for social purposes.[61] A promise-breaker who justified his action by claiming that he did not recognize the institution of promising might be at peace with his own conscience, but the rest of the community would react precisely as a lawyer would react to someone who claimed not to recognize the validity of the law of contract. In the colloquial usage the retort would be: 'Too bad'. I return later to this fundamental question.

WHY SHOULD THE RULES OF A PRACTICE BIND ANYONE?

Setting aside purely logical arguments of the kind pursued by Hare, it is interesting to note that the arguments which have been offered concerning the binding nature of practices or rules are closely parallel to the arguments which (I have suggested) underlie the binding nature of promises themselves. It is possible to identify four points, each of which has its parallel in this way. First, there is the argument that a practice only binds anyhow if (*a*) it is fair, and (*b*) operates in a fair society. Second, it has been argued that a practice may be binding if it involves mutual benefits to the participants, so that the party who receives or expects to receive benefits, must, in his turn, be willing to render benefits according to the practice. Third, it has been urged that practices give rise to expectations, and are relied upon, so that it would cause harm to violate the practice. And fourth, we find it argued—along traditional contractarian lines (and not necessarily for the logical reasons given by Hare)—that a practice may bind if one accepts it, or assents to it.

The first point concerns limits on the binding nature of the practice, rather than the reasons why it binds. But it is, in a sense, the negative aspect of the second point. The practice of promising binds because it is a practice involving co-operative activity among human beings, which is mutually beneficial; and promises are only binding insofar as the practice is a fair one and operates in a fair society. Both these points are, of course,

---

[61] See e.g. F. S. McNeilly, 'Promises De-Moralized', 81 *Phil. Rev.* 63 (1971), with which I am very largely in agreement. See further, Chapter 6 on this aspect of the question.

elaborated by John Rawls in *A Theory of Justice*,[62] where he sets out to answer Prichard's question, what is it, which looks like a promise to keep promises, which makes one bound to keep a promise? His answer, in effect, is: it is the existence of a just practice of promising together with the principle of fairness which creates the obligation. The 'principle of fairness' is a complex idea; but in essence it is a principle requiring that a person should play his part under the rules of an institution, when two conditions are satisfied: first, when the institution itself satisfies the principles of justice, and secondly, when one has 'voluntarily accepted the benefits of the arrangement or taken advantage of the opportunities it offers to further one's interests'.[63]

The full account is, of course, very tightly argued, and I do not profess to do more than pick out the essential points. Nevertheless, the more closely Rawls's account is analysed, the more evident it is that he is treating the voluntary acceptance of benefits under the practice of promising as the essential ground for regarding the practice as binding.[64] It is because many forms of human co-operation and exchange cannot be carried through by simultaneous performance on both sides, that promising is needed, hence the convention or practice arises. And a person who makes a promise does so for the purpose of obtaining some benefit under the practice, hence it is fair or right that he should be bound by it.

So Rawls's account comes in the end, to fastening on two aspects of promises: first that they are voluntary, and secondly, that they normally bring benefits to the promisor. It will be seen that these are two of the three grounds on which (as I have argued) the legal validity of contracts has always been based in the common law. But the legal view treats these two factors in connection with the individual promise, not with the practice of promising as a whole. If a promise is voluntarily made, the promisor consents to the proposed arrangements; and if he consents to them, then that may be, *per se,* a sufficient ground for holding him to them. Equally, if a promisor gets a benefit

---

[62] pp. 344-50; see also 'Justice as Fairness', 67 *Phil. Rev.* 164 (1958).

[63] A very similar argument is offered by Hart for justifying the recognition of certain obligations of a *non-promissory* character: 'Are there any Natural Rights?', 64 *Phil. Rev.* 175 (1955), reprinted in A. Quinton (ed.), *Political Philosophy* (Oxford, 1967), p. 53.

[64] See also David A. J. Richards, *A Theory of Reasons for Action* (Oxford, 1971), pp. 164-9; John Finnis, *Natural Law and Natural Rights,* pp. 301-8.

out of some arrangement, that may be, anyhow in appropriate circumstances, itself a ground for imposing some corresponding burden upon him.

If then, these two (out of three) grounds for regarding promises as constituting valid legal contracts turn out to be in essence the same as the two grounds Rawls is putting forward to justify the binding force of the practice of promising, has he really succeeded in answering Prichard's question without falling into the infinite regress? For where Prichard hankered after the idea that a promise only binds if one has promised to keep one's promises, Rawls seems to be saying that a promise only binds if one has voluntarily accepted the benefits of the practice of promising. But if (as I argue) one of the chief grounds on which promissory obligations are justified (or inferred) is that the promisor has voluntarily accepted a benefit from the promisee, how can it be argued that the promisor is bound by the practice of promising because he has accepted benefits under the practice? The latter reason is merely a generalization of the former, not a justification of it. To say that I have received benefits from promises in the past, and therefore I ought to perform my own promise now, seems to add little (except reiteration) to the argument that I have received a particular benefit from this particular promise, and therefore I ought to perform it.

But the negative aspect of Rawls's account seems in some ways to be more important, if only because it has received less attention from philosophers, and (perhaps inevitably) lawyers. The fact that promises only bind (roughly speaking) in a just society is a most important qualification on the sanctity of promises; and although lawyers perhaps cannot openly recognize that their own societies are unjust (for the law is a creature of that society and the lawyer must accept its premises), there is, I think, nevertheless a sense in which the law has sometimes come to recognize this. For the movement away from the ideal of freedom of contract during the past century and more has coincided with the move towards a greater economic egalitarianism. The sorts of contracts which were made in the last century between (for example) some of the worst factory owners and their workers, or between shipowners and Irish emigrants sailing to the New World, are today looked back upon with horror. They are felt to be unjust, and the injustice stems almost entirely from the extreme inegalitarianism of the society in which such contracts were made. And even today, many legal rules which have the result of making certain types of contractual provision simply void—no matter how solemnly and knowingly it has been promised—must, I think, be explained along these lines. Consider, for example, the protection accorded to tenants under rent control regulation; no matter what promises he may have made, the tenant is not bound to accept a notice to quit, for he may apply to a tribunal to grant him security of tenure; nor is he bound to pay the rent he has promised if the rent control officer finds it to be an 'unfair' rent. Legislators who pass such laws into effect must do so because they think it is unfair that tenants should be bound by promises of this kind; and although it is not always easy to understand (let alone justify) the reasons underlying Parliament's legislation, such legislation must, I think, in the end rest upon the belief that there is something unfair or unjust about a society in which some people own houses they do not need for their own occupation, while others do not own a house at all, and have to rent those of the former. None of this involves accepting that such legislation is wise or economically desirable, or even that Parliament's sense of what is an unfair society is acceptable.

Some legislation of this character may, of course, be motivated by other considerations. Legislation to regulate rents, for example, may be influenced by a desire to ensure some approximation to equality of benefit in exchange. If only a 'fair' rent is to be paid by a tenant, this may be because it is felt by our legislators that it is morally right that the exchange between landlord and tenant should be an exchange of approximately equal benefits. This assumes that legally controlled 'fair' rents are more likely to approximate the 'real' value of the premises being rented than a free market transaction. But it is difficult to understand how this could be so, unless it is further assumed that tenants as a class are incapable of judging their own interests, or alternatively that the 'real' value of something is not set by economic considerations at all. Since neither of these assumptions is easily defensible, it seems more likely that this kind of legislation is based on the idea that a 'fair' rent means a rent which is fair having regard, not just to the value of the premises, but also to the means of tenants, and the means of landlords. This does, therefore, seem to be an illustration of a situation where it has been adjudged by our legislators (wisely or not) that our society is sufficiently unjust to prevent free bargains, and promises made to give effect to bargains, from being binding.

We may be on firmer ground if we move away from the idea that the practice of promising is somehow underpinned by acceptance of, or consent to, the practice. It is, perhaps, safer to argue that those who participate in the practice agree *in* doing so, rather than agree *to* do so. The distinction between the two was first observed upon by Hume, who pointed out that people often do things in agreement without necessarily making any agreement.[65] Hume gave the example of language, which can scarcely be used except by those who agree in general with the meaning of the words they use; but any attempt to postulate an agreement as the basis of a language is clearly absurd. In modern times it has been argued by David Lewis that the concept of a convention which gives rise to norms, can best explain the institution of promising.[66] To Lewis a practice which is seen to be beneficial by many (or perhaps most) people, and which gives rise to expectations, leads to a convention, without any need to postulate an act of convening or agreeing. And such a convention can easily give rise to socially enforced norms, which may ultimately be felt to be moral norms. And the lawyer may add that once the sanction of the law is given to the convention (or some instances of it), it is likely to grow stronger and to reinforce the moral feelings behind it.

However, to some writers this explanation of promising is fundamentally a sociological one, rather than a moral one. The mere fact that it is widely appreciated that everyone's interests would be served by a convention cannot (so it is said)[67] actually give rise to such a convention without a promise or agreement to observe it. Conventions in themselves are merely arbitrary, and one cannot be bound to observe them without some promise or agreement to do so. Even in the case of language, it is argued that it is necessary to posit an agreement to speak the language according to the rules.[68] Arguments of this nature have a curiously unreal ring to them. Customs and conventions arise from what people do, not from what they agree or promise. It is difficult to understand why they should not be regarded as creating at least some form of obligation even without any agreement or promise to observe them, at any rate where there is some under-

---

[65] *Treatise on Human Nature*, III. ii. 2.

[66] *Convention* (Cambridge, Mass., 1969), especially at pp. 97-100; see too E. Ullman-Margalit, *The Emergence of Norms* (Oxford, 1977), pp. 85 ff.

[67] M. H. Robins, 'The Primacy of Promising', LXXXV *Mind* 321 (1976), pp. 332 ff.

[68] Ibid., p. 336.

lying purpose to the custom or convention. To the lawyer, the requirement of an agreement or promise is particularly odd, for he is acquainted with the simple fact that when it is widely appreciated that everyone's interests would be served by a convention, one of the simplest ways of bringing it about is to pass a law recognizing or creating that convention. Naturally, like all laws, such a convention will bind those who agree to it, and those who do not; and the lawyer finds it difficult to see why the moral position should be so fundamentally different from the legal position. I shall return to this point again, in Chapter 5.

Now that I have surveyed the various points of view about the binding nature of the 'practice of promising', it is worth pausing, before I pass on to examine the distinction between regulative and constitutive rules. We have seen that the sorts of reasons which are commonly given for regarding the practice of promising as creating an obligation to keep a promise are essentially the same as the reasons generally given by utilitarians for treating particular promises as morally binding. In both cases we have the element of consent, with the expectations to which that gives rise,[69] we have the fact that expectations lead to actions in reliance which may cause loss if the promise is not kept or the practice is not observed; and in both cases we have some element of benefit—in the one case, some actual benefit may be rendered which deserves a return, in the other case, the practice as a whole may be treated as beneficial to those who take part in it. This congruence in argument is not merely coincidental. Whenever a particular moral result is justified by generalization, the arguments in the particular case, and the arguments for some general practice or rule covering the particular case, are likely to be similar, if not always wholly identical. And the article in which John Rawls first developed the theory that the binding nature of promises derives from the existence of a 'practice of promising' was, in substance, a statement of the case for rule utilitarianism.[70] But the arguments for holding that a social 'practice' or convention may be binding extend, of course, far beyond the case of promising. Other

---

[69] Moreover, in both cases the question may arise as to the reality of that consent, or the freedom with which it was given. In particular circumstances this question has much agitated lawyers (and recently led to fundamental changes in the law); but the same issue arises with 'subscriptions' to the whole institution of promising, as I have argued above, p. 111.

[70] 'Two Concepts of Rules', 64 *Phil. Rev.* 1 (1955). Rawls, of course, ostensibly abandons the utilitarian position in *A Theory of Justice*.

practices and conventions can be justified by similar reasoning. Indeed, it could be said that many laws passed by Parliament create and are designed to create binding practices and conventions which those who pass them think to be morally right and just.

Now the importance of this lies in the fact that it raises doubts about the *peculiarity* of the case of promising. If indeed, there are huge numbers of practices and conventions which are adopted (morally, or legally, or both), if the grounds underlying such practices relate to the expectations and reliance they arouse, to the fact that they are (more or less) agreed to, or anyhow used by people in agreement, and to their mutually beneficial characteristics, then the notion that promising is *different,* or even in some sense *primary,*[71] must surely be abandoned. The importance of promising in any given society arises from the nature and values of that society, and not from the inherent moral nature or the logical character of promising itself.

THE DISTINCTION BETWEEN REGULATIVE AND CONSTITUTIVE RULES

How valid is the distinction between regulative and constitutive rules? Is it true that it is logically impossible to have promises unless one first has rules defining the concept of promising? This has proved a controversial question since the appearance of Rawls's paper on 'Two Concepts of Rules'. The distinction seemed at first sight to have powerful explanatory force when applied to the case of promising. Constitutive rules, unlike regulative rules, enable things to be done which could not logically be done at all in the absence of the rule; for example, they enable people to create obligations just by saying something. A person who makes a promise invokes the procedure of the constitutive rule; he uses the facilities provided by this set of rules to create the desired result. Moreover, the idea that one cannot logically make promises without a rule which defines and constitutes the concept of promising seems to fit in well with the critiques of Natural Law and intuitionist ethics which I referred to earlier. One of the objections made by modern legal theorists to the Natural Law approach has been that there is no such thing as an abstract or intuitive definition of concepts like promises. Thus, to a lawyer, a promise, if it has any legal significance, must be

[71] See M. H. Robins, op. cit., *supra,* n. 67.

a legal concept, with a legal definition. A lawyer cannot deduce the legal concept of what a promise is by the light of nature; it is for him, as a lawyer, to supply that concept. Nevertheless, this approach has also come in for much criticism. It has, for example, been argued that in one sense *all* rules are both constitutive and regulative.[72] An act of uttering a few words can be described as the subject of regulative rules, which determine that if a person acts in such and such a manner, he shall come under a duty to do so and so; or the act can be described as the act of promising, which is constituted by the rules of the institution of promising. Any act which is relevant for the purposes of a rule can be described in terms of its physical features (a man opened his mouth and made various sounds) or in terms of its relationship to the rule (the act amounted to a promise).

Consider the analogy of the trust. The legal institution of the trust came into existence because lawyers felt it would be (morally) wrong if a party entrusted with property for specified purposes used it for his own purposes instead. Once the institution of the trust exists, it becomes possible to set up a 'trust', deliberately invoking the institution. But the institution was not created in order to enable people to set up trusts, but to protect those who just trusted others. The fact of trust undoubtedly predates the institution of the trust.

Historically, it seems almost certain that the same sort of development lies behind modern contractual ideas, at least in the law. Much early contract law did not emerge out of the concept of a binding promise at all; on the contrary, there are well-known examples in early law of typical contracts which were not conceived by lawyers to be promissory in their nature. For example, a simple loan was not thought to be a promissory transaction: the borrower was indebted because he had received property of the lender, not because he promised to repay it.[73] The notion that the borrower was promising to repay was a consequence of his liability, not a cause of it. Of course this does not prove that, morally as distinct from legally, people did not conceive of loans as promissory in their nature. But it would be surprising if the early common lawyers adopted ways of thought so radically different from those governing moral ideas.

---

[72] See e.g. Raz, *Practical Reason and Norms,* pp. 108-9; Warnock, *The Object of Morality,* pp. 37 ff.; Hanfling, op. cit., pp. 18-19.

[73] See S. F. C. Milsom, 'Reason in the Common Law', 81 *Law Q. Rev.* 496, 501 (1965).

It is thus simply wrong to say baldly that promising is impossible unless one first presupposes an institution or practice of promising which enables promises to be made. It needs no institution and no rules (other than linguistic ones) for a person to induce another to rely upon him (or trust him) and then let the other down in such a way as to generate a sense of grievance. Equally it needs no institution and no rules for a person to render benefits to another in such a way as to raise expectations of reciprocity, so that again a sense of grievance may arise if no return is received. These are cases in which it would often be accepted today that an implied promise exists; and it is therefore clear that implied promises can be conceived without an institution of promising.

It may be less clear how an express promise can be created or made without first presupposing rules which determine what is to count as a promise, and since most people take the express promise as the paradigm case, it seems much more important if rules are needed for this case. I shall argue later that the implied promise may well be the paradigm in fact, but anyhow much depends on what one conceives as an express promise. If a person tells another that he intends to act in a certain way, and invites the other to rely upon him ('You can count on me'), many people would regard this as tantamount to an express promise. But this again does not need any rules, procedures, or conventions. The promisor is merely indicating in advance that he agrees that, should he let the promisee down, he will be deserving of moral or legal censure. The same can be said of the promisor who knowingly accepts a benefit (say a loan) without promising in so many words to repay it, but who indicates clearly enough that he understands that the transaction is a loan. It is part of the concept of a loan that it involves an obligation to repay; and since this is such a simple transaction, it seems irresistible to conclude that a promisor who understands the nature of the transaction must be in effect promising to repay the loan. But the conclusion is unnecessary, and (if the borrower is dishonest) may be mistaken. So long as the concept of a loan is understood, an obligation to repay a loan is intelligible without recognizing the institution of promising.

Nevertheless, although it seems to be possible to understand promising without presupposing an institution of promising, there is a grain of truth in the argument that the institution must come first. For if promising does not presuppose an institution of promising it does presuppose understanding of the concept of obligation. It is not sufficient for a person to complain that he has relied upon another, and been let down by that other, in order to justify the imposition of an obligation on that other. As I have previously suggested, this is, in effect, the argument which MacCormick makes, and which I criticized on the ground that it omits a crucial ingredient in the equation. For the complainant must be able to explain why he is entitled to rely on the other, and why he is justified in feeling a sense of grievance if he is let down; similarly, the person who renders benefits to another which are not reciprocated may have to explain why those benefits ought to have been reciprocated. If the obligation not to cause harm to others by letting them down, and the obligation to reciprocate benefits rendered, are the sources of promissory obligation, as I suggest, then something other than promising must underlie those obligations. In Chapter 5 I shall argue that, in modern times, what underlies those obligations is the social and legal morality of a group of persons. It is the judgment of the group which determines what kinds of trust and reliance ought to be protected, and what kinds of benefits ought to be reciprocated. To that extent it is true to say that criteria must exist for the creation or recognition of obligations before promises can even be implied; but if such criteria do exist, nothing else seems to be needed to imply the existence of a promise, or to decide what kinds of express utterances are to count as promises.

There is, however, one very limited class in which promising does presuppose more than this. It does seem necessary to presuppose an institution or practice of promising to explain the promise which is (in legal parlance) wholly executory—the unpaid-for, and unrelied-upon promise. If such a promise does create an obligation, it can only be because there are recognized procedures enabling this to be done. Promises of this kind cannot arise out of the fact of trust, or the rendering of benefits, for in these circumstances there is, by hypothesis, no trust and no benefit rendered. If it were not for the institution of promising, then, promises of this kind could not be made; whereas promises arising out of trust or benefits rendered could still arise without difficulty.

It is thus a great mistake to overstress the notion that when a person makes a promise he is consciously and deliberately choosing to make use of the facilities provided by the institution of promising. This is probably not how most contractual or promissory obligations are created. However, there are some, relatively rare, circumstances in which people do 'use' the institution (or the law) of promising to create obligations (or to try to create them) precisely because there is no other way of doing so. For instance, in the law, it is not uncommon to find attempts made to give gratuitous promises legal enforceability by stipulating for some nominal return, for example, a 'peppercorn rent', or a nominal sum of £1 in return for a binding option to purchase. Possibly the case of the manifestly illegal and immoral promise may be an example of the same kind of thing in the moral context; that is, it might be seen as an attempt to 'use' the institution (and language) of promising to create an obligation precisely because there is no other (legitimate) way in which one could do so.[74] It is, I think, even possible that the whole business of executory promises and contracts may at one time have involved a deliberate sort of 'use' of moral and legal ideas originally developed for different circumstances altogether.

---

[74] See J. Raz, 'Promises and Obligations', in *Law, Morality and Society*, ed. Hacker and Raz, pp. 212-13.

Chapter 5

The Social Context of Promising

As we have seen, none of the existing utilitarian or non-utilitarian accounts of promising is altogether satisfactory. A fresh start is needed, but before we can make any real progress a number of preliminary issues need to be considered. I shall begin in this chapter with some rather fundamental questions about the purposes of morality, or, if that seems to beg questions as to whether morality can be said to have any purposes, about the point of view from which moral questions are asked. These are very large questions, and it may seem inappropriate to embark on them in a book with the limited objective of clarifying our understanding of the moral basis of promising. But it is imperative that something be said about these large issues, because, as I shall hope to show, no progress at all is possible until we have settled one key question about the moral point of view.

A casual glance at the literature on promising will show that writers on this topic all begin from one or other of two diametrically opposed positions as to the whole purpose of the inquiry. On the one hand, there are those, who appear to be in the majority today, who look at the issues from an internal point of view, and who appear to think that the object of moral inquiry is to assist those who seek guidance as to the 'right thing to do'. And on the other hand, there are those who look at morality and moral rules from an external position, and who are more concerned with the question why people in general should observe moral rules, why it is socially desirable or necessary that moral rules should exist and be respected.[1] Writers in the first category[2] tend to begin by suggesting that morality sets out to answer such questions as: What ought I to do? Why should I keep my promises? Should I observe a moral rule for its own

---

[1] See generally G. Harman, *The Nature of Morality,* Chap. 8; Frankena, 'Obligation and Motivation in Recent Moral Philosophy', in A. I. Melden (ed.), *Essays in Moral Philosophy* (Seattle, 1956).

[2] See, e.g., B. Williams, *Morality,* pp. 17, 87-95; Hare, *The Language of Morals,* p. 1, and *passim.* More generally Phillippa Foot has recently observed that 'all [philosophers] are agreed in looking to the individual for [the] location [of moral issues].' 'Approval and Disapproval', in *Law, Morality, and Society,* p. 229.

sake, or because it is likely to produce the best consequences on the whole? Should I observe a moral rule where I think I can do more good by breaking it? And, more generally, why should I be moral at all? Those who take this position appear to think that the primary functions of rules about promising are, first, to instruct people in how to make promises,[3] and secondly, to give them guidance as to why and when they are obliged to observe promises.

Those who start from the second, more external position, amongst whom can probably be ranked all the classical utilitarians, begin by assuming the social context, rather than placing themselves in the position of the individual wrestling with his conscience. They tend to ask themselves why it is in general desirable for the social group that promises should be observed, or that moral rules in general should be observed. Their concern is with how people in general should be advised to behave, rather than with how a particular individual should behave in a particularly difficult moral dilemma. This does not mean that the moral rightness of an action is seen by an externalist as depending solely on external behaviour, and has no relationship to intention. But it probably does mean that intention only becomes important as a state of mind which tends to make certain actions more or less probable. The externalist's position is likely to be similar to the lawyer's who in the last analysis is concerned with behaviour, but who is therefore concerned with intentions insofar as they bear on behaviour.

To the externalist, thus, morality is fundamentally a social phenomenon. Moral duties arise out of the social moral sense. Generally speaking, this is greatly assisted by the crystallization of conventions reflecting that moral sense. Of course, it can be said that conventions are not themselves purely external. They arise from the moral sense of individuals who make up society, and in that sense can be said to have an internal element.[4] Perhaps one can even say that there is 'general will' which creates these conventions.

Much is implicit in the selection of one, in preference to the other, of these points of view. For example, those who write from the internal point of view (as I shall for convenience call it) often appear to assume that the individual in question *wants*

---

[3] For example, the main part of Searle's paper, 'What is a Speech Act?' (in *The Philosophy of Language*, ed. Searle), appears under the heading, *How to Promise*.

[4] See G. Harman, op. cit., p. 112.

to do his moral duty, but is unclear as to what his duty is; this explains the rather high moral tone of those writers. Some of them appear to dismiss, almost as though it is beneath their notice, the possibility that the agent does not *want* to be moral at all.[5] Another natural consequence of adopting the internal viewpoint is that the circumstances of a particularly difficult case appear to be more important than the application of moral rules in general. The internal position is thus more likely to be adopted by the act utilitarian, while the external position is more likely to find favour with rule utilitarians. Those who adopt the external viewpoint are also likely to have more serious doubts (to put it mildly) about whether people do (or at least would, in the absence of moral training) want to behave in a moral fashion. I do not mean that the internalist may not be deeply concerned at the social implications of morality, but these cannot be for him, as they are for the externalist, the only sources of moral principles. To the externalist the 'mystique' of morality (if any) is simply a way of fooling people, and so exercising greater social control over their minds, and hence their behaviour.

To the externalist, then, morality is a form of social control closely analogous to law, though one which is extremely cheap to operate by comparison with law, and hence, to the economist, 'terribly efficient'.[6] It would take me too far afield to get seriously entangled with these large questions, and I must simply assert my conviction that there are no insuperable difficulties in the way of those who find law and morality to be essentially similar methods of social control. I thus take my stand with those who stress the closeness of the analogy, rather than the differences.

One important consequence of adopting this approach is that it may become impossible for the lawyer to justify the law simply by appealing to moral rules. In particular, if the moral principle that promises ought to be kept, is analogous to, and serves similar purposes to, the legal principle that binding contracts

---

[5] Ross is perhaps the prime example of this approach. More recently Hare, too, has commended the 'high moral tone' of some writers on promising. Hare does take note of the person who does not want 'to be moral' and indulges in an imaginary argument with him, which concludes in Hare's conceding him the right to be 'immoral' so long as he is not also illogical. See *Freedom and Reason* (Oxford, 1963), pp. 160-85. (Hare would not agree that he is, in fact, being immoral, hence my use of inverted commas.) Of course the completely egoistical position is also an 'internalist' one. My use of the terms 'internal' and 'external' differs, of course, from that of Professor Hart, in *The Concept of Law*, pp. 138-44.

[6] Calabresi and Melamed, 85 *Harvard L. Rev.* 1089 (1972) at p. 1090, n.4.

must be performed, then the law cannot be justified by pointing to the moral rule. Something must lie behind them *both*; there must be some social purpose or purposes served by these closely related principles. Indeed, I am in this book arguing in the reverse direction. Just because it is found on inquiry that the social purposes served by the moral rules about promising seem very similar to the purposes served by the law of contract, it seems reasonable to argue that moral principles are indeed social principles.

Also implicit in the selection of the internal or external viewpoint may well be a bias against or towards consequentialism. Anyone who begins from the external viewpoint tends to assume that moral rules have a *purpose,* and since it is hard to conceive of this purpose except by assuming it has something to do with the welfare of human beings in the widest sense, it is easy to equate the external viewpoint with a broad sort of utilitarianism.[7] On the other hand, to adopt the internal viewpoint enables one to deny that morality has any purpose, or anyhow any *human* purpose at all. And if that sounds too extreme, it is certainly easier, from the internal viewpoint, to argue that particular moral rules do not necessarily have a purpose, or at least, are not necessarily congruent with any purpose.

Now I do not know that there is any way in which I can explain why I think the external viewpoint should be adopted in preference to the internal viewpoint. The internalist has many of the advantages of the intuitionist. He may appeal to an internal knowledge of a divine morality; or he may simply insist that, for him, the purpose of moral rules is to guide his behaviour. But it is, I think, legitimate to make two points, the first of a general nature, and the second having particular reference to the case of promising. The general point is that extreme internalism, like intuitionism, largely puts an end to rational discourse. Insofar as moral issues are thought to be worth writing and arguing about, it would seem reasonable to insist that the starting-point, at least, must be a viewpoint which takes account of more than one person. The point of view of the promisee, for example, and of neutral third parties would seem as important as that of the promisor. Moral obligations are, after all,

---

[7] Two modern works which seem to me largely to fall into this category are Warnock, *The Object of Morality,* and J. L. Mackie, *Ethics.* Curiously, given his general approach, Warnock fundamentally rejects the analogy between law and morals, on the ground that there are no moral rules at all, but only moral reasons for actions.

duties owed by one person to another, and it is hardly possible to conceive of moral obligations except as between the members of some social group (which might, in an appropriate context, be the human race as a whole).

But my second point, which is the more important, is that only the external viewpoint enables any rational explanation to be given of the binding nature of promises. This does not, of course 'prove' that the external point of view is 'correct'. All I assert is that it is not possible to give a coherent explanation of why promises should be morally binding unless one first posits a social context, within the framework of which obligations arise.

I have, in the course of surveying previous accounts of promising, indicated that many explanations appear to involve an infinite regress or a *petitio principii*. I want now to draw these cases together and to argue that only by stepping outside the internal viewpoint and taking account of the social dimension, is it possible to escape these difficulties. In discussing the utilitarian account of promising, we saw how many writers have pointed out that there is a logical difficulty in ascribing the binding nature of promises to the expectations and reliance to which promises lead. I also referred to MacCormick's attempt to escape from this difficulty by arguing that the binding nature of promises derives from the *fact* that they are relied upon or give rise to expectations, but I suggested that this argument proved untenable in the end. For what it fails to explain is why the harm which is suffered by the promisee from his disappointed expectations or reliance should be ascribed to the promisor. The mere fact that he has these expectations or has acted upon them cannot alone justify that ascription.

I now want to suggest that there is no way in which we can answer this question except by positing the social dimension. For there is an inescapable initial decision to be made as to the relative entitlements of the promisor and the promisee, and that initial decision can only be made by society. It is precisely similar to the initial allocation of property entitlements which must be made by a State before one can have any property laws. As Calabresi and Melamed have written:

The first issue which must be faced by any legal system is one we call the problem of 'entitlement'. Whenever a state is presented with the conflicting interests of two or more people, or two or more groups of people, it must decide which side to favour. Absent such a decision, access to goods, services and life itself will be decided on the basis of 'might makes right'—whoever is stronger or shrewder will win. Hence the fundamental thing that law does is to decide which of the conflicting parties will be entitled to prevail. The entitlement to make noise versus the entitlement to have silence, the entitlement to pollute versus the entitlement to breathe clean air, the entitlement to have children versus the entitlement to forbid them—these are the first order of legal decisions.[8]

Similarly, it seems to me, some initial decision must be made between the entitlement of a promisor to change his mind, and the entitlement of a promisee to have the promise performed; moreover, that decision arises in the moral dimension no less than in the legal one. There is simply no basis, unless and until that entitlement decision is made, for ascribing any loss or disappointment of expectations suffered by a promisee to the promisor. Once that ascription is made, or at least once rules for making that ascription are made or arise, it becomes possible to argue that a promisee is in appropriate circumstances *entitled* to expect the promise to be performed, and to act upon that expectation. And from there, it is an easy step to the conclusion that the promise creates an obligation. But there is, I suggest, no way in which the crucial element of *entitlement* can be explained except by a decision to adopt the external viewpoint and bring in the social dimension. For if we ask why a person is *entitled* to expect a promise to be performed, or to act upon it, a vicious circle is inescapable so long as we confine our attention to the promisor himself. If we say that the promisee's entitlement comes from the mere fact of the promise, the promisor can argue that this obviously assumes that the promise is binding by virtue of having been made, which is what in turn justifies the entitlement. And if we try to escape from this by seeking, with Prichard, for some sort of promise to perform one's promises, an infinite regress is still more apparent.[9] Similarly, the will theorists must all, in the end, face up to the same logical impasse, from which Grotius could only escape by invoking Natural Law. No person can bind himself by an 'act of will' unless it is first admitted that an act of the will can bind the will. No person can bind himself merely by intending to bind himself, if we stick rigidly to the internal viewpoint. No matter how often, or emphatically, a person may proclaim his intention, and his further intention not

---

[8] *Supra*, n. 6, at p. 1090.

[9] Prichard in fact denies (*Moral Obligation*, p. 173) that the idea of a promise to keep one's promises leads to an infinite regress, though his denial may seem unconvincing to some; and he anyhow admits, of course, that some explanation of the prior promise is still required.

to alter that intention, nothing can prevent him from doing so, or explain why he should not.

The same impasse, I have suggested, faces those (like Hare) who have sought to explain the binding nature of promises by invoking the existence of the practice of promising, and then requiring that the practice *be accepted* before it binds. It is clear that the explanation of the binding force of promises in terms of the existence of a practice is a significant move towards the external viewpoint, and for that reason it is a move in the right direction. But the argument that the practice binds only if it is accepted is a move straight back to the internal viewpoint, and lands one immediately in the infinite regress once more.

So, at the end, I suggest, the assumption that promises do in general create binding obligations entails (if one rules out of account divine morality) a social group whose judgment determines the initial question of entitlement. The fact of expectations (and of reliance) may well be a necessary condition in practice for the social group to make determinations of entitlement, but the fact alone, without the judgment, does not suffice.

If we proceed then to ask how society determines the question of entitlement, how the social group in fact faces these questions, the answer is largely a sociological one. But it can be said that the question can be determined in a variety of ways. Like conventions—and perhaps these *are* conventions—questions of entitlement can be determined by social agreement, or by rule or by custom and precedent, or perhaps even by simple coincidence of behaviour.[10] Hence, once we adopt this external viewpoint and recognize that these entitlement questions must be socially determined, we have solved the sort of difficulties which Prichard and Hare in their own different ways found in the idea that obligations can just be created. Obligations within the social group *can* just be created because the social group is in charge of the rules of the group, and does just create the rules. Since the rules are designed for regulating the relations between members of the group, it naturally is for the group to create the rules. The position of the individual thus differs from that of the group. He cannot just create moral rules or moral obligations by what he does, because he is not in charge of relations between himself and other members of the group.

---

[10] See D. Lewis, *Convention*, pp. 85-6.

Now, if we look at what our lawmakers are doing and have recently been doing in the case of promises, we shall find a number of interesting things. First, that the circumstances in which it is felt desirable that promises should not create legal obligations are today far wider than is generally recognized in the literature on promising; and secondly, that there are a great many circumstances in which no explicit promise is given, but in which obligations are imposed because of the recognition of entitlements in respect of expectations, reliance, or unjust enrichment ideas. Full examination of these two trends in the law would be inappropriate in this book, but taken together they amount, without question, to a diminution in the importance of promissory obligation, and to a growth in the importance of other sources of obligation.[11]

We thus find a decline in the belief that the individual has the right to determine what obligations he is going to assume, and an increased strength in the belief that the social group has the right to impose its own solution on its members, dissent as they may. In this respect the changing ideology of contract law (and, I repeat, that means also the moral foundations of contract law) closely parallels the weakening (at least until very recent times) of the social contractarian theories of political obligation. The idea that individuals can stand aside from the social group, insist upon their own sovereignty, whether in the political sphere, or in the contractual sphere, is untenable. The social group may, indeed, pay great attention to the desires and interests of its members in determining what obligations it should impose upon them, and what entitlements it should recognize: but it is the social group which makes the decisions and creates the obligations or entitlements.

It may be said that this merely describes a trend in the positive morality of modern England, but scarcely justifies it. What right does the social group have to impose its decisions on the dissenter who does not accept the group? And anyhow what *is* the morality of a social group? If the morality of the group is to be identified with that of a bare majority, it may become still more difficult to justify the right of the group to determine how moral obligations are to be created. Where is the legitimacy which justifies the majority in simply overruling the minority? Much could be said on this question, though it would take me too far afield to explore it at length. But two things at least can be said.

---

[11] See my *Freedom of Contract,* Chap. 22.

First, that he who relies on the legitimacy of assent as a source of obligation (whether in political theory or in promissory and contractual theory) may be the slave of a value system as much as the majoritarian who simply insists on the right of the majority. The difference is that the former is relying on the value system of a traditional and liberal ideology, while the latter is relying on the value system prevalent in modern England. And secondly, that there is at least one plausible argument which can be made to give legitimacy to the rights of a majority, which is the traditional utilitarian case for democratic government. It can be urged that majority rule is likely to maximize the total utility of the group as a whole, and so it is for the benefit of the whole group that individual dissent should be overridden, so long as the group has a firm conviction to this effect. Now it is desirable at once to qualify this by pointing out that this is a *likely* consequence of a majoritarian system, not an inevitable one; in certain circumstances it may be found that limits on the power of the majority will actually maximize total utility. I do not wish to pursue this immensely large theme; but I do want to point out that all this is just as true of acceptance (or assent) as a legitimating factor. The fact of assent to an arrangement (whether in political or in contractual affairs) is *likely* to maximize utility, if one assumes even minimum rationality on the part of the person concerned. But again, this is far from being an inevitable result. The experience of the past hundred years (especially the experience of contract lawyers) has shown that, although the power to give a permanent and binding assent to future arrangements may often, perhaps even usually, maximize utility, it does not always do so. Indeed, there is a significant proportion of cases in which it manifestly fails to do so. Too many people have entered into too many foolish, unreasonable, unfair, and even unconscionable contracts in the past 150 years for any lawyer to doubt this. It could be said, then, that assent as a legitimating factor is evidentiary, rather than conclusive in its own right. It is because assent to arrangements is likely to maximize utility that it is so often an important justifying factor in law, morals, and politics. But if it is found that utility is not in fact maximized, then assent can be (and increasingly is) put aside as not in itself a sufficient factor. As will be seen later, I will argue that both in law and in morality, this is the key to understanding the source of promissory liability.

The consequences of adopting the external viewpoint in the

way I have suggested are immensely liberating. A number of difficulties very largely disappear (or, anyhow, are side-stepped) when we do this. Let me take, for a start, the problem about inter-personal comparisons of utility. Now it is well established that one cannot *prove* that different individuals derive the same utility from the same good; but as soon as one adopts the viewpoint of a moral legislator it is clear that moral rules must normally be based on the assumption that one *can* make such inter-personal comparisons. A legislator who represents, and is legislating for, the group as a whole, plainly must, both as a matter of principle and of practice, legislate on the basic assumption that different people derive the same utility from different goods. Of course, since he knows that the assumption may be unfounded, he may well be wise to permit people sufficient freedom of choice, so that each person may attempt to maximize his utility with an optimal mix of goods. But legal or moral rules, framed from the external viewpoint, as they must be framed, need not themselves pay any further regard to the problem of inter-personal comparisons of utility.

Let me next consider the generalization problem, which we found earlier to raise insuperable difficulty to a whole-hearted acceptance of a utilitarian account of promising. The problem, of course, stems from the fact that there are many situations in which it seems best on the whole if a promise is broken, and yet in which this is only true if promises are generally observed. How does one recognize the conflicting demands of the rule and the instant situation? The solution, I suggest, lies in adopting the external viewpoint. If we recognize that the purpose of morality is to guide the behaviour of members of that moral community, that moral rules have a very similar function to legal rules, then we must approach this sort of problem as a moral legislator might. Now a moral legislator would find much to assist him in the law, because the law does have a number of subtle and flexible techniques which go a long way towards solving the generalization problem; and insofar as it may fail to solve the problem in a number of residual cases, the moral legislator may well accept that he fails to solve it also.

Let us look first at the cases where the law does provide some means of dealing with the generalization problem. I do not pause to examine the obvious and straightforward possibility of making laws more detailed, of having more and more sub-rules, exceptions, provisos, and so on: this goes without saying. But the lawyer also has many other techniques to cope with this problem.

For example, he has the possibility of using Equity, Mercy, or some other form of discretionary adjustment. By such means he retains the applicability of the rule for future cases, but sets it aside in the instant case.

A second possibility is to leave the rule apparently standing, but to graft on to it exceptions or modifications which do not appear as such. The use of fictions is an obvious example, but there are other more subtle cases, such as rules which preserve an apparent legal liability but effectively eliminate any sanctions behind that liability. As we have seen, this is a common device in the law of contract where it often happens that a promise is 'binding' in theory, but its breach would lead to no legal sanction because no 'loss' would ensue. More generally, the infliction of carefully graded sanctions (for example, nominal fines, or even 'absolute discharges' in the criminal law) goes a long way towards reconciling the need for the general rule, with the recognition that in appropriate cases, adherence to the rule may not be justified. Even a discretion not to prosecute can be seen in the same way.

Now the result of these techniques is that the law manages to a substantial degree to avoid the generalization problem which has troubled philosophers. It does not, however, wholly dispose of the difficulty. Residual cases may remain in which it would be best to break a rule, but in which, for one reason or another, the law remains unable to recognize that it is best. If that happens, the lawyer can but regret the result, but he must also recognize that it is part of the price which is paid for the benefits of a greater conformity with the rule in cases where conformity is desirable. The lawyer's aim must be to attain that optimal mix which ensues from (*a*) the good flowing from adherence to a rule, and (*b*) the harm which flows from over-adherence where, in one instant case, breach might be more advantageous. If the legislator can improve the balance by redrawing the rule more narrowly, or by recognizing some discretion in the judge to depart from the rule, or by adopting some other technique, he should then do so. But once he has arrived at what appears an optimal situation, it becomes, by definition, more harmful to permit departure from the rule than to require adherence.[12]

---

[12] It will be recalled that I have previously rejected the argument that in the last analysis this is not possible and that an optimal rule cannot recognize *any* case in which more harm than good flows from adherence. This is because it is empirically false to suppose that a rule has no deterrent effect outside its correct sphere of application. See *supra*, p. 52.

It will be seen that in these residual cases the law in no way attempts to answer the dilemma of the good citizen who honestly and perhaps reasonably thinks that breaking the law may in some cases do more good. Adoption of the external viewpoint to moral problems leads, I suggest, to the same result for morality as for the law. Moral rules simply provide no answer to the problem of what the citizen should do when breaking a rule appears to do more good than harm. If we once adopt the viewpoint of the moral legislator, then it is clear that his position must be to insist upon compliance with the rule, while, at the same time, making adequate provision for exceptions, discretions, mitigating penalties, and so on. Of course, the moral, like the legal, legislator may in practice prefer that the rule be broken where better results actually do, in the result, flow from the breach. But he will certainly not wish to say this, or admit it publicly (for that would show that his rules are not optimal); and he would also insist that the rule-breaker acts entirely on his own responsibility and at his peril. If it turns out that more harm than good follows from the breach, the breaker can expect little sympathy.

No doubt it will seem odd to some that there may be *no* moral answer to questions which some philosophers have regarded as lying at the very heart of morality. But the oddity is, I suggest, more apparent than real. In one sense, there is always at least one moral answer to the question, namely to obey the moral rule. But if the questioner is really seeking an answer to the question whether there are unformulated or even unacknowledged exceptions to the rule, it does not seem very odd if there is no moral answer to give him. If the problem was a relatively simple one, there would be a moral answer. It is precisely because these questions are put in unusual situations, where the application of moral rules is peculiarly difficult, that morality is unable to supply an answer at all. In this respect morality is in precisely the same position that the law would be in if there were no judges. Without judges, difficult legal questions would also lack any authoritative answer. No doubt there would be no shortage of unauthoritative answers, but if the problem is a difficult one, these answers will assuredly conflict. Likewise, with morality: in the absence of authoritative moral judges, moral judgments on difficult issues will conflict, and there is, and can be, *no* single moral answer to the question.

Let us now apply some of these ideas to the case of promising.

One must begin with the fact that keeping promises is a rule which in many cases is likely to produce results which both the legal and moral legislator would approve. Social co-operation will be encouraged by the rule, to the great advantage of human beings in general. Now it is wrong to think that social co-operation will not occur without the institution of promising. Indeed, as we have seen, the institution of promising is a relatively late arrival in the development of modern societies. The fact is that much social co-operation can take place without promising, so long as there is a sufficient degree of trust. For example, voluntary exchanges can be made, either simultaneously, or by one person trusting the other, 'giving credit' to the other. Logically, it has been argued that even a simultaneous exchange may imply a promise,[13] but that may well be to read into a relationship of trust or confidence ideas derived from a different cultural tradition. But it is at any rate clear that relying on trust alone as an instrument of social co-operation has great weaknesses. There is the obvious case where one party breaks his trust, but there are also less obvious cases, such as those where there is no trust in the first place. There are also cases of the 'prisoner's dilemma' type where it is in the interests of all that all should do something, but each person may be even better off if everybody else does the thing in question and he alone abstains. The example of vaccination is often given: if everybody else is vaccinated during an epidemic, there is no danger of my catching the disease, and I may therefore reason that I will be better off by not being vaccinated. But if everybody reasoned in this way, the vaccination programme would fail. Promising and contracting can also be seen in the same way. Although I am better off if everybody except myself observes the rule that promises and contracts be kept, this is not an argument which can be generalized. Once the external viewpoint is adopted, the difficulty disappears. The social group will decide that vaccinations, or promise-keeping is in the interests of all (on the whole) and will adopt moral and legal principles which encourage the members of the group to behave in the socially desirable manner.

It is thus a mistake to see promising as an exercise of an autonomous power in which society has itself no (or very limited) concern. One of the lessons of games theory is that there are

---

[13] H. A. Prichard in *Moral Obligation*, p. 180.

circumstances in which the original collective decision to create or recognize norms, like those of promise-keeping, is a necessary prerequisite for individuals to achieve their own greatest advantage. This is the explanation of contract which Hobbes gave in *The Leviathan*[14] and it remains valid today. It has, too, the merit of showing that promising, laws, and the institution of the State all perform a similar function in this respect. For if it is lack of trust that prevents social co-operation, one way of encouraging greater trust is by punishing those who betray a trust and rewarding those who keep faith. To do this requires that an authority be created with power to administer punishments and rewards, and that this authority should then take steps to encourage the keeping of faith. Similarly, legal and moral rules can be seen as alternative ways of encouraging trust and co-operation. For there are many situations in which individual transactions cannot in practice achieve the desired results: in economic terms, this is because 'transaction costs' are too high. If I wish to exchange my house for your money, promise-keeping norms (and legal rules) suffice to overcome the problem of lack of trust. But if I wish you to respect my right to drive across a busy road junction today, in exchange for my recognizing your right to do the same tomorrow, it is impossible to achieve this result by voluntary exchange, and it is necessary for the social group to act in a more collective fashion by making laws, or recognizing similar social rules such as queuing, or respect for traffic lights.

Now, although the recognition of norms requiring promises to be kept will usually encourage social co-operation and, to that extent, help to optimize human welfare, in some broad sense, it does not always do so. The law recognizes this in various legal rules, and also by the use of such legal techniques as those mentioned earlier. Because the law has authoritative and impartial judges to decide cases of this nature, it is able to insist that promise-breakers *usually* act at their peril: if they are justified in the view of the law, as interpreted by the judge, then they will be retrospectively vindicated in breaking the promise. If they are not justified, then they will be subject to penalties. But the penalties may be nominal, or mitigated by discretions. However, these equitable and discretionary modifications are not allowed to detract from the continued vitality of the general principle that

---

[14] See in particular Chap. 14; see too C. B. Macpherson, *The Political Theory of Possessive Individualism* (Oxford, 1962), pp. 97-8.

promises (or at least contracts) must be observed. In this way the law seems to reconcile the desirability of maintaining the generality of the rule unweakened, while in practice allowing for many mitigating or modifying factors. But even so, the law may and often does overshoot the mark. Legal principles and rules may be wider than is necessary to give effect to particular policies. This may be intentional, because the lawmakers wish to maintain the strength of the principle or rule and think it is optimal to accept some overkill; or it may be done by inadvertence because the lawmakers are simply mistaken, and have invested a principle with a sanctity of its own, failing to perceive the original or underlying purpose.

Unfortunately, the vocabulary and techniques of traditional morality are in some respects less rich and flexible than those of the law. There is, for example, no moral language adequate to convey the notion of a promise which is binding, and yet breach of which is not visited by any sanctions. In ordinary moral discourse, to say that a promise is 'binding' is to say that it ought to be kept. And to say that it ought to be kept implies that *some* sanction is appropriate if it is not kept, even if the sanction is only the limited one of moral criticism. Moreover, even if morality is created like law (as I have argued), it is created more slowly, less consciously, and perhaps less precisely. There is therefore a greater danger that morality will overshoot the mark in encouraging too great a degree of respect for the rule that promises should be kept; the law may overshoot the mark also, but given the discretionary and mitigating techniques used by the law, this is less likely to happen.

Chapter 6

The Practice of Promising

From time to time I have commented critically on the methodology
of various writers who have sought answers to questions about
the nature and sources of promissory obligation without any
sociological inquiry into the institution of promising as it cur-
rently exists in a modern Western society. I have commented
that this approach seems particularly odd when it comes from
philosophers who argue that promises derive their binding force
from the 'practice of promising', but make no attempt to inquire
into the rules of this practice. In this chapter I propose to make
some preliminary inquiry into the 'practice of promising' as it
exists in modern England. This in no way professes to be a
serious sociological study of promising; in particular, my data
come mainly (though not exclusively) from the Law Reports
and are no doubt unrepresentative for that reason. This is conceded without reservations; but it remains true that much may
be learnt about the morality of promising from some acquaint-
ance with the law, and the legal treatment of promises. It is
right to stress that, when people's interests are seriously affected
by what they regard as a breach of a promise, they can and do
have recourse to the Courts for justice; and although judges are
not free to do justice precisely as they please, there is no doubt
that in most cases of this nature, the justice which the Courts
administer is very largely congruent with the moral sense of the
community. Although it may differ from the sort of verdict often
to be found in philosophical writings, this is, I believe, because
lawyers and judges are more aware of the complexity and subtlety
of the problems which are involved. The law is thus more sophis-
ticated in its morality than many non-lawyers might think; it
is difficult to substantiate this assertion without a substantial
treatment of the law of contract and this is obviously not the
place for that. But it is a place for a beginning to be made.

The Strength of the Promise-Keeping Principle

I want to begin by suggesting that the strength of the principle
that promises must be kept is not nearly so great as seems to be

assumed by many writers. Neither in the community at large, nor in the law, I suggest, is the principle accorded that sanctity which many philosophers still think is due to it.[1] Historically, it is of course true that in the middle of the last century the sanctity of contract was widely regarded, by lawyers and others, as the keystone of the social and legal edifice. But the law has moved a long way since then, and this movement certainly appears to have been a response to changing social attitudes; philosophers who still write about the duty to keep promises with the high moral tone that one often finds (for example in Ross, Hare, Hart, Warnock, or Rawls[2]) appear to be reflecting the moral attitudes of the last century rather than those of the present day. It is perhaps significant that a philosopher who has recently made a serious attempt to study the law of contract discovered somewhat to his surprise that in the law, 'the opprobrium attached to [promise breaking] is not often great'.[3]

So far as the rules of law are concerned, it must be stressed that the sanctions for breach of promise, or (contract) are usually very mild by comparison with many of the sanctions at the law's disposal. It is very rare that the law provides for the *punishment* of the contract-breaker. Neither imprisonment nor fines are available as remedies for breach of contract, nor is it customary (except in certain limited categories) for Courts actually to order contracting parties to perform their contracts.[4] In the great majority of contractual actions the law merely provides for the payment of sums which are due, or for damages in default. And damages are almost invariably assessed on purely compensatory principles, that is to say, they are limited by the extent of the promisee's loss. They cannot include an element of 'exemplary' or 'punitive' damages such as are sometimes allowed in other kinds of actions. It is true (as we have seen) that the promisee's 'loss' is understood sufficiently widely to encompass his lost

---

[1] A few writers have themselves criticized the general philosophical tradition on this point, e.g. Narveson, *Morality and Utility*, p. 193; John Finnis, *Natural Law and Natural Rights*, p. 308.

[2] Even J. L. Mackie, *Ethics*, p. 123, surprisingly argues that 'Hobbes's third law of nature, that men perform their covenants made, is an eternal and immutable fragment of morality.'

[3] R. Bronaugh, 'Contracting: An Essay in Legal Philosophy' (unpublished Oxford B. Litt. thesis, 1976), p. 29.

[4] In practice, contracts for the purchase and sale of houses, or land, are normally 'specifically enforceable' by order of the Court: failure to comply is punishable by imprisonment.

expectations, but that is normally the limit of the promisor's liability.

But this is not all, because (as I have also pointed out) where the promisee has not relied upon the promise, and no payment has been made to the promisor, so that the promisee's claim is purely for his loss of expectations, it will often happen that no damages are recoverable at all. If the promisee can obtain substitute performance elsewhere at no additional cost, he is expected, as a reasonable man, to do so, and not to insist upon performance by the promisor. This explains why, in cases like *Lazenby Garages* v. *Wright,*[5] to which I referred earlier, a car dealer who is able to resell a car which the buyer has refused to take and pay for, may be unable to claim any damages at all. So in cases like this the sanction for breach of contract is, in fact, nil.

Moreoever, empirical studies of business attitudes to contracts and contract-breaking, both in England and in the United States, suggest that business men in fact expect and tolerate a considerable amount of contract-breaking, at all events on matters which they do not regard as of fundamental importance. A leading American contracts scholar has recently been moved to say that 'it is perfectly clear that a great deal of promise breaking is tolerated and expected. Indeed, it is so widely tolerated that a realist would have to say that beneath the covers we are firmly committed to the desirability of promises being broken, not just occasionally but quite regularly.'[6]

This kind of evidence may not tell us much about social attitudes to the morality of promising. But there is also evidence from other legal cases that public bodies, at least, appear to have less compunction about promise-breaking today than perhaps they would have done a hundred years ago. Promises are frequently made by corporate bodies or other associations of people (such as Governments) as well as by individuals. And when there is a change in those who represent such bodies, personal moral scruples about promise keeping may be non-existent. Thus (for example) where a local council contracted (that is, promised) to sell council houses to certain tenants, and then, following an election, a new council took office pledged to a new

---

[5] *Supra*, p. 6.

[6] I. Macneil, 'The Many Futures of Contract', 47 *Southern Calif. Law Rev.* 691, 729 (1974). Indeed, Holmes, J. used to argue that a contracting party was *entitled* to break his contract and pay damages in lieu, if he chose. This view did not win many adherents among lawyers, but in particular circumstances it reflects the reality of legal rules.

policy, the new council declined to fulfil these contracts. They were sued by one tenant and put up a manifestly untenable defence; they appealed to the Court of Appeal where again, they strenuously defended on the flimsiest of grounds; and when they lost again, they sought leave to appeal to the House of Lords—unsuccessfully.[7] And it is, perhaps, not irrelevant to remember also that in 1975 the Labour Government invited the people of Britain to decide, in the Common Market referendum, whether they wished to affirm or repudiate the treaty obligations solemnly entered into by their elected representatives only a few years earlier. One factor which played virtually no part in the public debates[8] was that the country's representatives had actually signed the Treaty of Accession, and thus pledged the nation's word. The public debates treated the whole issue as though the question was one which arose *de novo,* and as though the merits of joining the Community were up for discussion.

When we turn to the actual rules of law for the 'enforcement' of promises, we also find (as I have previously mentioned) that there are different degrees of bindingness. As was stressed in a seminal article on the theory of contractual liability, 'the "binding" effect of a promise is a matter of degree, proceeding in an ascending scale which embraces, in order, the restitution, reliance and expectation interests.'[9] If this sounds a little cryptic for those unacquainted with this legal terminology, all that it means is that the legal right of a promisee to obtain recompense for value actually rendered to the promisor ranks highest, that his right to be compensated for loss incurred through reliance on a promise, ranks second, and that his right to compensation for his disappointed expectations ranks lowest in the scale. Some philosophers have recognized that the binding force of promises may vary in a similar sort of way,[10] but the implications of this have not (I think) been properly grasped. At the lowest, recognition of these differing degrees of bindingness must involve acceptance that pure expectations are not generally thought

---

[7] *Storer* v. *Manchester City Council* [1974] 1 WLR 1403.

[8] So far as I am aware, the only prominent figure to raise this issue (in a televised debate at the Oxford Union) was Mr Heath, who had personally signed the Treaty.

[9] Fuller and Perdue, 'The Reliance Interest in Contract Damages', 46 *Yale Law J.* 52 and 373, 396 (1936); cf. John Finnis, op. cit., pp. 308 ff., for a very different view.

[10] For example, Ross, *The Right and the Good,* p. 100. Warnock (*The Object of Morality,* p. 94) attempts to distinguish *obligations* (which one is *bound* to perform) and other 'duties' (which one *ought,* but is not bound, to do). This distinction seems untenable: the bindingness of *all* oughts is surely a matter of degree.

deserving of a high degree of protection, and in some cases are not thought worthy of protection at all. On this view, the breach of a promise which has not been paid for or relied upon is a relatively venial wrong, and in some instances (for example where alternative arrangements can readily be made by the promisee), not of sufficient importance to warrant legal protection. But the point may involve deeper implications, as can be seen if we turn to examine some of the generally accepted justifications for breaking promises.

Justifications for Promise-Breaking

Few philosophers have attempted to analyse the circumstances in which a breach of promise may be found morally justifiable. When they discuss this question at all, it is usually in terms of trivial cases such as a social promise to meet or dine with a friend, which is broken because the promisor's son is taken ill. Now in law, by far the most important justification for breaking a promise is that a return promise has itself been broken in whole or in part. It is the breach by one party of his contractual duties which is the principal justification for breach by the second party of *his* duties. This was originally justified by lawyers at the end of the eighteenth century in the same way that they (and the Natural Lawyers) explained why promises induced by fraud or supervening events might be discharged; that is to say, they argued that it was 'impliedly' intended that the promises were conditional upon mutual performance. Thus if one party refused to perform, the other party's promise did not have to be performed, because he had not promised to perform in that event. It later came to be felt that this argument from 'implication' was too fanciful to explain the many difficult situations which had to be differentiated by law, and that other considerations explained the legal approach. In particular, judges were, and are, much influenced by the belief that it is *unjust* for a party to be compelled to perform a promise if he has not received (or may not receive) substantially the benefits that he has bargained for.[11]

---

[11] Patterson, 'Constructive Conditions in Contracts', 42 *Columbia Law Rev.* 903 (1942). In modern English law, it is well established that a breach of contract by one party discharges the other, *either* (1) if that is the effect of the agreement, expressly or by implication, *or* (2) if the breach substantially deprives the other of the benefit he expected to receive under the contract.

It thus seems that not only is the receipt of a benefit itself one of the principal grounds for holding a promise to be binding, not only that the duty to recompense for benefits is a strong source of legal obligation even in the absence of a promise; but also that the failure to receive an anticipated benefit is a strong ground for treating the duty to perform a promise as no longer binding. So here too there seems confirmation for the idea that perhaps it is not the promise itself which creates the obligation, so much as the accompanying incidents, such as the rendering of benefits, (or in other circumstances, acts of detrimental reliance).

Why are Promises Made and Kept, or Broken?

The above discussion serves as a convenient link to some other questions which are little discussed in the philosophical writings about promises. Why do people make promises? Why do they keep them? Why do they break them? It is evident from the previous discussion that one common reason why people break promises is that a return promise has been, or is likely to be, broken by the promisee. And this itself is some indication of the fact that people who make promises very often—perhaps usually—do so because they want to get something from the promisee which they can only get by doing so. It seems too often to be assumed by philosophers that the paradigm of a promise is the charitable or wholly benevolent promise, the promise which involves no return at all.[12] This is surely wrong. It is of course difficult to be sure, in the absence of empirical research, what are the most common types of promises, and why these are given, but it seems highly probable that they are promises given as the price of something the promisor wants. Promises of this kind do not confer an uncovenanted benefit on the promisee. On the contrary, it is the promisor who often benefits from such a promise, for it is a means of deferring a liability, rather than of creating an obligation. To take a simple illustration, a person wishes to buy goods but has not the cash to pay the price; he asks the seller to give him credit, that is to say, to accept a promise of payment in lieu of actual payment. In a case of this nature, the buyer's obligation to pay the price surely derives from his purchase of the goods, rather than from his promise; and, as I have previously argued, the implication of a promise

---

[12] Rawls, *A Theory of Justice*, at pp. 344-50, rightly stresses that promises are ' often' made to secure something which the promisor wants. I believe this is a major understatement.

to pay the price may be the result, rather than the cause of holding the transaction to be a purchase. Of course, it must be clear that the transaction is not a gift (and that no doubt depends on the intentions and relationship of the parties), but once this possibility is ruled out, the voluntary acceptance or receipt of the goods by the buyer is the necessary and sufficient condition for his liability. An explicit promise alone is neither of these things. If the promise was given and the seller failed to deliver the goods, the buyer (as explained above) would not be bound to perform his promise; and if the buyer requested the seller to supply the goods and voluntarily accepted them when supplied, he would be liable to pay the price even in the absence of an explicit promise. No doubt it would be said that he had 'impliedly' promised, but it is not clear why the implication needs to be made, and the buyer's obligation to pay the price would exist even if he promised without any intention of keeping his promise.

Cases of this nature—that is the giving of promises in lieu of immediate performance of a duty—are very common indeed. But there are other similar cases where the promisor's duty is not deferred, and yet he makes the promise to obtain some benefit which he desires. Two parties enter into a contract on 1 January for the purchase and sale of a house on 1 February. Each promises something to the other because he wants what the other is willing to give. The case differs from that discussed in the previous paragraph because the performance of the two promises is intended to be simultaneous; neither party will perform before the other, and no credit is to be given. But this does not alter the fact that each promise is given because of what it brings; and this also is borne out by the rule that prima facie a failure by one party to perform will discharge the other. Thus many promises are given because the promisor expects to derive some benefit from the promise. But it may be possible to put the matter more generally: promises are given to induce people to act upon them. In the cases so far discussed, the action which the promisor wants is something beneficial to him. In these cases, the promisor *wants* the promisee to act in reliance on the promise. But there may be cases in which the action will be of little or no benefit to him except in the trivial sense that if he wants it, it must be assumed that it will be *some* benefit to him. Because this case is conceptually wider than the previous one, it is the one which lawyers and philosophers have tended to concentrate upon. Action in reliance is more generally recognized as a 'consideration' in the law than conduct beneficial to the promisor; and a parallel is to be found in much philosophical writing. But it is important to appreciate that in a large proportion of cases, perhaps most cases, the action in reliance which the promisor seeks to induce the promisee to undertake, is something beneficial to the promisor, directly or indirectly.

Now it is apparent that where the promisor has not yet actually obtained what he wants at the time when performance of his promise is due, he will (unless he has changed his mind in the interim) normally be motivated to perform his promise for precisely the same reason that he originally gave it—namely, that he wants to induce the promisee to act in some way likely to be beneficial to him. Thus, in the example of the contract for the purchase and sale of the house, both parties will normally be motivated to perform their promises on the day set for performance for the same reason that they originally gave their promises, that is the seller wants money in preference to the house, and the buyer wants the house in preference to the money.

It should, I hope, be apparent now why it seems to me idle to discuss the source of the moral obligation to perform a promise without having some regard to the question *why* promises are given, and *why* they are (normally) performed. If we assume that promises are binding because of some inherent moral power, or even if we assume that they are binding because of the expectations they rouse, or that they are binding because of the existence of a practice of promising, we are in danger of overlooking that *most* promises are performed because it is in the interests of the promisor to perform. The legal and moral sanction thus turns out to be needed for some cases only; and (I would venture to guess) for a small minority of cases. It is needed for those cases where the promisor has obtained credit, or full performance of what he sought to obtain by his promise; and it is needed for those cases where the promisor changes his mind after giving his promise, and before he performs it. Of course, even in these cases, it may be in the long-term interests of the promisor to perform. As many writers have observed, the loss of credit and trustworthiness which results from promise-breaking may make it in the long-term interests of the promisor to perform, even in the two situations I have mentioned.

The importance of this, I suggest, is that it should influence our view of the paradigm case. In much philosophical writing, it seems to be assumed that the paradigmatic case is of a promise which is wholly gratuitous and is given for charitable or benevolent purposes. It seems to me far more likely that the source of both legal and moral obligations concerning the binding force of promises is derived from the more common case where the promisor obtains, or expects to obtain, some advantage from his promise, and that cases of charitable and benevolent promises are the result of extrapolating from the common case. I will return to this point in Chapter 7.

The Intentions of the Promisor

I want now to draw attention to certain difficulties which arise concerning the intention of the promisor. There is, of course, the obvious and initial difficulty arising from promises which the promisor has no intention of performing. Are these to be called genuine promises? Those who believe that the essence of a promise is the intentional commitment, the intentional acceptance of an obligation, plainly have difficulty with the case of the fraudulent or dishonest promise. I have previously pointed out that there would in fact be no insuperable difficulty in arguing that the promisor in such a case is under a duty, not because he has promised, but because he has deceived. However, this is certainly not the legal approach. A lawyer would unhesitatingly say that a dishonest promise was a promise, and that the promisor is liable because he has promised, and not because he has deceived. Hence he is legally liable for disappointing the promisee's expectations, and not just for loss incurred in reliance. If the dishonest party had not made an apparent promise, but a dishonest statement of a different character, this would not be so. I think it probable that current English 'positive' morality would broadly agree with the law in regarding a dishonest promisor as bound because he had promised, and not because he had deceived, though obviously that point cannot be settled by general argument.

Nevertheless, the nature of the intention which a promisor must have—even leaving aside this particular problem—is a much more difficult question than seems to be generally assumed. One of the few writers to discuss this issue is Searle,[13] who argues that a promisor must intend that his words 'will place him under an obligation' to do what he promises. Thus, he says, Mr Pickwick

---

[13] 'What is a Speech Act?', in *The Philosophy of Language*, pp. 50-1.

did not promise to marry Mrs Bardell because 'we know that he did not have the appropriate intention'.[14] A lawyer's reaction to this would be that although *we* may know that he did not intend to marry Mrs Bardell, (because the author has told us) Mrs Bardell did not know this fact. And since, in everyday life, there is no benevolent author to tell us what other people's intentions are, we are in fact entitled to assume that their intentions are what they appear to be. The jury's verdict in *Bardell* v. *Pickwick*—if we can assume that they honestly thought that Mrs Bardell had reasonably construed Mr Pickwick's words as an offer of marriage—was thus sound in law.[15] This may be thought to show that a promisor must at least intend to act in such a way as to make it reasonable to construe him as intending to promise, rather than that he should merely intentionally act. But the significance of this distinction depends on what 'reasonable construction' involves. It may involve merely implying a promise because the kind of conduct in question usually is accompanied by an intention voluntarily to assume an obligation. But it may, *per contra,* involve 'implying' a promise because the neutral, impartial judge thinks that in all the circumstances, an obligation ought to be imposed on the promisor.

No doubt Mr Pickwick's was an extreme case. But there is also no doubt that it is very common for the law to hold a person bound by a promise when he never intended to give one. Sometimes, as in Mr Pickwick's case, this may well be because the promisee has reasonably understood the words and conduct of the putative promisor as indicating that the promisor does mean to make a promise. Even here, of course, if no such intention is actually present, it is not self-evident what is the source of the obligation. Some moralists, while agreeing that in such circumstances, a duty or obligation may rest on the promisor, would derive the duty from some other source than a promise.[16] And it is perhaps significant also that some legal writers think that the law goes too far in protecting pure expectations when they are the result of a mistake or misunderstanding of this kind. If, for instance, the mistake is discovered before the promisee has

[14] Searle also says that even an insincere promisor must intend that his words 'will make him responsible for intending to do' what he has said he will do. I must confess my inability to understand the state of mind of a promisor who has this intention: see above, p. 102.

[15] I said as much in my *Introduction to the Law of Contract* (2nd edn., Oxford, 1971), p. 4.

[16] For example, Sidgwick, *Methods,* p. 304.

acted on the promise, and before any payment has been rendered for it, it is not obviously just that the promise should still be held binding. In legal theory, the promise probably is still binding, but I think it fair to say that a Court would probably find that theory unpalatable, and would strive to avoid it if it could do so. But, in light of what has already been said in this book, this does not show a legal hankering after a subjective theory of liability. What it shows is that—here as elsewhere—the protection of those who have paid for, or relied upon promises, is generally accorded a much higher priority, than the protection of bare disappointed expectations.

It must now be noted that in the law there are many circumstances in which a promise is implied, not only where there is probably no intention to give one, but where it cannot even be said that the words and behaviour of the promisor, reasonably construed, would give rise to the inference that he intended to give one. A simple example arises in the law of sale, where a seller is often treated as 'impliedly' promising to supply goods of merchantable quality, goods fit for their purpose, and so on. Obligations of this kind appear to be imposed on sellers as an expression of the sense of justice arising from social policy; they appear to have little to do with the real intentions of most sellers.

PROMISES WITH VARIABLE CONTENT

I now want to say a little about a variety of other difficulties which experience with the law shows to be involved in the notion of intention in this particular sphere. Too many writers appear (at least in dealing with promises[17]) to assume that the state of mind of a person who promises to do something is a relatively simple matter; whether he is honest or not, it seems to be widely assumed that sharp lines can be drawn between the person who intends to do something and the person who does not. Unfortunately this is not the case. There are many acutely difficult questions here. For example, a person may sign a written document which contains many printed clauses, and which purports to be a contract. Each clause may even begin by saying 'I hereby promise' or words to that effect. The promisor may, or may not read all or part of the document; he probably has some understanding of the general nature of the document, but it is unlikely that he knows in any detail what the clauses contain or what they mean

[17] Of course, in dealing with the criminal law, a considerable literature (both legal and philosophical) has grown up around the question of intention.

or what is their legal result. I find it very difficult to say what this person's intentions are in relation to such matters. Lawyers have in the past tended to assume (with little articulated justification) that to sign a document is, in a sense, to indicate one's acceptance of all that it contains. The signer, by placing his signature at the foot of the document, *intends* to bind himself to all that it contains.[18] He may thus be said to promise to do whatever the document requires him to do. But this conclusion creates great difficulties. Suppose the document contains some wholly unexpected and grossly unfair clause, such as has never been included in contracts of this nature, would it still be said that the signature amounts to a promise to do whatever the document requires? Or suppose that the document contains clauses which are today declared to be void by Act of Parliament, for the very purpose of protecting unwary customers who sign such documents without reading them? To the lawyer it matters little whether or not one says that the signer has promised to perform the void clause, because in either event, it is not binding. But to the moralist, it may matter whether we say, 'there is no promise here at all', or, 'there is a promise but the promisor is legally relieved from performance.' And surely the moralist needs to be aware of these problems. Can he really assert that clauses made void by Parliament under consumer protection legislation, are still morally binding and ought to be kept? But if such promises are not morally binding, while other promises (of whose content the promisor is equally ignorant) are binding, how can the explanation be sought in the intention of the promisor?

There are other difficulties. Contracts sometimes contain clauses under which one party may vary the duty of the other party. An example only too well known to many householders today, is the power of a building society to alter the terms of a mortgage by increasing the interest rate payable, after due notice given. Suppose a person has entered into a mortgage of this character, at an initial rate of 7 per cent, but ten years later finds himself paying 12 per cent. Would it be said that he has promised to pay 12 per cent? Or that he intended to pay 12 per cent? Certainly, he is legally bound to pay 12 per cent; he is treated as having contracted to pay for it, but it is not clear to me whether one would say that he had *promised* to pay it, still less that he

---

[18] See for example, Lord Pearson in *Saunders* v. *Anglia Building Society* [1971] AC 1004 at 1036.

intended to pay it. The reality would seem to be that he intentionally entered into a certain transaction and that one of the consequences of that transaction, to which he is committed, is that he
is now bound to pay the higher interest rate.

Stronger cases can be found in the law. For example, a person
joins a club or society, or takes shares in a company. The association (whatever its form) will have rules which bind the members,
and the person joining will be bound by them, even though he
does not read them or know anything about them. Thus far the
case is no different from the one discussed earlier. But the rules
of an association will almost always contain procedures for their
own alteration, and frequently these procedures will envisage
alteration by some majority vote of the members. Suppose that
a person joins a tennis club with an annual subscription of £5;
we may readily agree that he has promised to pay £5 a year, and
that he fully intends to do so. But suppose now that the club,
by majority vote, with our friend dissenting, increases the subscription to £10. Are we to say that, so long as he remains a
member, he has promised to pay £10 annually; are we to say
that when he joined he intended to pay whatever subscription
was due, from time to time, as duly required by the club rules?
Of course, a member may resign from a tennis club, and if he
does not resign, we may say he must be 'assumed' to have acquiesced in the new subscription and so has impliedly promised to
pay it. For most practical purposes this is no doubt legitimate
enough; but what is not legitimate is to *equate* this person's state
of mind with that of the man who says, 'I promise to pay £10.'
Still more difficult cases can be found where the opportunity to
escape the consequences of the new rule by resignation does not
exist. For example, a member of a company who holds shares
of class A is outvoted on a resolution which has the result of
reducing the value of class A shares and increasing the value of
class B shares. To 'resign' or sell his shares is no solution to this
person's problems. The reduction in the value of his shares is
already an accomplished fact. Is he bound by the result? Are we
to say that, when he joined the company, he must be deemed to
have accepted the consequences of any change duly passed by
appropriate legal procedures?

Now all these cases raise questions as to the precise relationship which subsists between the intentions of the promisor and
the content of the promise. These illustrations show that, in law
at least, a person who enters into a transaction may be held bound

by many consequences of the transaction even though he does
not intend those consequences. Obligations of this kind surely
cannot be justified by saying that the promisor 'intended' to
assume them. The reality is that he intends to enter into a transaction, the consequences of which are imposed upon him by
the law. It seems difficult to argue that, in principle, the moral
solution to these cases differs from the legal solution. No doubt
there may be moral dissent from some extreme legal cases; but
it surely cannot be doubted that (for example) a mortgagor is
morally, no less than legally, bound to pay the interest rate
properly required of him, even though it is far higher than the
one he originally promised to pay.

One further problem needs mention. In law, breach of a contract often has the result of making the promisor liable to pay
damages. The way in which the damages are assessed often
depends on a number of legal rules which may, in some situations, involve much complexity. If, in the cases discussed in
the previous paragraphs, we are willing to say that all the consequences of the original contract, or promise, must be 'deemed'
to have been covered by the promise, or by the promisor's intentions, are we now to say the same for the legal consequences?
It would seem remarkably odd to say that a person who is guilty
of a breach of contract must be deemed to have promised (and
intended?) to pay damages for breach, as assessed by the Courts.
Yet the total consequences of the promise are an elaborate mesh
of the actual words used (particularly written words) and of the
law. Some promises are read in by the law which are not explicitly stated; some promises which are explicitly stated are
struck out by the law as void; other promises are subject to
legal interpretation which may alter their literal or prima-facie
import; and the calculation of the damages, as I have said, may
involve some complex legal rules.

Who Makes Promises, to Whom, and Who is Bound by Them?

There are further sociological matters about the practice of promising on which the law provides some guidance; and here again,
I believe, it will be found that some of the assumptions made
in much philosophical writing are too simplistic, for lack of
attention paid to these data. Let me begin with the question,
Who makes promises? Philosophers nearly always assume that

promises are only made by individual human beings. But this is not true. Promises are made by people acting collectively in all manner of institutional groups. Promises are made by companies, associations, schools, hospitals, universities, Governments, and many other institutions. This fact is relevant to the moral issues arising from promising for a number of obvious, and perhaps less obvious reasons. First, it makes it necessary to recognize that one person (the agent) can make a promise which binds another person (the principal), something which many philosophers seem reluctant to recognize. Second, it is much more difficult to attribute a 'real' intention to a collective group than to a single individual promisor. For one thing, the intentions of (say) the members of a Board or a Committee, acting on behalf of an institution, may not all be the same. For another thing, institutions often act through agents (in the legal sense) such as executives, directors, secretaries, and so forth. Agents sometimes commit their principals by promises which the principal (or superior agents) did not wish, or intend, to make. Legally, there are rules for determining when a principal can be bound by an agent who thus acts in excess of his authority, but there is no doubt that this is a common legal phenomenon. All this naturally strengthens the legal tendency to ignore 'real' intentions, and focus on apparent intentions—on what is said and done, rather than what was 'actually' intended.

A second reason why the nature of institutional promisors is often relevant to the moral issues is this. Institutions often have specified formal procedures for making decisions. Boards of directors, College Governing Bodies, Committees of various kinds, normally have formal meetings, and keep records of their decisions. When a body of this kind announces its intentions, or makes a decision which it then communicates to the persons concerned, the line between a mere statement of intent and a promise becomes somewhat blurred. A public announcement in the form 'The Committee [Board, Government, etc.] has decided ...' is much closer to being a promise than a comparable statement by a private individual. Decisions of this character are usually more trustworthy than declarations of intent by a single individual, because the former are so much more difficult to change than the latter. An extreme example of this may, perhaps, be found in legislative procedures. There is a sense in which an Act of Parliament is a declaration of Parliament's will and intention that the persons concerned should behave in the manner laid down in the Act. In the British constitutional system, such a declaration of intent does not preclude Parliament from changing its mind tomorrow and repealing the first Act. But parliamentary procedure is a formal process, governed by many technical rules of procedure, and, in the majority of cases, taking several months to transform a Bill into an Act. It is, in the result, reasonable to assume that laws will remain unchanged, save at longish intervals (except of course after an election!), and the public are generally entitled to adjust their conduct on the assumption that they can rely upon the existing law. Indeed, we can go further, because it is reasonable to say that legislation tells the citizen how he must and also how he may behave. Those who adjust their behaviour in reliance on the legality of a course of conduct are entitled to feel aggrieved if they are not given adequate time to adjust to changes in the law. It would indeed not be wholly fanciful to suggest that the legislature, by laying down the lines of proscribed behaviour, is impliedly promising that those who do *not* cross the lines will not be subject to penalties.[19] The implication of a promise in such a case arises from the nature of decision-making procedures, and the way in which Parliament declares its intent. It may, of course, be said that any such implied promise would be fictitious, but that depends upon the nature and purpose of implied promises. No doubt it would be fictitious to impute to Parliament any actual intent to assume a legal obligation not to change the law without adequate notice. But it would not be a fiction to argue that Parliament passes laws in order to tell citizens how to behave in various respects; and that if the citizen complies with these instructions, and assumes that if he observes the law he will not be subject to penalties, it would be morally wrong for Parliament to punish him. If we think that that would be morally wrong, it is because we think that people are justified in relying on the law as from time to time enacted, and that such reliance should be protected. So Parliament may well come under a moral obligation to respect such reliance. It seems to be largely a matter of taste whether we say that such an obligation derives from an 'implied promise'.

One final point may be made here about the parties to a promise. It is not uncommon in law for a promise to become binding on some third party, other than the promisor. For example, contractual promises may bind the executors of the

---

[19] L. Fuller, *The Morality of Law* (New Haven, 1964), pp. 61-2.

promisor after his death; in effect the promisor's successors take his property burdened with his liabilities, and these liabilities include promissory, or at least contractual liabilities. Or, again, it is sometimes possible for an owner of a piece of land to burden the land with a promise (for example, not to build on it, or not to build certain types of property), and this promise will bind subsequent owners of the land provided that certain simple formalities as to registration have been complied with. Cases of this nature may be of some importance to the basis of promissory liability for the moralist as well as the lawyer. For one thing, they illustrate what is often thought to be an impossibility, namely that a promisor can promise that someone else will do something; but they also illustrate cases where it is plain that the liability of a person on a promise must be based on something other than his consent. The third party who succeeds to, or buys, property thus burdened with another's promises, will often know of the burden when he takes the property, and may in some sense be assumed to acquiesce in it; but this is not necessarily the case. The purchaser of land burdened with a registered covenant is bound by it even if he knew nothing of it at all: the onus is on him to discover it by searching the register. Of course, it can be said that the reasons for holding such a third party bound by a promise may be quite different from those affecting the promisor himself. But in practice it will usually be found that, in the absence of consent, there will be present one or both of the other two bases of contractual liability, viz. that the third party has derived some benefit, for which the promise is, in a broad sort of way, the *quid pro quo*; or alternatively that the promisee has acted upon the promise in such a way that it would seem unreasonable and unjust if the third party was not bound by it. So once again, it seems that the duty to recompense benefits and to compensate for losses incurred by actions in reliance may actually embrace liabilities thought to be promissory, and which certainly are promissory in origin.

The Content of a Promise

I want here to examine a number of related issues concerning the content of a promise. Most of them are questions which have been extensively canvassed by philosophical writers who have, unfortunately, paid little or no attention to the experience provided by the law.

IMPOSSIBLE PROMISES

Can a person promise to do the impossible? There is a long-standing belief, shared by many legal systems, as well as by many philosophers that this is somehow impossible. For the moralist, the underlying rationale for this belief may well be the Kantian idea that 'ought' implies 'can'. If you cannot do something, it is futile to say you ought to do it; and the fact that you have promised to do it cannot alter this basic futility. But any legal system which consistently holds that all impossible promises are quite void rapidly creates difficulties for itself, which it must then try to solve; and in the end, it is usually found that the solution involves recognizing that the promise has, after all, some legal validity. For the rule that an impossible promise is void is a rule of logic (if that) rather than one of convenience or justice. There are many situations in which it leads to serious injustice to hold a promise to be void. For example, in a famous Australian case in 1951, a Government Commission had advertised for sale an oil-tanker thought to contain salvageable oil, and believed to have been wrecked on a reef in the Pacific.[20] The buyers bought the ship, and proceeded, at considerable expense, to fit out a salvage expedition. But when they arrived at the place mentioned in the advertisements they found no tanker and no reef. The ship had never existed at all; the sellers had acted on totally inadequate information (as the Court found) in advertising the ship. But when the buyers claimed damages for the losses they had incurred, the sellers argued that they had entered into an impossible contract (to sell a non-existent ship) and that the contract was in consequence void. This plea was rejected by the Court which held that the sellers must be taken to have contracted (that is *promised*) that the tanker existed, roughly at the point stated.

Another case where impossibility—if seriously pressed as a defence—would have caused grave injustice, arose out of the old action for breach of promise of marriage. In *Shaw* v. *Shaw*[21] the plaintiff had gone through a marriage ceremony with Shaw when he was (as he knew, though she did not) already married. She had lived with him for many years as his wife, but when he died, his real wife, now his widow, appeared on the scene and claimed to be his legal heir. The plaintiff claimed damages

[20] *McRae* v. *Commonwealth Disposals Commission* (1951) 84 CLR 377. The case is discussed by A. M. Honoré in 'References to the Non-Existent', 68 *Philosophy* 302 (1971).
[21] [1954] 2 QB 429.

against Shaw's estate for breach of his promise to marry her; it was argued that this was an impossible promise, and perhaps also an illegal one. But in the manifest interests of justice, the Court evaded the plea, holding that Shaw had, in effect, contracted that he was able to marry her.

The decision in this last case actually proceeded on the theory that Shaw's estate was liable, not on the main contract, but on a subsidiary implied promise. Shaw 'impliedly' promised that he was capable of marrying the plaintiff. In this way the result may seem less offensive to the traditionalist (lawyer or philosopher) who believes that there is something just impossible in the nature of things about a promise to do the impossible. But the argument, as a realist would see it, is surely one for Occam's razor. For an implied promise of this kind can always be imported into a contract. If a promise to do X is impossible, we can imply that the promisor has promised that he is in fact capable of doing X, or that the facts are such that X is capable of being done. What is the purpose of this circumlocution?

In any case, there seems no general doctrine of English law that impossible promises are void. In 1850 a judge declared that a man could if he chose, contract 'that it shall or shall not rain tomorrow'.[22] And in practice it not uncommonly happens that a man contracts to do something which he cannot do, for example, convey a piece of land to which he has no title. Lawyers have little difficulty with such cases although it is no doubt true that a person would normally be assumed not to have *knowingly* made an impossible promise. There are, I think, two related reasons why impossible promises seem to have caused less difficulty to the lawyers than to the philosophers. The first is that the lawyer is well aware that many legal obligations are constantly violated, and he is armed with weapons to deal with the consequences of these violations. As I have previously pointed out, a great deal of law is concerned with such consequences. Philosophers, on the other hand, have devoted little attention to the moral consequences of a breach of a moral obligation. The second reason is that so much philosophical writing on promises adopts what I earlier called the internal point of view, while lawyers almost of necessity adopt the external viewpoint. If a person conceives

---

[22] Maule J. in *Jones* v. *How* (1850) 9 CB 1, 137 ER 790. Maule J, seems to have meant that a man could promise 'that it shall rain tomorrow' or the contrary, not that a man could make a single promise 'that it shall or shall not rain tomorrow.'

of moral rules as guides to assist him in wrestling with his conscience, it is perhaps natural to think that he feels under no
duty to do that which he cannot do. But the lawyer who adopts
the external viewpoint takes a more jaundiced look at this kind
of question. He is, in the first place, apt to be much more sceptical
about the plea of impossibility, as a matter of fact. What is possible is often a relative matter: with the necessary expenditure
of money and effort many things are now possible which seemed
unthinkable a little while ago. Moreover, the fact that the defendant *has* promised to do the thing in question is, to the lawyer,
at least some evidence that the defendant thought he could do
it, and perhaps, therefore, the promise is some evidence of what
is in fact possible. But even if the lawyer is in the end quite satisfied that the defendant promised to do something impossible,
he feels no immediate need to absolve him from all liability.
True, he might feel disinclined to award the promisee damages
for his lost expectations, but if, as in the Australian case previously referred to,[23] he has incurred losses by acting in reliance
on the promise, or if he has paid for the promise, it is today
almost inconceivable that some legal remedy should not be made
available to the promisee.

THREATS AND UNWANTED PROMISES

The formal similarity between a threat and a promise has been
the subject of some dicussion by philosophers,[24] though not by
lawyers. Both threats and promises are commonly made in the
form, 'I will ... if you ...', that is to say, both are commonly made
with a view to inducing other people to behave in certain ways.
I have already stressed that promises are normally made because
the promisor *wants* something, and this is no doubt true also
of threats. But it is possible to make promises *or* threats which
do not seek to induce conduct, though it is hard to conceive any
reason for *communicating* a promise or threat unless it is at least
intended to induce expectations, pleasant or unpleasant. It has

---

[23] Honoré, op. cit., argues that the Court's reasoning was faulty and that what is
needed is the notion that the defendants had authorized or mandated the plaintiffs to
act on the assumption that the tanker existed. The view for which I am contending
is that to authorize someone to act on a certain assumption is one way of making a
promise.

[24] See e.g. J. R. Searle, 'What is a Speech Act?', in *The Philosophy of Language,* pp. 48-9;
Pall Ardal, 'And That's a Promise', 18 *Phil. Q.* 225 (1968); Michael Clark, 'Obligations',
Proc. Arist. Soc. 53 (1972/3); Vera Peetz, 'Promises and Threats'. LXXXVI *Mind* 578
(1977).

also been argued that to a utilitarian, there is no distinction between a promise and a threat and both should be equally binding; this (it is assumed) is absurd, and consequently a way of
disproving the utilitarian account of promising.[25]

One possible source of confusion should, perhaps, first be
cleared out of the way. A threat is often the mirror image of a
promise; thus it has been said that every promise implies a threat,
and every threat implies a promise,[26] though it is plain that this
is only true of promises and threats which are made to obtain
something from the other party. This is reflected in the legal
rules governing the admissibility in evidence of confessions in
criminal trials. It is a fundamental rule that if the confession has
been made as a result of either an inducement *or* a threat, it will
not be admissible. It is obviously immaterial whether a suspect
has been persuaded to confess by being told he will be bailed
when he has made a statement, or by threats that he will *not* be
bailed *until* he has done so. The only point of importance about
this type of case is that it illustrates how a promise can be implied
from a threat.

But in cases of this nature, what is promised is not what is
threatened, and there is no danger of confusing the content of
the threat with the content of the promise. More puzzling is the
question whether a threat is not, in some respects, like a promise
in that it can actually create an obligation with respect to the
action threatened. Is it possible to conceive of circumstances in
which a threat creates an obligation on the part of the threatening
person? A number of writers have wrestled with highly fanciful
examples designed to show that, even if a threat is made which
the threatened person subsequently would like performed, the
threatener is either under no duty to perform it, or at least under
a lower duty than holds with promises; and examples have also
been given of circumstances in which a promise may be unwanted
by the promisee, although it does not amount to a threat, for
example where a rich man offers money to a friend as a gift,
but the friend insists on treating it as a loan and promises to
repay it.[27]

Once again, the legal perspective may help resolve some of

[25] Michael Clark, op. cit.
[26] H. Havighurst, *The Nature of Private Contract* (Evanston, Ill., 1961), p. 33.
[27] On threats, see Michael Clark, op. cit.; Ardal, op. cit.; and on unwanted promises,
see W. R. Carter, 'On Promising the Unwanted', 33 *Analysis* 88 (1972/3).

these problems; in both cases it can offer much less fanciful examples than those which philosophers have dreamt up.

The first case concerns threats. We can start by noting that even an unperformed threat may have legal consequences: it creates, or is liable to create, unpleasant expectations, and—at least where there is no justification for doing so—this may amount to a crime such as blackmail, or even assault. To threaten someone with immediate bodily attack is an assault, even if no force is actually applied. But there is case law to show that, if the threat manifestly cannot be carried out, or if the words uttered, though in form a threat, show that the speaker does not mean to inflict any harm, then no assault is committed. This is particularly interesting having regard to the parallel with promises, for it suggests that expectations are (anyhow usually) a necessary condition for the making of a threat. The parallel with promises also arises where the threat is acted upon. A person who acts upon a threat may suffer loss or commit himself to an irrevocable course of conduct which would otherwise involve loss, in precisely the same way as a person who relies upon a promise.

In law, the binding effect of threats can be seen with what lawyers call repudiations. Suppose *A* and *B* have entered into a contract whereby *A* is to supply *B* with certain goods. *A* later informs *B* that he cannot or will not perform his contract unless *B* pays a higher price than agreed in the contract. *B* remonstrates, and demands performance according to the contract, but *A* threatens to abandon the contract unless *B* agrees new terms. This is, in law, a repudiation of the contract by *A*. *B* now has a choice, in precisely the same way as he does with a promise. He may refuse to accept *A*'s repudiation, and insist that the contract remains binding (although, of course, in the end, such a refusal will probably be pointless); or *B* may 'accept' the repudiation, and treat the contract as terminated, while reserving his right to claim damages from *A*. 'Acceptance' of a repudiation clearly parallels 'acceptance' of an offer (or a promise which is treated as an offer by the law). Thus, *B*'s acceptance may be treated as completing an 'agreement' by which the old obligation is discharged, though *B* retains his right to sue for breach. Alternatively, *B* may 'accept' by relying on *A*'s repudiation, for example, by purchasing the goods elsewhere. If *B* does this, it is clear law that *A* cannot thereafter insist on resuming to supply *B* under the original contract. *A*'s threat will thus be 'binding' on him. He will be 'taken at his word', not permitted to 'go back upon' his threat. The words and underlying ideas are precisely the same as those used in the case of a promise.

The second case concerns the unwanted promise, as where a rich man makes a gift to a friend who insists on treating it as a loan. In fact a recent case from the Law Reports raised this issue in a very practical way.[28] In this case a mother provided £500 to her son to help finance the purchase of a house in which he planned to make a home for his own family, as well as his mother. The mother went to live with the son, and eventually died. The question then arose whether the money was a loan, and so repayable to the mother's estate (in which case another son would have had rights arising from it) or a gift. The evidence showed that the mother had intended the money as a gift, but the son had insisted on treating it as a loan. In the High Court, Goff J. held that the money should be treated as a gift. His reasoning is not entirely clear, but seems to have been based on the view that the only requirement of a valid legal gift is that the money should be handed over and received by the donee, and that the donor should intend to make a gift. The recipient's insistence on promising to repay it does not create an obligation to do so because it has not been accepted by the donor. The reasoning seems perfectly sound, and it is not evident to me that a moral obligation should be attached here where there is no legal obligation. The mother, after all, did not expect to receive the money back.

All this may be thought to support the utilitarian case for treating the justification for the binding force of a promise as resting on the expectations and/or reliance which the promise is designed, or at least, likely, to produce. But as with the case of promises, this justification may sometimes overshoot the mark, that is to say, even where there is no expectation, and no reliance, we may sometimes feel the desire to stigmatize some conduct as a threat, because it is the kind of conduct which often does produce expectations or reliance, for example, a 'threat' which in the particular case manifestly cannot be carried out. Thus we cannot say that, strictly speaking, expectations and/or reliance are necessary conditions for utterances to count as threats; but it may still be the case that we wish to discourage threats because normally they produce expectations and/or reliance of a kind we think unjustified.

---

[28] *Dewar* v. *Dewar* [1975] 2 All E.R. 728.

PROMISING A FACT

Is it possible to promise that something is so? Many philosophers insist that it is not possible to promise that a fact is so, or that the promisor has done something.[29] Promises, it is widely assumed, must relate to the future. Now—like so many questions of this kind—it is not at all clear what is meant by assertions of this nature, that promises 'cannot' assert a state of facts, or 'must' relate to the future, and so on. As I have argued, if promising is derived from the rules of a social practice of promising, one might have thought that the answer to these questions must be found in the rules of the practice; and the law of contract is the nearest thing we have to a statement of those rules. Now in the law, there is no serious difficulty about promising facts. A promise of this kind is known in law as a warranty, and warranties, in this sense, have been recognized in the common law for over 300 years. A person who sells a horse and warrants the horse to be sound is, in law, promising that the horse is sound; just as, in the Australian case referred to earlier, the Court held that the seller had promised that the oil-tanker actually existed.

It is true that, in common linguistic usage, it might seem odd to say that a person promises that a fact is so; but there is nothing odd about analogous expressions, such as, 'I give you my word that this is so'. Nor would it be odd for a person to promise to tell the truth and then to make a statement that a fact is so. Indeed, since it is generally accepted that a person has a moral obligation to tell the truth, and it has even been argued that, by the mere use of language, a speaker impliedly promises that he will tell the truth, it seems odd to insist that his factual assertions cannot in themselves be promises. If a person says: 'I promise to tell the truth. This horse is sound.', he would seem to have promised that the horse is sound; certainly if he knows the horse is not sound, it seems plain that he has broken his promise. What difference, then, does it make if he omits the first sentence?[30]

Moreover, if we consider the purposes of making assertions of fact, we shall see that they are often the same as the purposes of a promise as to the future. Both are often made for the purpose of inducing conduct in others. The would-be borrower who promises to repay a loan is seeking to persuade the promisee to

---

[29] For example, J. R. Searle, 'What is a Speech Act?', op. cit., p. 48.

[30] Consider too the possibility of the seller saying, 'I promise to deliver a horse *which is sound.*'

lend him the money; the would-be seller of the horse who asserts that the horse is sound is seeking to persuade the other party to buy the horse. This is why it would be perfectly normal to use such expressions as, 'You can count upon it' or 'You may depend on me' indifferently, whether or not the speaker is referring to a promise as to the future or a statement of fact.

The belief that a statement of fact cannot be a promise seems to me to stem from two sources. First, there is the impossibility problem. If the horse is in fact unsound, what does the buyer *mean* when he says, 'I promise that it is sound'? He cannot by his words convert an unsound horse into a sound horse. But the answer to this, I suggest, is broadly the same as the answer to the general difficulty about impossible promises. If the horse is unsound, the seller cannot alter that fact; but he can pay compensation to the buyer for his loss, or perhaps he can take the horse back and return the buyer's money. There does not really seem to be any great problem here. It can, of course, be argued that a warranty is in substance a promise to indemnify the promisee against the consequences if the warranty is untrue;[31] this promise relates to the future conduct of the promisor and thus disposes of the difficulty. But this seems unreal and artificial. The legal result of a breach of warranty is to impose a duty to indemnify on the promisor, but that is also the legal result of a breach of a promise to do something in the future. Does a promise to do X, then also have to be interpreted as a promise to indemnify the promisee if X is not done?

The second difficulty seems at first more serious. A statement of fact does not *look* like a promise in most contexts. An explicit promise carries the stamp of obligation on its face; but statements of fact do not seem to involve this element of commitment in most circumstances. Many assertions are made in the course of ordinary conversation without the speaker having any intention of assuming a commitment, and without the listener thinking that he thereby acquires any rights. However, on further analysis, many of these differences melt away. Much of the difficulty arises because of an attempt to equate explicit promises as to the future on the one hand, with mere statements of fact on the other. But statements of fact are as variable in their content, emphasis, and purpose as statements as to the future. In both cases there is a conventional way of making the assumption of

---

[31] This is the explanation given in Corbin on *Contracts* (revised edn., St. Paul, Minn., 1963), §14.

obligation explicit—by using the word 'promise' or 'warrant'. Perhaps because the latter has largely fallen out of ordinary use in this context, there is a tendency to equate explicit promises as to the future with casual statements as to existing fact. That is an illegitimate equation. Casual statements as to existing fact match casual statements as to the future. And non-explicit promises as to the future match statements of fact which are held by impartial third parties (such as judges) to create an obligation. We thus have a threefold classification which fits both statements as to the future and statements as to existing fact:

(1) Explicit assumptions of obligation, by promising or warranting.

(2) Casual statements as to the future *or* fact which give rise to no obligation, for example, because reliance on them would be unreasonable.

(3) Statements as to the future or fact which are not explicit promises or warranties but are nevertheless held sufficient to justify the creation of an obligation on the speaker, having regard to the content, emphasis, and context.

But, having said all this, it must now be admitted that there is at least one respect in which the law does distinguish between statements as to the future and statements as to the present. A bare expectation is sometimes legally protected, if it relates to some future action; but (so far as I am aware) bare expectations arising from statements of facts are never legally protected. Thus an exchange of promises as to the future—a bargain or mutual agreement—creates expectations which are legally protected even prior to performance, reliance, or rendering of benefits. But an assertion of fact, even if made in return for some contemplated future action, does not create legal liabilities, unless and until it is acted upon. Even in the extreme case of deliberate deceit, the mere expectations of the deceived party are not legally protected. If he acts upon the statement and suffers loss, he may claim damages; but if (for instance) he discovers the untruth before he thus acts, he will not obtain any compensation for his disappointed expectations.

Curiously, this distinction has not been observed or commented upon by lawyers, and it is therefore unclear what legal justification there may be for it. Naturally, the conventional legal or moral theorist is entitled to argue that the distinction supports the simple idea that a promise is *per se* a morally binding commitment, and thus differs from a statement of fact. And the utilitarian who justifies the enforcement of promises by reference to the expectations (and/or reliance) to which they give rise, must find some explanation for this distinction. But he may, of course, prefer to argue that the distinction is unjustified, and that both types of expectation should be equally protected, or alternatively, that neither should be. He may argue that the distinction has been recognized by the law simply because it would be unusual for parties to make a bargain, comprising a bare assertion on one side, in return for a promise as to the future on the other side. And Courts have, therefore, not had to articulate any principles to deal with such cases in any systematic way. The bare assertion of fact which is *not* part of a bargain resembles the bare statement or promise as to the future which is likewise one-sided. Neither of these raises legally protected expectations.

PROMISES AS TO THE FUTURE CONDUCT OF THIRD PARTIES

Another common assumption made by many writers[32] is that one cannot promise that a third party will do something: promises must relate to conduct of the promisor. To a lawyer, this seems to confuse a number of issues. There is a distinction between a promise which imposes an obligation on the promisor that a third party will do something; and a promise which imposes an obligation on the third party himself, that *he* should do something. The latter is by no means impossible in law, though certainly unusual. I have given above a number of illustrations.[33] But the former is not only perfectly possible, but quite common. A contract of guarantee, by which a person stands surety for the performance of a third party's obligations, is sometimes treated in law as a promise *that* the third party shall perform his obligations.[34] Of course, it can be said (and some lawyers prefer to say) that such a contract imposes an obligation on the promisor to see that, or to ensure that, the third party performs. But nothing seems to turn upon selection of one or other of these phrases, and in some respects the first formulation seems the more accurate.

It is right to add that even ordinary business contracts usually involve significant obligations as to the conduct of third parties. When a builder contracts to erect a large office block, nobody

---

[32] For example, J. R. Searle, 'What is a Speech Act?', op. cit., p. 48; C. K. Grant, 'Promises', LVIII *Mind* 359 (1949).

[33] *Supra*, p. 154.

[34] *Moschi* v. *Lep Air Services* [1973] AC 331, especially the judgment of Lord Reid, at p. 345.

expects him to do the whole work unaided. It is manifest that he is undertaking to do something which involves a great deal of work by a labour force which may extend to thousands of men. By making the contract, the employer, or company, *contracts,* or *promises*, that he will find men who will do the necessary work. The idea, occasionally to be found in articles on promising, that a promise must relate to something wholly or exclusively within the power of the promisor,[35] seems quite extraordinary to the lawyer. What justification is there for imposing arbitrary limitations on the concept of a promise which run so counter to experience of everyday business activity?

STATEMENTS OF INTENTION

I have previously said that there is a fundamental division of opinion among philosophers as to whether a statement of intention can amount to a promise.[36] On the one hand, there is the broadly utilitarian approach which treats statements of intent as implicit in all or nearly all promises, the question whether it amounts to a promise depending on emphasis and context;[37] on the other hand there is the approach of those who stress the 'speech act' nature of promising, and insist that to promise is to place oneself under an obligation which is an entirely different matter from declaring one's intention.[38]

It will probably be evident from much that has previously been said that, as a lawyer, I am firmly committed to the view that promises and statements of intent do not fundamentally differ, and that the distinction between them, in any given case, is a matter of degree. However, before I attempt to justify this viewpoint—which would be generally shared by lawyers—it is necessary to recall that I have argued that one can promise that a fact is so, and also that a third party will do something, or even that a state of affairs shall come about. Thus it would not be correct to say that a promise always implies a statement of

[35] Grant, op. cit.

[36] *Supra*, pp. 25, 50-1, 100.

[37] See e.g. Hanfling, 'Promises, Games and Institution', *Proc. Arist. Soc.* 13 (1975); McNeilly, 'Promises De-Moralized', 81 *Phil. Rev.* 63 (1971); MacCormick, 'Voluntary Obligations and Normative Powers', *Proc. Arist. Soc. Suppt.* (1972), 59.

[38] See e.g. Ross, *The Right and the Good*, p. 77; J. L. Austin, 'Other Minds', *Proc. Arist. Soc. Suppt.* XX, 148 (1946); Searle, 'How to Derive "Ought" from "Is"', 73 *Phil. Rev.* 43 (1964); J. Harrison, 'Knowing and Promising', LXXI *Mind*, 443 (1962), reprinted in A. Phillips Griffiths (ed.), *Knowledge and Belief* (Oxford, 1967); R. G. Durrant, 'Promising', 41 *Aust. J. of Phil.* 44 (1963).

intent; it may imply a statement of fact, or a prediction about a future act by a third party, or a natural occurrence. The one point in common between these possibilities is that they all involve that a promise has some propositional content: it contains, expressly or by implication, a statement of present or future fact which can be true or false.[39] No doubt, the most common of these is the statement of intent, and I shall therefore concentrate upon that possibility. The basic thesis for which I am contending here is that it is a matter for the social group to determine (legally and morally) whether an obligation should be imposed on a person as a result of words or conduct; and it is largely immaterial whether his words appear to be a promise or a mere statement of intent or of fact. His own desire to impose an obligation on himself (or to avoid doing so) is a relevant factor in the social group's ultimate decision, but is certainly not conclusive.

An illustration may be in order here. It would not be difficult to find many examples from the cases on the law of contract, but I have selected a decision of the International Court of Justice to illustrate this point. In 1974 the Governments of Australia and New Zealand sought an order from the International Court of Justice declaring that the conducting of atmospheric nuclear tests in the Pacific by the French Government was illegal under international law. In June 1974, prior to the Court hearing, the French President made a public statement declaring that, after the series of tests then in contemplation, the French Government would be able to move to underground testing, and that this series would therefore be the last involving atmospheric tests. Later statements of the French Government confirmed this statement of policy. When, after this series of tests was completed, the case came up for decision before the Court, it was held that these public statements by the French Government were binding in international law.[40] Consequently, the Court declared that there was no longer any contestable issue before it, and it dismissed the case. The interesting part of the judgment concerns the status of the declarations of the French Government's policy as to future tests. It is most unlikely that the French Government had any intention of actually binding itself by anything in the nature of

---

[39] Lawyers have a peculiar assumption that a statement of fact must relate to the present or the past. They assume that a statement as to the future cannot be a statement of fact. This is a mistake which has sometimes led lawyers astray, but, in general, nothing turns on it.

[40] *Nuclear Tests Case, Australia* v. *France*, ICJ *Reports*, 1974, p. 253.

a Treaty (or a less formal promise) not to undertake such tests as it saw fit. But the Court nevertheless imputed to the French Government an intention to bind itself by these statements. It seems clear that the majority of the Court accepted the fictional nature of this imputed intention to be bound. Having announced its intentions in a public manner, the French Government, said the Court, 'was bound to assume that other States might take note of these statements and rely on their being effective. The validity of these statements and their legal consequences must be considered within the general framework of the security of international intercourse and the confidence and trust which are so essential in the relations among States. It is from the actual substance of these statements, and from the circumstances attending their making, that the legal implications of the unilateral act must be deduced. The objects of these statements are clear and they were addressed to the international community as a whole, and the Court holds that they constitute an undertaking possessing binding legal effect.'[41]

The process of reasoning is typical of that employed by lawyers generally. The Court declares that it is searching for an 'intent to be bound' but in effect imputes such an intent on broad grounds of policy and fairness in international relations. The truth is that the obligation was created not by the French Government, but by the Court; or more strictly it was the Court which decided that a moral/legal obligation arose out of the circumstances. It is easier to understand why the Court should go through the process of finding an 'intent to be bound' in a case of this character, where it may be assumed that the Government concerned might have repudiated the notion that the Court was empowered to impose obligations upon it, *ab extra,* as it were. In a domestic context, there is today no particular reason why Courts should still strive to impute the consequences of their decision to the intent of the parties concerned. Doubtless, it may seem to some to have a legitimating purpose, but it is possible that this is a legacy of the liberal heritage of the last century.

I can summarize what I have said so far thus: a declaration of intent may be treated by the law as binding if there are grounds upon which it can be said that an obligation should be imposed. The terms of the declaration are one of those grounds, but not the only one. Likewise, the intentions of a speaker to assume

[41] At p. 269.

(or not to assume) an obligation is a relevant but not a conclusive factor. Other relevant factors would be that the speaker was already morally obliged to do what he has said he intends to do, and the degree of emphasis with which he has spoken. Even repetition may be a relevant factor. When in *Richard II,* the Duchess of York seeks mercy for her son from Henry IV, she is not satisfied with the royal pardon, unequivocal though it seems. 'Speak it again', she demands,

> 'Twice saying "pardon" doth not pardon twain,
> But makes one pardon strong.'[42]

It remains to make a number of other points. First, precisely because declarations of intent so often leave it doubtful how far others are justified in relying upon them, explicit disclaimers, as well as explicit promises, may determine the issue. A person who says 'I intend to do such and such, but, mind, I make no promises' may be able to claim that nobody was entitled to have any expectations, or to act in reliance upon them as a result of such a statement. However, I do not accept, and the law today does not accept, the notion that this sort of disclaimer is always conclusive.[43] No doubt there are circumstances in which such a disclaimer may be legitimate, but there are also many circumstances in which it is not. The putative promisor may well be attempting to have things both ways in speaking thus: on the one hand, he wants to raise expectations in the minds of his hearers—what, indeed, is the purpose of making statements of this kind if he does not want them to raise expectations? And on the other hand, he wants to reserve complete freedom of action. In some circumstances this sort of disclaimer is thus a disreputable attempt to obtain the benefit of raising expectations and inducing actions in reliance without accepting the corresponding obligations. Until recently such disclaimers were commonly found in the 'small print' of many consumer contracts under which business firms sought to exclude their legal responsibility for all kinds of expectations and reliance. Today, such disclaimers are widely prohibited by Act of Parliament. It is not evident to me that the legal solution to such problems is not also—in broad terms—a moral solution.

---

[42] Act IV, scene iii.
[43] This is the answer to the objection put by J. Raz, 'Promises and Obligations' in *Law, Morality, and Society,* ed. Hacker and Raz, p. 216.

Conversely, explicit promises may also not be conclusive that there *is* a legal (or moral) obligation. Often, there are factors which nullify the force of even the most explicit promise. Quite apart from the traditional legal defences such as coercion, fraud, or breach of promise by the promisee himself, there are today many circumstances in which a person may be relieved from an express promise in law. Often this is because the law seems to have doubts about the underlying distributional justice of our social system (as in the case of protected tenants), sometimes it is because promises are given (especially in writing) by people who do not understand their implications; sometimes it is because, taking the circumstances as a whole, a more just result seems to require that the promise be disregarded. I have referred to many illustrations of legal rules designed to achieve these results earlier in this book. Here it is enough to stress that—especially as many of these legal rules are of relatively recent origin—there must be a strong presumption that most of them are, at least in broad outline, in accordance with current moral ideas. Certainly, anyone who accepts that positive social morality is the only kind of morality (other than a Divine morality) about which much can be said must surely accept the moral basis to many of these modern derogations from the old liberal ideology of freedom of contract. And even those who do not accept this starting-point must, I would urge, be prepared to offer some comment or criticism of the modern trend away from freedom of contract in the law. It is not by chance that the law has moved so far away from freedom of contract; it is because those responsible found the old law excessively unjust in a large variety of situations.

How Promises are Made

To read the literature about promises, one would assume that typical promises are made by use of explicit words, such as 'I promise', or 'I undertake', etc. In fact, use of these terms tends to be unusual except in formal and legal documents, or in formal ceremonies, such as the swearing of an oath. Most promises are made by much more general language than this. It is in practice much more common to hear expressions like, 'I can't promise' or 'Mind, I don't promise', than to hear the affirmative form. So that, when disputes or arguments subsequently arise as to whether one party was under an obligation to do something, it is necessary for the lawyer (as for anyone else who wishes to offer a moral judgment) to look at the matter retrospectively. It is also necessary to look at the matter from the external viewpoint. The question now is not, how to make a promise, or how to use the facilities offered by the legal or social institution of promising, where one wishes quite deliberately to create an obligation; the question is whether one party, by his words and conduct, acted in such a way as to create an obligation.

In addition there are many aspects of social and legal policy which may influence the decision. Many of these factors will be largely a matter of intuition, and tradition. Certain types of statement are simply not thought of as promissory or contractual. Particularly where it is customary to use special forms or ceremonies to create binding obligations their very absence may often lead to the conclusion that no obligation was created. Thus (for example) governmental declarations of policy which are not enshrined in the special form which gives them legal validity will often be thought non-promissory. Other factors may well arise from an unarticulated belief that certain types of expectation or reliance, though not in themselves unreasonable, cannot conveniently be made the subject of legal redress. For example, reliance on bus or train timetables is perfectly normal and reasonable conduct, but for a variety of reasons it is extremely doubtful whether it would be desirable on policy grounds to afford any legal redress to those whose reliance causes them loss. So it is probable that (even in the absence of disclaimers in small print) such liability would not today be imposed. Timetables would not now, I think, be regarded as promissory or contractual documents.

Similarly, for other reasons, judges are often reluctant to interfere in domestic quarrels or disputes, and they are, therefore, likely to find that declarations of intent in this sphere create no obligations on the ground that they are non-promissory or non-contractual. The parties, it is said, 'do not intend to create legal relations'. But the position is nearly always different once significant acts of reliance have occurred. The gravity of the resultant loss may well be such that the Court feels bound to interfere, and it may do this by imposing, retrospectively, an obligation which it treats as promissory or contractual. To take a recent example, in *Tanner* v. *Tanner*[44] a married man became father of twins by another woman with whom he had been having

---

[44] [1975] 3 All E.R. 776.

a liaison. He bought a house for the occupation of the woman and the children, and the woman gave up her (rent-protected) accommodation to move into the house. Later the liaison came to an end, and the man sought to evict the woman and children and recover possession of the house. It was held by the Court that the man's conduct and words amounted to a contract (or promise) that the woman and twins should be entitled to live in the house indefinitely. It will be noted that the woman had given up a secure home to move into the new house, and thus acted in reliance on her expectations, and on the man's words and conduct. The precise words, as is to be expected, were not recorded and could not be recalled anyhow. It was enough for the decision that the man had made it clear that he intended the house to be a home for the woman and her children. Whether he 'intended' to bind himself by a promise, whether he gave the matter any thought at all, was in the end irrelevant. It was the view of the Court that justice required that his statements and conduct should be treated as sufficient to create a legal obligation. It would be strange, I think, for anyone to argue that such a decision is a matter of technical, dry law, which has no bearing on the moral issues involved.

Cases concerning warranties, that is statements of fact which are treated by the law as promissory, or contractual, involve much the same issues. Here too one has the possibility of using the express language of warranty, or of expressly disclaiming that a warranty is given; neither is conclusive in law. But far more common in practice than an attempt to settle the issue expressly is the mere use of language to make assertions or statements of fact which are then acted upon in ways which are more or less probable, more or less invited by the speaker, more or less serious in their consequences. Here again, it is up to some judge (whether he is a legal or a moral judge) to look at the facts retrospectively and externally, and ask himself whether what was said *ought* to be treated as promissory or contractual. Should an obligation be imposed as a result of what was said? A seller of a horse says, 'The horse is sound'; is that a warranty or not? The answer may depend partly, but certainly not conclusively, on what the parties intended. It also depends upon the Court's view of what is just. If the buyer has paid a price which would be a fair price for a sound horse (which suggests that he believed and acted upon the statement), most modern judges would say without hesitation that it ought to be treated as a warranty.

Now it is important to appreciate that whether a statement of intent or a statement of fact is treated as promissory is, in the last resort, dependent on the value systems influencing the judge. This is perhaps particularly obvious when dealing with the question whether a statement of fact is a warranty or not. At one time it was widely thought desirable that buyers should be encouraged to stand on their own feet, examine the goods they bought themselves, rely on their own judgment. This led naturally to the doctrine of *caveat emptor* which was widely enforced in the Courts (though never as widely as commonly believed) between about 1830 and 1870. But today there is very little left of this doctrine because Courts (and the public) no longer believe that there is anything wrong or unreasonable in buyers relying upon the reputation and competence of manufacturers and sellers rather than on themselves. Much the same is true of statements of intent. At one time it was thought that such statements should not be interpreted by the Courts as promissory unless the intent to be bound was plainly present, or at least appeared to be present. But today Courts decide for themselves whether they think statements of intent should create obligations, and, in deciding that question, express promises or disclaimers are only of prima-facie value.

It needs to be stressed that cases of this general nature are very common indeed. It is misleading to start with the assumption that promises are typically the actions of careful, rational, calculating individuals who pause and deliberate before deciding to say anything as to their intentions, and make up their minds whether they wish to announce these intentions in promissory form or not. No doubt, in some spheres of life people behave in this way—for instance, in entering into important business transactions. And in the last century it was widely thought desirable by utilitarians, economists, and lawyers that people should be trained to think and calculate rationally before acting in all spheres of activity. It was under their influence that freedom of contract became the ideology of the times; and it is the influence of that ideology that makes lawyers and philosophers today still write as though this was the typical way of making promises. But this is an idealized version of what (in the view of some) ought to happen; it is fantasy to suppose that it is the common course of life to behave in this way.

IMPLIED PROMISES

I come now to the problem of implied promises. Both in ordinary discourse and in law (as well, of course, as in traditional political theory) the concept of implied promises plays a large role. In law and, I think, with most contemporary writers on philosophy, the traditional explanation of an implied promise assumes that the explicit promise is the paradigm case. The implied promise is then treated as a case where no explicit promise is made in so many words, but where, from his words and conduct, it is plain that the party intends to bind himself.[45] Simple examples, regularly given to law students, concern contracts made by boarding a bus, placing money in an automatic vending-machine, or ordering a meal in a restaurant. In none of these cases does anyone say 'I promise' or anything remotely resembling it. In the second case, nothing is said (orally) at all. Yet the lawyer, and the common man, would agree that legal obligations plainly ensue. The lawyer explains these obligations by saying that there are implied promises. The common man may be less sure, although he probably would agree that these implications exist. But there are difficulties with this traditional explanation. What of the person who does not intend to pay his fare on boarding the bus, or pay for the meal supplied to him in the restaurant? The lawyer brushes aside this difficulty, appealing to what he calls the 'objective test' of promise or assent. There is the appearance of a promise and that is enough. But this explanation is not very satisfying. For it dismisses what is—on the traditional view—the very central requirement of a promise. If a person who intends to steal a ride on a bus is liable to pay his fare in exactly the same way as the person who intends to pay his fare, it seems odd to say that it is the intention which creates the liability in both cases.

However, although it may well be true that a person who boards a bus, or orders a meal in a restaurant, creates an expectation that he will pay an appropriate charge, and may, in that sense, be taken to have made a promise, there may still be something misleading about the conventional implication of promises here. For to imply a promise suggests that it is because of the promise that the relevant party is bound by an obligation. He is obliged to pay for the meal or pay the bus fare *because* he has promised. However, it seems quite plausible to suggest that

[45] For example, Ross, *The Right and the Good*, p. 27.

the truth is the other way round. It is because he is bound by an obligation that we generally feel impelled to imply a promise. Naturally, if that is right, the source of the obligation cannot lie in the implied promise itself, but must be sought elsewhere. It is not difficult to suggest alternative sources of the obligation. For whenever promises are implied from conduct, it is often, perhaps always, the case that the conduct itself justifies the creation of the obligation. A person orders a meal in a restaurant and the meal is laid before him, and he eats it. Surely these facts alone suffice to create an obligation to pay. There is a legal duty, and a socio-moral duty, requiring those who order and eat meals in restaurants to pay for them. Naturally, when the facts are highly stereotyped, and of frequent occurrence, the existence of the obligation is always known on both sides. It is scarcely possible that a person could order a meal in a restaurant without realizing that he thereby comes under a legal and social duty to pay for it; and the restaurant is equally aware of the normal understandings governing its own business. In the great majority of cases of this nature, therefore, the intention to pay will exist, and so will the intention to assume or accept the legal obligation. But we must never forget the defaulter. Occasionally people do order meals in restaurants without any intention of paying. Nobody doubts—least of all the lawyer—that this makes not the slightest difference to the obligation to pay.

I have previously pointed out that, as a matter of history, we know that generally speaking concepts of property, of debt, and of obligation antedate the concepts of promise and contract.[46] Thus, whereas in modern times we say that a person who borrows money impliedly (if not expressly) promises to repay it, in earlier times the borrower's liability was placed on different grounds. He was liable because he had received the lender's money (and the lender did not intend to make a gift). Thus, obligation comes first, and the implication of a promise later. Moreover, this kind of development still occurs where new social or legal obligations are thought to arise, on one ground or another; and then, once they have been justified, it comes to be said that they are supported by an implied promise. Let me give an illustration. A manufacturer of a product (say a drug) places it on the market and it turns out to have serious ill effects on some users. Let us further assume that this is the result of some wholly unknown

---

[46] See J. C. Smith, *Legal Obligation* (London, 1976), pp. 62-3; see also, p. 119, *supra*.

and unforseeable medical condition, and that the manufacturers, in the existing state of scientific knowledge, could not have discovered the dangers. Thus, in law, they would be found not to have been negligent. Are they, nevertheless, under any obligation to compensate those who have used and bought the drugs from retail chemists? If we attempt to answer that question by asking whether the manufacturer impliedly promises (warrants) that the drug is safe, merely by placing it on the market, or perhaps by advertising it, it is evident that no easy answer is available to the question. The manufacturer probably does not have any definite intentions on this question at all: if asked whether he intended to promise or warrant that his drugs were safe, he would probably want to consult his lawyer to find out what his legal obligations were before replying. It is certainly unlikely that he would answer with an unequivocal, Yes. The man in the street, I suspect, would also be hard put to it to say whether there is an implied promise in such circumstances. Now the lawyer would say that there was no such implied promise, but what enables him to say that with confidence is his knowledge that there is (at present) no legal liability on the manufacturer in the absence of negligence. Thus, to the lawyer, the implication or non-implication of a promise follows from the determination of legal liability, and does not, itself, determine that liability.

However, there are many proposals to change the law on this point. It is widely felt that manufacturers of drugs (and other products) should be obliged to compensate those injured by their products even if they have not been negligent and are in no way to blame for the defective or dangerous nature of the product. Now if these proposals come to fruition, it will become possible to say, without serious solecism, that a manufacturer *does* impliedly promise, or warrant, that his goods are safe. And, once the change in the law becomes thoroughly established, and well known to manufacturers, it might come to be said that a manufacturer *intends* to assume this liability. In a hundred years' time, the existence of this obligation may be so well established, and taken for granted, that people may come to feel that the obligation arises from the implied promise or warranty.

I have not so far discussed a question about implied promises which is often thought (by lawyers and others) to be of some theoretical importance, namely are they 'genuine' or 'fictitious' promises? There are, I think, three possible views on this question. The traditional legal (and perhaps philosophical) view, which is still widely held, is that the justification of the obligation arising from an express and from an implied promise is the same: in both cases, it is the intention of the promisor which justifies the liability. The second view, advanced by many modern lawyers, is that this is only true of express promises and *some* implied promises; other implied promises, on this view, are 'fictitious'. They are invented promises designed to legitimate the imposition of an obligation which does not arise from the intention of the 'promisor', but for other reasons of fairness and policy. But there is a third possible view, which is the one I am contending for. On this view, as with the first, the justification for the obligation arising from express and implied promises is the same; but that justification is in both cases derived from an amalgam of ideas of fairness and policy created by the social group.

The role of explicit promises, on this view, is not so much to create obligations as to provide evidence to clear up what would otherwise be doubtful issues. It is precisely because it is often difficult to say whether an obligation arises in certain circumstances that explicit promises are useful. I will explore this evidentiary theory of promising further below. Here I want to stress that this theory involves a completely different perspective on the relationship between explicit and implied promises. This theory, in effect, takes the implied promise as the paradigm case; it assumes (for instance) that the obligation to pay a debt for services rendered is a paradigm of legal or moral duty and that the presence of an explicit promise in this situation does not affect the fundamental nature of the obligation. The explicit promise which creates a wholly new obligation, on this approach, is an oddity, and very far from being a paradigm case.

Chapter 7

Promises and Other Sources of Obligation

Promises as Consent

It will be apparent from what has so far been said, that a central part of my thesis is that promises cannot be understood except in the context of obligations generally. In particular, I have devoted much time to the legal 'doctrine of consideration' which provides that, in general, promises are only binding if they are in some sense paid for, or relied upon, or if a counter-promise is given in return. It goes without saying, of course, that these legal ideas have their parallel in the moral world. It is universally agreed that moral obligations can arise from the receipt of benefits, or from the causing of harm or injury to others, as well as from promises. In this chapter I propose to analyse the relationship between these three sources of obligation. I do not mean to imply that there are not other possible sources of obligation, for example, that of a parent to its child, but these three are so closely related that promising cannot be studied apart from the others.

I must begin by suggesting that promising may be reducible to a species of consent, for consent is a broader and perhaps more basic source of obligation. Consent is in particular a more extensive factor in negativing or discharging the existence of obligations than in their creation; but the denial or discharge of one obligation often entails the recognition or creation of others. If I give you permission to picnic on my land, I remove the obligation which you formerly had of not entering my land, but I also create a new obligation in myself not to throw you off without first revoking my permission. Now one can, of course, eliminate or discharge an obligation by giving an express promise, but debts and other obligations are often waived without anything in the nature of an express promise. A person who waives a debt, for instance, is simply expressing his consent to not receiving it. He can, of course, be said to be impliedly promising to forgo it, impliedly promising not to claim payment or to sue for it, but it is not clear what such an implied promise adds to the mere expression of consent. Of course, some waivers are not legally binding (at least prior to reliance), and this may be said to be precisely because a waiver is not the same as a promise; only if we can imply a promise, it may be argued, is a waiver binding even before it has been acted upon. But (as I have previously argued) implied promises are often thought to arise because we have already determined that there is an obligation. So here too, it may be that a waiver would be construed as amounting to an implied promise where it is felt that the waiver ought to be binding.

In any case there are many circumstances in which it would seem grotesque to insist that the efficacy of a consent depends upon the implication of a promise. For example, acts of physical intimacy which are indulged in by two consenting adults manifestly create no right of complaint against the other, whether in law, or in morality. The fact of consent (absent, of course, any negativing factors such as coercion, etc.) is a sufficient explanation of the result. Nobody would feel any need to say that the parties impliedly promise not to complain, or sue one another for assault.

Where an obligation is created, rather than discharged, it may be less obvious that promising is a species of consent, even though (as I have said) the discharge of one obligation often entails the creation of others. But it is true that in many cases the verbal formula 'I promise to ϕ' cannot, as a matter of language, be easily reduced to anything like 'I consent ...'. And this is perhaps still more difficult where it is a promise of a fact, or a third party's behaviour, or a state of affairs which is in question. But the fact surely is that an explicit promise is an expressed willingness or consent to the state of affairs which the promise posits, or which will be required by its performance. So, for instance, if I promise to deliver my car to you under a contract of sale, I am expressing my willingness to part with my car. In the case of a simultaneous exchange, rather than a contract made for future performance, the transaction indeed may not really involve promises at all. Each party simply consents here and now to making the exchange.[1] A contract for future performance may, it is suggested, involve two separable elements, (1) the consent to the terms of the exchange, as in the case of a present or simultaneous exchange, and (2) the element of commitment between the time

---

[1] This view is challenged by Prichard in an interesting paper in which he argues that even a simultaneous exchange logically involves mutual promises (see *Moral Obligation*, pp. 180-1), but the argument is fallacious. If a third party, X, is in possession of A's book and B's money, it seems quite clear that A and B could agree to an exchange without making any promises.

of making the arrangement and the time scheduled for performance. This latter may look more like a promise which is not reducible to any form of consent, but it too can be seen as an indication of present willingness to maintain one's consent to the arrangements; indeed, the second element is simply a way of saying that the first element (consent to the exchange) is irrevocable.

The view that promising is, in essence, reducible to a form of consent is to be found in *The Leviathan*, where Hobbes argues in effect that a promise is an expression of consent not to interfere with others in their enjoyment of their natural rights. Similarly, he sees a sale of property as a form of consent or renunciation of the property owner's rights to prevent the buyer from helping himself to the property.[2] A rather similar idea seems to lie at the root of a suggestion made by H. L. A. Hart.[3] For although he was one of the originators of the idea that promises depend upon the existence of a practice, Hart does not seem to have regarded this as the source of the moral obligation created by a promise. This he rested upon the idea that a promise is a surrender of the promisor's freedom in certain respects; by thus surrendering his freedom he legitimates the conduct of the promisee in now having the right to demand something from the promisor. It is this emphasis on the *special* rights of the promisee which, Hart stresses, explains the puzzling idea that one can, by a promise, change one's moral obligations. For, he agrees, 'it would be mysterious if we could make actions morally good or bad by voluntary choice'. It is because a promise has a special effect on the relations between the parties to it, that it affects the moral result: as between *this* promisor and *this* promisee it now becomes legitimate to do, or demand, something as morally right which was not so before. As the argument is put by Hart, it seems to be manifestly incomplete. For what Hart has here justified is not the binding nature of a promise, but the validity of a consent. For, as I shall argue later, the difficulty with promises seen as a species of consent is to understand why they are irrevocable.

Now consent takes many forms, of which the explicit promise is only one; other types of consent may sometimes be regarded as justifying the implication of a promise, but they are often more naturally described without reference to the concept of promises

---

[2] Chapter 14.
[3] 'Are there any Natural Rights?', 64 *Phil. Rev.* 175 (1955).

at all. We use many linguistic forms in ordinary discourse to describe those various ways of consenting. For instance, we may say that a person has done something voluntarily, that he has agreed to do something, that he has acquiesced in something; we may say that a person has permitted, or given leave to another to do something; that he has abandoned, or renounced something, a right for example, or even an expectation; we say that a person has accepted something (an offer, for instance, or a service); we may say that a person has admitted something, or confessed to a charge. Each of these verbal forms describes a different way of indicating consent, or assent, to something, and this list is very far from being exhaustive. In particular, it makes no mention of another variety of words whose primary purpose is to indicate a person's desires, wants, or aims and goals; these ideas are not precisely the same as those involved in the notion of consent, but they are closely related, and each of them may well entail *some* basic element of consent.

Now the peculiarity of promising is that it is so often concerned with a future, rather than a present consent; indeed, except in the case of the warranty, this is perhaps always so. Most, if not all, other forms of consent *can* relate to the future, but they can also, and perhaps more commonly do, relate to the present. And because they commonly relate to the present, they rarely seem to call for any justification. Prima facie, at least, if a person consents to do something here and now, it is not normally felt necessary to explain why that consent should be 'binding' on him. Indeed, the word 'binding', which plainly has future connotations, is inappropriate when used of a present consent; it would be more apt to speak of a 'valid' consent, when it is a present consent which is in question. The general presumption that a person is the best judge of his own interests is normally a sufficient starting-point for dealing with a present consent. However, even this is very far from being always conclusive. The increasing paternalism of modern societies means that laws and regulations of various kinds are deliberately designed to prevent people from doing what they want to, from validly consenting to treatment of a kind believed to be harmful or exploitative.

Now a consent to something in the future does not have this powerful prima-facie presumption in its favour, at least when looked at from the point of view of the consenting party. For if the consenting party changes his mind, and does not maintain his consent when the future has become the present, then the presumption must, it seems, be that his present state of mind, whether of assent or dissent, should govern. And there is no doubt that, if we put explicit promises on one side, many other forms and ways of expressing consent to not involve any kind of commitment to maintain that consent in the future. A person who has given another a *permission* to do something in the future would not normally be thought to have committed himself not to revoke that permission; such a commitment would indeed *be* an explicit promise not to revoke the permission. No doubt such a promise might be implied in appropriate circumstances; and it may well be explicit where it is part of some contractual arrangement under which the person giving the permission is paid for his consent. So too, where the other party has acted in reliance on the permission, it would probably be widely agreed that the permission should not be revoked, at least without giving adequate notice. But if there is no payment, and no action in reliance on the permission, it would be generally thought that the permission can be freely revoked on reasonable notice. This is, indeed, what the law generally provides.

Or take another type of consent—a renunciation or abandonment of a right. Here, too, questions may arise as to whether the renunciation is final and irrevocable. No doubt there may be certain formal procedures for renouncing certain types of right, and, if complied with, these may be regarded as final—just as (say) an actual transfer of a piece of property might be final. But other rights may be renounced in ways which involve no set procedure, and in these cases it is very likely that, if any payment is involved, or if any other party has acted to his prejudice in reliance on the renunciation, it will be held irrevocable. On the other hand, where the renunciation is purely intended to operate *de futuro,* and there has been no element of benefit or reliance, it may seem perfectly reasonable to allow it to be withdrawn. Thus, in *Re Cranstoun's Will Trusts*[4] it was held by Romer J. that a beneficiary under a will which had formally renounced its right to take out probate, and claim its legacy, could withdraw this renunciation. His decision was quite specifically placed upon the ground that no other party had changed his position in reliance on this renunciation, and there was, in the circumstances, no question of payment.

Many other cases of a present consent being perfectly valid,

---

[4] [1949] Ch. 523.

while it stands, but freely revocable as to the future, can be found. A patient may, for example, validly consent to a surgical operation, but such consent is, of course, revocable. Indeed, such is the value placed upon a person's rights over his own body that it cannot be doubted that, in this instance, the right to withdraw the consent would be conceded even if others had acted in reliance upon the consent—for example, if a hospital has made arrangements for the operation to be performed. So, too, many examples can be found from the law of a consent which can be validly given but which is not binding so far as concerns the future. For instance, a tenant protected under the Rent Acts can actually surrender his tenancy (for payment, if agreed) but cannot *bind* himself as to the future (even for payment). An accused person can validly admit his guilt by a plea of guilty in the face of the Court; but he cannot bind himself to plead guilty by any sort of agreement or contract or admission made out of Court. What he says out of Court (for example in police interrogation) is admissible in evidence against him; it is of evidentiary value since it may help to prove that he was indeed guilty. It is a reasonable presumption that people do not normally confess to crimes which they have not committed. But this is far from being an irrebuttable presumption, since we know nowadays that innocent people do sometimes confess, for a variety of reasons, to crimes which they did not commit.

Now in all these and many other cases, a consent may be given which—as I have said—is revocable. And whether it is in any given case revocable is a matter which depends only partly on the intention of the party giving the consent. No doubt, if he expressly reserves his right to revoke his consent, that tends to settle the issue; and no doubt if he expressly disclaims any right to revoke his consent, that too may tend, in some cases at any rate, to settle the issue. That, indeed, would amount to an explicit promise. But in most cases, no thought is given to the question of revocability. And if it arises, it has to be settled on a basis which pays little weight to the intention of the consenting party. When it does come to be settled, it seems natural that a variety of factors should be taken into consideration. For example, there are important questions concerning the particular interest of the consenting party. Thus, as I have suggested, anything which involves the consenting party's own bodily integrity is likely to weigh heavily against the view that a consent should be irrevocable. And a man's right to plead Not Guilty of a charge before a Court is also likely to be highly valued in our sort of society, and hence to be treated as not being open to an irrevocable waiver or consent.

But where overriding considerations of these sorts are not in question, it seems clear that the revocability of a consent must involve a balancing exercise which can only be conducted from the external point of view. On the one hand are the interests of the (formerly) consenting party who now wishes to change his mind, and consent to something quite different, perhaps the reverse of what he previously consented to. On the other hand are the interests of those who are, or may be, in various ways affected by the revocability of the consent. For example, there are those who may have paid for the consent, there are those who may have acted upon it, or, strictly, acted in the belief that it would be maintained. And there are those who have merely had expectations that the consent would be maintained.

In order to understand when, and why, a consent becomes irrevocable, it is therefore necessary to look at the rendering of benefits and acts of reliance as sources of obligation, and that I shall shortly do. But it is first necessary to ask whether this line of argument does not apply to promises themselves. If a promise is a species of consent, and if the revocability of a consent is a matter which depends only partly on the intention of the person giving the consent, why should this not also be true of promises? There certainly seems no problem about holding this to be true of implied promises where (as I have argued) the implication often follows the determination that an obligation exists. But even with explicit promises, there is no reason why the same analysis should not be applicable. An explicit promise, seen as a species of consent, carries with it (as I have argued above) a second factor, namely, an intimation of willingness to maintain one's consent. And here we come back to the logical problem posed by the difficulty of seeing how one can prevent oneself from revoking one's consent, merely by saying that one will not revoke it, even by saying it in a form which is normally thought to be promissory. And anyhow, as I have repeatedly stressed, a promise is by no means always binding in law, or morality. We thus find that, whether a consent is or is not expressed in a form which amounts to a promise, its revocability is a matter to be settled by external factors: a decision by the social group (or the judges appointed by the group) is necessary before one can say whether the consent is irrevocable. The expressed willingness of the party concerned to treat his consent as irrevocable is neither a necessary nor a sufficient condition for the social group to hold the consent to be irrevocable.

Promises as Admissions

I have said there are many different ways of expressing consent, and that one way of expressing consent is to make an admission. If A claims a debt of £10 from B, and B admits the debt, he agrees that he owes it, and he consents to the fact that A has a claim on him. I now want to argue that a very common justification for treating a promise as binding is that the promise is evidence, is an admission, of the existence of some other obligation already owed by the promisor. By making an explicit promise, the promisor concedes or admits the existence and extent of the pre-existing obligation. Indeed, I shall argue that this is in truth the paradigm of an explicit promise. On this view, an implied promise is either an implied admission of the existence of a prior obligation, or it is merely a way of describing a situation in which such a prior obligation arises even though there is no admission.

Now, other sources of obligation can arise from a great variety of circumstances, but legal experience suggests that most of them fall under one of two heads. Obligations arise, firstly, because one person has done good, or rendered some benefit, to another; and secondly, because one person has done some harm to another, and in the context with which we are concerned, the type of harm which commonly arises is harm following some action (detrimental reliance) induced or encouraged by another person. These obligations, it would be widely agreed today, can arise without any intention of assuming an obligation, without any consent or express promise. But they very frequently coexist with express promises, and wherever an express promise coexists with some other ground of obligation it is arguable that the primary function of the promise is—in legal language—evidentiary. The purpose of the promise, on this view, is to provide evidence about some of the issues involved in determining precisely what obligation arises from the *other* grounds of obligation. In the great majority of cases, the other ground will be some element of benefit or reliance, and for that reason I have concentrated on these two. But there are other possible sources of obligation which may coexist with promises, and where the promise may similarly have an evidentiary function.

It is perhaps worth beginning by giving illustrations of simple cases where promises coexist with other sources of obligation. Let me first take cases where the other ground of obligation (which it will be convenient to call 'prior') does not involve any element of benefit or reliance. One important group of cases which the lawyer calls readily to mind are cases where one person has caused injury to another, say in a road accident, and a claim for compensation is made. Now if one party (I will call him the defendant) has been guilty of fault, or negligence, as the law defines that term, he is legally liable to pay compensation to the other (the plaintiff). Nobody would doubt that there is likewise a moral obligation in this situation, though some may feel that there is also a moral obligation even where there is no negligence and no legal liability. Now, when a claim for compensation is made following a road accident, the customary procedure is for negotiations for a settlement to be conducted between the plaintiff and his advisers on the one hand, and the defendant (or his insurers) and his, or their, advisers on the other. In the great majority of cases (of which there are many thousands every year) an agreement will in due course be reached, under which the defendant promises to pay a particular sum of money and the plaintiff agrees to accept this in full satisfaction of his claim. Once this agreement has been made, the actual payment will normally follow quickly enough, but between the making of the agreement and the payment, the matter rests upon the promises of the parties.

In this type of case it seems clear that once the promise of payment is made by the defendant, the promise coincides with, or overlaps with the prior duty to make compensation which is anyhow imposed by law. It is, in this sort of case, easy to see what is the purpose of the promise. This is to dispose of matters of doubt and controversy arising from the uncertainty of the prior ground of obligation.[5] For although the law is in theory plain enough that the defendant has to pay damages for his negligence, the application of this legal rule in practice causes much trouble. In the first place, it is often very difficult to say whether the accident was caused by negligence, or even how it was caused at all. Moreover, the plaintiff may himself have been partly to blame (in which case his entitlement to damages in law is reduced under the rules of 'contributory negligence') and this too will

---

[5] See MacCormick, op. cit., p. 72, where the same point is made.

add to the uncertainty. Then also, the measurement of the compensation is an equally difficult problem. Complex rules exist for the purpose of fixing the amount of 'pecuniary loss' which the damages will include, and still greater difficulty arises when some attempt is made to fix a sum by way of compensation for non-pecuniary items, such as pain and suffering and loss of faculties. Thus the attempt to value the plaintiff's claim leads into many difficulties even in relatively straightforward cases. If no agreement is reached between the parties, the plaintiff will have, in the end, either to drop his case, or take it to Court. If the case gets into Court, the Court will, of course, have the task of deciding all the uncertain issues, such as whether there was negligence, and how much should be awarded in damages. This is naturally a slow and expensive process. It is very much quicker and cheaper for the parties to agree on these matters if they can.

Now it may be argued that parties can *be in* agreement on such matters without *making* a binding agreement, or exchanging promises. To admit that you were to blame for an accident does not, it may be said, imply that you are promising to pay for the consequences. But this does not mean that promises are not admissions; what it means, or what it shows, is that admissions are of varying degrees of conclusiveness. To admit that you are to blame for an accident is less conclusive than to promise to pay for the consequences. Legally speaking, however, the admission, even without the promise, would be a highly relevant fact in any legal proceedings. In the absence of any explanation, it is likely that a Court would readily conclude that a person who admitted his fault was indeed to blame for the accident, and consequently came under an obligation to pay for the consequences. However, an admission is rebuttable: perhaps it can be shown that the party making the admission was greatly shocked by the accident, and did not really understand what he was saying, or perhaps it can be shown that the accident was due to something for which he was not responsible (sudden brake failure) and his admission was not really intended as a confession of guilt, but as an exoneration of the other party from any responsibility. Obviously, these and other possible explanations may help to rebut the effect of an admission of fault.

A promise to pay for the consequences of an accident differs only in that it is less easily rebuttable. Indeed, in most ordinary circumstances, it is not rebuttable at all. But it is vital to note the qualifying words, 'in *most ordinary* circumstances'. For there are some (fairly) ordinary circumstances where a promise is re-buttable (or not binding) and there are certainly many extra-ordinary circumstances where this is the case. In the particular example under discussion, it is not indeed clear how much more conclusive a promise is than a bare admission on its own. Thus, if the evidence is that the promisor was greatly shocked and did not really know what he was doing etc., it would seem un-likely that a promise would be any more conclusive than a bare admission of fault.

Now there may, of course, be serious questions about how conclusive a promise ought to be, but that is also true of bare admissions. For example, a troublesome problem of criminal procedure has been whether a defendant who has pleaded guilty to a charge should be entitled to appeal. But what I am trying to show is that, in any case of this nature, that is, where a promise coexists with other obligations, it is a mistake to think of the promise as *creating* a wholly new obligation where none existed before. Of course, if we do treat a promise of this kind as (more or less conclusive) of the issues left doubtful without it, then there is a sense in which the promise *has* created the obligation. Perhaps, if the case was tried out, it would be held that there was no negligence and no liability at all. And if that *were* the case, then the promise would have created liability out of nothing. But the promise is not made in order to create an obligation; it is made in order to settle a dispute, which it does by precluding the promisor from (generally) reopening issues which he has admitted against himself. It may, no doubt, be argued that a promise may be just as vague and uncertain as the prior obliga-tion, but that does not seem to be correct. If it really is just as vague as the original obligation, it surely adds nothing to it at all. If a person who is involved in an accident says to the other, 'I promise to pay whatever compensation I may be legally liable to pay you', it seems to me very doubtful whether (at least in law) this would be regarded as a promise at all. If the injured party actually sues for damages in such a case he would probably sue on the original obligation (claiming damages in tort for the injury) and not for breach of contract.

The example I have been discussing is merely one well-known species of agreement, a compromise agreement. But compromises are not the only examples of promises being used where some other, prior ground of obligation, may exist. For the fact is that a great many promises are made to do things where some prior obligation already exists. People promise to pay their debts, for instance; and it is possibly significant that such promises are more commonly encountered *after* the debt has been incurred; indeed, perhaps most commonly when the debt is overdue. It is the fact that it is overdue which makes a creditor begin to wonder about the reliability of the debtor, and to demand payment or some reassurance that payment will indeed be forthcoming. The promise to pay is then not designed to create the obligation which of course already exists, but to make it clear that the debtor admits it, and (perhaps) to place some time-limit on the indulgence requested. Or again, consider formal promises, such as oaths. Promises to tell the truth by a witness in a Court, or in an affidavit sworn for legal purposes, oaths of office or of allegiance, and such like, are rarely made except where there is already some prior obligation. In such cases the promise adds emphasis and ritual to an existing obligation. It also makes it more difficult for the promisor subsequently to deny that he owed the prior obligation at all. Here too, therefore, the promise has this evidentiary character. In modern societies, this purpose of ritual and ceremonial promising has become almost obsolete, for it has largely been replaced by the written record. To obtain a person's signature to a written promise or contract is generally found to be much the simplest and most efficient way of having an indisputable record which the promisor cannot subsequently deny. But in primitive communities, many forms of ritualistic promising appear to have as one of their primary purposes the desirability of making it as difficult as possible for a promisor subsequently to deny the existence of a prior obligation which was confirmed by the promise.

Where a promise is used to add weight to a prior obligation, or where some ritual, such as an oath, or other ceremony, is used to reinforce a prior obligation, it may seem that the purpose of the promise is not so much to clarify doubts (as with compromises) but rather to reinforce the existing obligation. No doubt it may have this effect, but the purpose of solemn and ritual promises may still be thought to be largely evidentiary. Although the position at the moment of the promise may be clear enough, experience shows that in later times, doubts may arise about the existence and extent of the prior obligation. In years to come, some of the parties may be dead, and anyhow memories fade. It is to help fix things in the mind that ceremonies and ritual so often surround the making of formal promises and oaths; and the greater the ceremonial, the greater also is likely to be the number of witnesses. In time, it may happen that more attention comes to be attached to the ritual itself; and in primitive societies, much attention may come to be paid to allegations of technical flaws in the ritual, which may be alleged to negate the obligation. All this may have helped to obscure the fact that the real obligation in such cases does not come from the promise or the oath. The point is well taken in *Julius Caesar*,[6] when Casca suggests that the conspirators should swear an oath, and Brutus replies:

> No, not an oath: if not the face of men,
> The sufferance of our souls, the time's abuse,
> If these be motives weak, break off betimes,
> And every man hence to his idle bed;
> So let high-sighted tyranny range on,
> Till each man drop by lottery. But if these,
> As I am sure they do, bear fire enough
> To kindle cowards and to steel with valour
> The melting spirits of women, then countrymen,
> What need we any spur but our own cause
> To prick us to redress?

Now in all these cases, a promise is made when some prior obligation already exists. But there is no doubt that promises are also made when no such obligation exists, and it may seem then that the promise must be designed to create a new obligation. However, even in a case of this nature a promise may have the character of being largely evidentiary. For although there may be no prior obligation, a promise is very often given (as I have previously emphasized) in exchange for some return. Traditionally, the paradigm of a legal contract has been regarded as created by an exchange of promises. Suppose, for example, that *A* and *B* 'agree' on the sale of *B*'s house to *A* for £20,000. *A* promises to pay the price, and *B* promises to convey the house. Now it may seem at first sight as though each promise creates a new obligation which did not exist before, and this indeed is how a lawyer would perceive the situation. But it may be suggested that this is to telescope two separable elements in a transaction of this character. As I have previously argued, an arrangement of this kind can be broken down into two elements, (1) consent to the terms of the proposed exchange, and (2) the binding

---

[6] II. i. 114 ff.

commitment to consummate the exchange. These really are quite separate things. It would be perfectly possible, indeed it is the usual course, to agree to the terms of the exchange before there is any element of commitment, and it is also possible to have the commitment without a full agreement on the terms of the exchange.[7] Now so far as the first of these elements is concerned, it seems to be still the case that each promise is nothing more than an indication of the party's willingness to exchange on the terms proposed. And each promise is thus evidence of the nature and terms of the transaction. Further, each promise is evidence of the fairness and justice of the transaction. The promises do not simply create obligations, on their own as it were. *A*'s obligation to pay the price will not arise just because he has promised: it will arise if and when he receives a conveyance of the house. *B*'s obligation to convey does not arise just from his promise: it arises if and when he receives the price. That this is so can be seen clearly enough by asking what would happen on breach by either party. If *B* fails to convey the house, *A* is not bound to pay the money. If *B* does convey the house, *A* is indeed bound to pay, but is it obvious that he then has the obligation to pay solely because of his promise? If he gets the house, he surely has an obligation to pay, irrespective of the promise: it is not *A*'s house, and *B* has no intention of making a gift, so *A* would seem to be under a plain obligation to pay for the house anyhow. The amount to be paid, of course, can hardly be *less* than he has promised; his promise is an admission of the fairness of the price agreed. He may, indeed, be required to pay *more* than he promised, for example, interest and legal costs may be added to the £20,000 if they are not paid on the due date, and the duty to pay these certainly does not derive from the promise.

Now it will be seen that the intention of the parties (or at least their apparent intent) is far from being irrelevant to the result. If there is a clear intent to make a gift, for instance, it is plain that *A* comes under no obligation to pay anything for the house, though, at least morally, he may come under vague duties of reciprocity in the future. But the degree to which parties are permitted by law to commit themselves by mere intent is limited, often for paternalistic reasons, sometimes for general reasons of justice. In the case of house-purchase transactions, for instance, the present legal procedure is generally designed to prevent parties

---

[7] See further below, p. 205 ff., where I discuss this more fully.

becoming bound merely as the result of their intention to buy
and intention to sell. In the first place, written evidence is necessary for the legal enforcement of such contracts, but secondly and
more fundamentally, agreements of this kind are nearly always
made, in the first instance, 'subject to contract'. The effect of
this formula, and indeed its very purpose, is to prevent a legal
obligation arising, mainly in order to protect the buyer from com-
mitting himself until he has secured his financial position and
had an opportunity to consult his solicitor. This is therefore a
classic instance of an 'agreement' which is an agreement on the
terms of a proposed exchange without any commitment to make
that exchange.

In a case of this kind, therefore, there is no difficulty in treating
the promises as still having an evidentiary character. Insofar as
the agreement is constituted by an exchange of promises, the
parties are merely saying, in effect: 'If the proposed exchange
takes place, I promise to [pay the agreed price] [tender a conveyance of the house].' The promises are not commitments to
consummate the exchange, but admissions of the fairness of the
terms proposed, and therefore of the obligation that each will
come under, if and when the other's performance is accepted.

The position is, perhaps, even clearer in cases of what lawyers
call 'unilateral contracts', where a person promises another some
payment if, but only if, some condition is satisfied. For instance,
a person may invite an estate agent to find a buyer for his house,
and may promise to pay the agent a commission of, say, £500
if the agent finds him a buyer. The legal interpretation of this
arrangement is that the house owner remains free to sell or not
to sell, and the agent takes the risk that he may spend money
without earning his commission. The house owner's promise
only comes into play in the event of a sale actually taking place.
If that does actually happen, it will be clear that the house owner
has received a benefit through the efforts of the agent, and both
morally and legally, he will then be obliged to pay some fair
recompense for the agent's services. It is at this point that his
promise can be seen as binding the house owner, but the nature
of its binding force is appreciated most clearly if it is seen as
amounting to a conclusive (or more or less conclusive) admission.
The house owner admits that the agent's services were not designed to be gratuitous, and he admits what is a fair recompense
for the value of the benefit he has received. The promise does
not create the obligation, which would arise from the fact that

benefits have been rendered without any intent of conferring a gift. Of course, it may be said that there would be an implied promise, in the absence of an express promise; but *this* kind of implied promise is clearly a result of the obligation, and not its source. It certainly does not perform the evidentiary function which an express promise serves. Indeed, to say that there is an implied promise is often to say no more than that there is an obligation; and it is precisely because such assertions may be arguable, and because the nature and extent of even admitted obligations may be still more arguable, that explicit promises are often made.

Let me now move to the case where a promise is given which is subsequently relied upon by the promisee. This case raises a number of difficulties not involved in the benefit case previously discussed. We must first of all admit that reliance on the *binding nature* of a promise cannot justify recognition of that binding nature. But I have argued that all promises have some assertion content;[8] they all involve a statement of intent, or a statement of fact, or perhaps a prediction about the conduct of a third party or of some state of affairs. If the promisee relies upon the assertion implicit in the promise, the next question (as I have also argued)[9] is whether he is *justified* in so relying. That, I have argued, is a question for the social group to answer: it must be so, for this is a social question. But in answering the question the group nevertheless pays close attention to the behaviour of the parties in question, as well as to what it perceives to be normal behaviour. So here, too, it can be seen how the purpose of an explicit promise is (as in the previous case) evidentiary or clarificatory. If I merely declare my intention to act in a particular way, it will often be unclear whether you are justified in acting on that declaration, so that, if you do act on it, and suffer loss, that loss is fairly attributable to me. To make an explicit promise is one way of helping to clear up the doubt which would otherwise arise. The promisor, by explicitly promising, is *admitting* that (insofar as it is for him to decide) he thinks the promisee will be justified in acting in reliance on him.

All this surely helps to explain why one of the commonest ways of making an explicit promise in practice is by telling the promisee that he can 'count upon' the promise, that he can 'depend upon'

---

[8] *Supra*, p. 166.
[9] *Supra*, pp. 66, 127 ff.

it, or rely upon it, or act upon it. The confusing thing is that the promisee appears to be invited to rely upon the promise itself. That is wrong. He is really being invited to rely upon the proposition inherent in the promise.

Of course, in a society where explicit promising is thought to be a well-recognized way of creating obligations, the promisee may come to rely, not only on the proposition implicit in the promise, but also on the binding quality of the promise itself. And when we have a legal system which is widely seen as independent of the moral system, we can even get the case of the promisee who relies exclusively on his legal remedies in respect of a promise, and has no faith at all in the assertion content of the promise. As we have seen, this kind of case may be possible in law, though it fits uneasily with legal rules designed primarily for cases where the promisee does rely on some assertion implicit in a promise.[10]

To sum up my argument so far: I have been suggesting that a promise is an admission concerning the existence and extent of other obligations which either pre-exist the making of the promise, or which anyhow would arise before, or at the same time as, the promise becomes obligatory. These other obligations can arise from many sources but most of them arise from benefits rendered to the promisor, or from acts of detrimental reliance performed by the promisee. In the former case, the promise is usually evidence that the transaction is an exchange and not a gift, and it is evidence of the fair value of the exchange; in the latter case, the promise is evidence that the promisor himself thought that the promisee would be justified in acting in reliance on the assertions expressed or implicit in the promise. Two concluding objections need to be considered before I go on to the more fundamental problem of why promissory admissions should generally be treated as conclusive.

It may, in the first place, be objected that promises just differ from admissions; the act of admitting, it may be said, is just different from the act of promising. If this is meant to imply that the act of promising creates an obligation, rather than that it admits the existence of an obligation otherwise created, the answer must be sought by reverting to the distinction between the internal and the external viewpoint. If, as I have argued, moral rules and moral obligations are the creation of the social

---

[10] *Supra*, p. 56 ff.

group, then it must be the group which ultimately decides what conditions justify the creation of moral obligations. The group may permit individuals to admit (more or less conclusively) that the conditions necessary for the existence of moral obligations are satisfied; but it is a much more serious matter for the group to permit individuals actually to create their own obligations. Of course, this is perfectly possible as a matter of logic. The social group may simply decide that moral obligations attach to whatever individual members of the group decide they should attach to. But that is (roughly speaking) the morality of liberalism. It is also the morality of a much looser social group than we are accustomed to in the present day. In modern times, the morality of social groups tends to be more pervasive, and more cohesive. The social group today is still willing to delegate considerable autonomy to its members; and it does this (in this sphere) largely by enabling them to admit, more or less conclusively, that circumstances exist in which the group recognizes the existence of obligations. But the modern social group has much more difficulty in recognizing the right of individuals to create obligations in circumstances where the group itself does not recognize the existence of obligations.

The second point to be dealt with here concerns the argument that even if a promise has primarily the evidentiary function I have allotted to it, it may also have further, reinforcing functions of its own. This objection falls into two parts. First, even if it is conceded that a promise may simply be evidence of the value (etc.) of benefits rendered, or of the justification of acts of detrimental reliance, where benefits *are* rendered, or acts of detrimental reliance actually *do* take place, what of the case where there are no benefits and no acts of reliance? Suppose the promisor breaks his promise prior to any benefits being rendered to him, or to any acts of reliance by the promisee, is the promise not, in some sense, still binding? That is a difficult and central question, but I will postpone any attempt to answer it until a later point. The second half of this objection raises the possibility that, even where some benefit is rendered, or some act of reliance takes place, the promise may have more than evidentiary value. It may reinforce, or enhance, the obligation that would otherwise arise. This argument may gain some support from the law of damages, because (for instance) it is often the case that a promise to pay a sum of money is enforceable as a result of an act of reliance, even though the promisee's costs or expenses as a result of the reliance are far lower than the value of the promise. Thus, in the famous case of *Carlill* v. *Carbolic Smoke Ball Co.*,[11] a company advertised a reward of £100 to anyone who used its anti-flu 'smoke-ball' as prescribed for a period of three weeks and still contracted flu; it was held liable to the plaintiff for the £100 despite the fact that her acts of reliance may have been much less valuable than that. One answer to the objection is to suggest that, in this sort of case at any rate, the promise is held binding in order to penalize rash and reckless (if not fraudulent) promises and advertising. In effect, the company was ordered to pay £100 in damages as a sort of fine, and not because its promise to pay the £100 was morally obligatory. That answer may not meet all cases, however, and it may be necessary, if the evidentiary argument is to be maintained, to argue baldly that there is no justification for treating promises as wholly binding in such circumstances.

WHY SHOULD ADMISSIONS BE CONCLUSIVE?

If promises are admissions, they are admissions of a peculiar sort. For they are irrevocable and conclusive admissions, at any rate in many ordinary circumstances. The question may now be posed, why does an admission conclusively determine so many issues? Why is the promisor not entitled to reopen them, and argue that, despite his admission, no obligation already existed, or the promisee was not justified in acting in reliance? Now it must first be remembered that the admission is, indeed, not always conclusive. There are a great many situations, especially in the modern world, where excuses, justifications, explanations are permissible. And if the law is any guide to these moral issues, as I have argued that it should be, we must bear in mind the modern legal changes which remove the conclusiveness from so many forms of promise.

But it remains, of course, the case, that many promises in law, and in morality, *are* conclusive; that, insofar as they are regarded as admissions, they are conclusive admissions. In asking why this should be so, it may help if we take a look at the law relating to admissions. Generally speaking, admissions in law are presumptive rather than conclusive evidence of what is admitted. An admission out of Court, for instance, can be cited as evidence against the party making the admission, and will carry varying

---

[11] [1893] 1 QB 256.

weight according to the nature of the admission and the circumstances of the case. Now the admissibility in evidence of such out-of-Court admissions is prima facie an exception to the hearsay rule, and lawyers have sometimes attempted to justify this exception in one of two ways.[12] On the one hand it is sometimes argued that an admission is admissible in evidence because it is likely to be true; although it is hearsay, and therefore shares the general weakness of hearsay evidence, the fact that the admission was made by a party to the case, and that it tells against his interest, is thought to make it sufficiently trustworthy to overcome the ban on hearsay. The other explanation sometimes proffered is one which basically rests on the notion that it is somehow *unfair* that a person should be permitted to deny (or even exclude from consideration) what he has formerly said. This is sometimes said to be an application of the legal principle known as 'estoppel' whereby a person is (in some circumstances) unable to deny the truth of what he has formerly asserted.

The first of these two reasons is relevant to the case of promising. Insofar as I have correctly assimilated a promise to an admission, it is plainly arguable that the promise is treated as conclusive partly at least because the admission implicit in it is likely to be true. If *A* promises to pay £10 to *B* in return for some service to be rendered by *B*, *A*'s promise is an admission that the service is worth £10 to *A*. As such, it is likely to be true. Similarly, if a person invites another to rely upon him by making some explicit promise and saying, 'You may count upon me', it may be said that he has admitted that the promisee will be justified in relying upon him. That admission is likely to be true. But this still does not take us to an explanation of why the admission should be conclusive. For the mere fact that it is an admission makes it probable that it is true but it is not, in itself, a ground for treating it as irrebuttable. However, there are many circumstances where the admission relates to something which is not a pure matter of objective fact. To promise £10 for a service is an admission that the service is worth £10 to the promisor; but that is not a simple question of objective fact. It may be an entirely subjective valuation. And the question whether one person is justified in relying upon another is even more obviously an evaluation, rather than a question of pure fact. In both these cases, therefore, there is some reason for treating the admission as conclusive.

---

[12] See M. Pickard, 'Statements of Parties', 41 *Modern L. Rev.* 124 (1978).

But there are two important qualifications to be made to this. First, it is not now generally regarded as necessarily true (except in a trivial sense) that a person's judgment of the value of something to him is wholly conclusive. No doubt this is often still the case with particular types of goods or services which do not have a readily available market. But with goods and services which do have a normal market price (or a price which normally falls within a fairly well defined range) it is usually thought that a person's own judgment of what something is worth (even to him) is fallible. And secondly, we still have the problem that even an admission of the value of something, as evidenced by a promise, seems only to be conclusive at the time the promise is made. For if a person changes his mind as to the value to him of some good or service, there is no obvious reason why the former, rather than the latter valuation should be treated as conclusive—and they cannot both be conclusive. The only argument that can be used to justify selection of the former valuation rather than the latter, is that the promisor now has (or may be assumed to have) reasons for dissembling. When he first made the promise he can be assumed to have directed his attention to the need to decide whether the promise was a fair return for whatever he was seeking to obtain with it; now, he may no longer be in this situation, for he may already have obtained his return. And much the same argument can be constructed with regard to reliance. But arguments of this nature obviously have many weaknesses. They certainly cannot be valid in all cases.

The second argument which lawyers have offered for treating admissions as an exception to the hearsay rule does not, I think, help us at all. For this argument is based on fairness, and is associated with the legal idea of estoppel. But estoppel is a reliance concept, and I have been arguing that reliance is one of the bases of promissory liability. So to justify the legal treatment of admissions as a species of estoppel is uncomfortably close to an attempt to reduce the concept of an admission to that of a promise. As I have been engaged in the reverse exercise, it is clear that no help is to be found here.

But there is one further argument which is of some importance. Where benefits have been rendered, or reliance has taken place, questions are bound to arise about the proper recompense for the benefit, or the possible responsibility of those who have relied. These questions are bound to arise at any rate in a society which accepts the obligations to render good for good, or to avoid injury to others. And if they arise, they have to be solved somehow. They could, in theory, be solved by methods which did not involve the choice of the parties. All prices of all goods and services could, in principle, be fixed by State decree, for example. In very many cases, this could be done in advance. In the case of less standardized goods or services, it might have to be done retrospectively. And this could also be done wherever one person has relied upon another, and suffered injury or loss in consequence. But it is obvious that a vast judiciary or bureaucracy would be needed to make all these decisions if they were not largely left to the parties themselves. Consider, for example, the simple problems which arise from those who cause physical injury to others by negligence—a limited class of cases where injury is caused, certainly far fewer in number than those where reliance of some kind causes financial or other loss. Even in this limited class of case, the great majority of disputes are (retrospectively) settled by agreement between the parties. Only some 1 per cent of these cases is tried by Courts. If we refused to accept the parties' own assessment of the amount to be paid by way of compensation in these cases, a huge extra flood of litigation would pour into the Courts. The same would obviously be true if people could not, by promising, make (more or less) conclusive admissions of the value of the goods they seek to obtain. So, too, if a person could not bind himself by a conclusive admission that what he says to another justifies the other in relying upon him, a great many more disputes would inevitably arise which would need some sort of judicial resolution.

These practical arguments about the need to allow parties to make their own decisions, when combined with some of the other arguments mentioned below, and, in particular, the argument from principle, may be thought to carry a good deal of combined force. For even if, on some occasions, it proves hard to hold a promisor to his promise as a form of conclusive admission, it may be felt that he is not deserving of much sympathy. Perhaps the promisor later comes to think that the benefit he has received is not worth as much as he promised to pay, and perhaps he may sometimes be right. In extreme circumstances we will now usually (anyhow in law) allow the admission implicit in the promise to be rebutted by extraneous evidence. But in less extreme circumstances, we will not allow this, even though we may think that it is quite possible that the promisor's second thoughts are right. If the promisor is thus caught by the rules overshooting the mark, it may be felt that he has brought his troubles upon himself. But we need to beware of assuming that everyone will agree on this point. The more paternalist a society becomes, the less common will this attitude become, and the less binding or conclusive a promise will be felt to be. As our society has become a great deal more paternalist during the course of the past century, I have argued elsewhere[13] that the result has been a great resurgence in benefit-based and reliance-based liabilities, and a corresponding decline in promise-based liabilities. This is only another way of saying that the conclusiveness of admissions has become gradually weakened in a great variety of circumstances.

THE TRUE BASIS OF LIABILITY ON A CONCLUSIVE ADMISSION

I have argued that, where promises coexist with an element of reliance or benefit, the promise is best understood as a conclusive admission. The question may now be asked whether, if this is right, the liability is 'truly' based on the promise, or on the element of benefit or reliance which the promise evidences. One short answer would be to dismiss the question as a purely verbal one. But there may be a number of real issues involved in this question which are worth further consideration.

I have at various points in this book, and still more elsewhere,[14] related the conclusiveness of promises as admissions with the doctrines of the classical economists and the Benthamite utilitarians, and with the general liberal heritage to which they gave rise. One of the fundamental tenets of early nineteenth-century thought was that the individual is the sole judge of what is in his best interests. An individual who makes a promise which coexists with some element of benefit or reliance, is therefore conclusively determining, as a third party judge might, if the issue came before him, a number of important issues about the benefit and/or the reliance. Thus (as I have suggested) he is determining what is in fact beneficial to him, what benefits are worth, whether his pronouncements are rightly to be depended upon, and so forth. Now it becomes possible to see that the conclusiveness of a promisor's decisions on various issues resembles the conclusiveness of ordinary judicial decisions. And it is possible to invoke the illuminating discussion of the conclusiveness, or finality, of

---

[13] See my *Freedom of Contract*, Chap. 22.
[14] See my *Freedom of Contract*, especially Chapters 13, 14, and 15.

judicial decisions, which is to be found in Hart's *Concept of Law*.[15]
Hart here demonstrates the importance of distinguishing between
internal and external viewpoints in analysing the finality of
judicial decisions. From the outside, it is possible to equate the
decision of the judge—because it is final and authoritative—with
the matter to be decided. Thus it becomes possible to say, 'The
Constitution of the United States is what the judges say it is.'
From the external viewpoint, this is accurate, but this is only one
perspective. There is also an internal viewpoint, that of the judge
himself, and of those who are thinking or arguing from within
the system. The judge does not conceive himself free to decide
what the Constitution of the United States is without constraint.
And others operating within the system, such as lawyers analysing or criticizing decisions of the Courts, also operate from the
internal viewpoint. A lawyer may recognize the finality of a
decision, but may criticize the grounds for it, which he could not
do if the external viewpoint were the only possible perspective.
For if the Constitution of the United States was, from the internal
viewpoint, what the judges say, then it would be impossible to
criticize a decision on the ground that the judges *should* have said
something else.

Hart's distinction between the internal and external viewpoints
is not the same as that which I myself have used in Chapter 5.
But his analysis of this distinction as applied to the finality of
judicial decisions appears to me to be transferable to the sphere
of promising. A promisor who promises to pay for some benefit
received is, I have argued, conclusively admitting a number of
vital issues. From one, external viewpoint, that admission can
be taken as the very ground of his liability. By promising to pay
for the benefit, he *admits* conclusively that it *is* a benefit, and he
admits conclusively what the benefit is worth to him. Since he is—
within limits—the sole judge of these matters (a person is 'the
best judge' of his own interests), his decision is final; he is liable
because he has promised. But there is also another, internal, viewpoint. This does not correspond wholly with what I called the
internal viewpoint in Chapter 5, for that was a viewpoint internal
to one individual. The present internal viewpoint is internal in
a slightly broader sense. It is internal to the promise, or the con-
stituents of the promise, in the same sense that Hart's viewpoint
of judicial decisions is internal to lawyers and others operating

---

[15] At pp. 138-44.

within the system. From this, internal viewpoint, we can see that the promise is not the *reason* for the obligation any more than the judge's decision is *to him* a reason for the law which he declares. The oddity is that the promisor is himself the judge, but he also retains his character as promisor. Thus, having in his capacity as judge conclusively determined what is beneficial, and how much it is worth, etc., he thereafter becomes bound, in his capacity as promisor, by his own decision as judge. Hence the external viewpoint may become appropriate even for the promisor himself, once he has made his promise. This explains why, once the promise is made, even the promisor may come to see himself as bound just because he has promised, and for no other reason. His position can be compared to that in which a judge might find himself if he became personally involved in a dispute on a point of law which he had formerly resolved in his capacity as judge. As a judge, various reasons would have underlain his decision on what the law should be (or was); but as a citizen, the judge would become bound by the law, irrespective of the reasons, and even of whether they were good or bad reasons.

As I have said, the internal viewpoint is not internal only to the promisor. It is internal to anyone operating within the system, as it were. So, for instance, if the question arises in any given case whether a promise *is* conclusive, whether there are grounds on which the promisor should *not* be bound by his promise, either in law or on morals, it is evident that the reasons underlying the promise will have to be examined. Then the fact that the promisor has received some benefit (or what prima facie appears to be a benefit), or that the promisee has acted in reliance, is a good reason for upholding the conclusiveness of the promise.

The notion of treating a promisor's conclusive admissions as though they were decisions made by the promisor as a sort of judge is, no doubt, strange. Perhaps the initial strangeness arises from the strongly held ideal that no person should be a judge in his own cause. The reason why this maxim does not bar the present perspective is that the promisor is treated as a judge *only against himself.* He is held liable on the promise because, *by his own admission,* what he has received is a benefit worth what he has promised for it. Thus, even if we treat him as the judge to decide what is beneficial, and what value benefits have, the decision he has made is *against* himself. Although speaking prospectively, no man should be a judge in his own cause, speaking retrospectively, a person who has decided against himself is the best of all judges. Once again, it is necessary to make the caveat that this represents a powerful value-position; and that many people today would find that position one that must be hedged around with many limitations and qualifications.

This discussion may suggest that—where some element of benefit or reliance is involved—no final answer can be given to the question, Is the promise itself the source of the obligation? It is no more possible to give a simple answer to this question than it is to ask what is the source of a rule of law laid down by a final Court. From the external viewpoint, the source is the promise, or the decision of the Court. From the internal viewpoint, the source is the reasons which have led to the promise or the decision of the Court.

Mutual Executory Promises

Nearly all that I have so far written in this chapter about the evidentiary nature of promises appears to make good sense where promises are actually followed by benefits or acts of reliance. If *A* promises to pay £1,000 for *B*'s car, then *A*'s promise may be treated as evidentiary once the car is delivered to him. But what of the position prior to any performance of the contract? If *B* has not acted in reliance on *A*'s promise, and *A* has not yet received the car, what is the source of *A*'s obligation to fulfil his promise? At this stage, surely, the evidentiary theory will not hold. This is correct, but it is right to stress that the problem we now have to encounter is of relatively minor dimensions. What we have to explain is why wholly executory mutual promises should be binding prior to the rendering of any benefit, and prior to acts of reliance. This is likely to be a short period in most circumstances, for although arrangements may sometimes be made a long while in advance, this is usually done in order that the parties, or one of them, can plan and adjust their conduct in reliance on the arrangements. Thus reliance normally follows hard on the heels of the making of mutual executory promises.

Moreover, (as I have previously suggested) mutual executory promises are not normally treated as creating very powerful obligations prior to acts of reliance, or the rendering of benefits. Even in business matters there is evidence that this is the case, and in social relationships it seems no less true. To break a social engagement, for instance, is not usually considered a very heinous offence provided that due warning is given so that no reliance will take place. So also, in law, as I have shown, there are many rules relating to the assessment of damages which show that the bonds which are created by mutual executory promises are not very powerful. Indeed, it is probably no exaggeration to suggest that non-recognition of the moral or legal obligation created by mutual executory promises would not lead to very disastrous results. It *is* quite possible to consider rationally the question which some philosophers appear to have thought inconceivable,[16] that is, whether bare mutual promises should create moral (or legal) obligations, whether we actually need that part of the practice of promising at all. Obviously there is a conflict between the desirability of retaining the right to change one's mind and the desirability of treating mutual promises as obligatory in their inception. It may be that the arguments for the present position outweigh those against it, but the arguments deserve rational discussion. This discussion should both help to place the problem in perspective and show that the moral obligatoriness of bare promises (even bare mutual promises) surely cannot be treated as paradigmatic of obligations generally.

It is, of course, the case that current moral codes do treat mutual promises as morally binding, and that the law generally treats them as legally binding. If the present position is to be justified, some explanations are called for, but it should first be said that there are a number of different *types* of explanation. The first type of explanation may be sociological, or historical, in nature: how has it come about that mutual executory promises have come to be regarded as morally (and sometimes legally) obligatory? Other types of explanation may relate to the grounds (e.g. economic or ethical) on which it is today felt that mutual executory promises should create obligations.

With regard to the first type of grounds, it may well be that the binding force commonly thought to attach to executory exchanges of promises is a result of simple extrapolation. For example, the mere receipt of a counter-promise may have been thought a sufficient benefit to justify treating a promisor as bound by his own promise; if he had actually received the benefit promised by the counter-promise, his own promise could have been treated as an admission, and so binding. Perhaps it came to be felt that mere receipt of the counter-promise was enough. Alternatively,

---

[16] See e.g. Hanfling, 'Promises, Games and Institution', *Proc. Arist. Soc.* 13 (1975), and Midgley, 'The Game Game', 49 *Philosophy* 231 (1974); cf. Rothbard, op. cit., (p. 34).

it may be that treating promises as binding where actual benefits were rendered to the promisor came gradually to have the effect of persuading people that promises always involved an obligation, even if they were not rendered in exchange for benefits. Thus, even gratuitous promises came to be thought morally obligatory, so that *a fortiori* an exchange of promises would be seen as binding.

It is not difficult to see how this sort of extrapolation might have occurred, particularly given the likelihood that it served a useful purpose in certain cases and that people would have been deliberately striving to encourage the extrapolation. The parallel, in modern law, with irrebuttable (or even rebuttable) presumptions and admissions is plain enough. People are sometimes encouraged to make admissions even when they are not true, and are known not to be true, in order to prevent future arguments. For instance a person buying some expensive item may be required to sign a form saying that he admits that he has examined the goods, and that various defects have been pointed out to him. This may be untrue, and may be known to be such, but it is nevertheless easy to see why such forms are used. Similarly, a person may falsely admit to having received something that he has not received, by giving a receipt, or making a false acknowledgement. Again, it is easy to see the purpose of this. The parties want their rights to be regulated as though certain facts were true which are not true. If the law, or the moral code, always respected people's intentions, it would be unnecessary to resort to these subterfuges. It is precisely because law and morals do not always (and have not in the past always) recognized the right of individuals to bind themselves merely because they intend to do so, that false admissions of this kind are used. If promises historically grew out of the notion of admissions, if they were normally conceived as binding because they normally were given as admissions of benefits received or of justifiable reliance, then it is easy to see how promises, even without benefits or reliance, may come to be thought to be binding. A parallel may be found with modern coinage and paper money: originally, the State stamp or certification of the coinage was a conclusive determination that valuable metals were of a specified weight and value. Later, it came to be possible to attach this conclusive stamp or certification to totally worthless bits of paper.

With regard to the second type of ground, it needs first to be stressed that the equation of the concept of 'an agreement' with mutual promises is not necessarily legitimate. I have previously pointed out that an agreement for future performance may involve two separable elements, (1) agreement on the terms of a proposed exchange, and (2) an obligation to consummate the exchange. I have given examples showing how the first element may be present without the second, as for instance, with non-binding agreements for the sale of a house. Now it follows from this that we cannot assume, without more, that every agreement on the terms of an exchange involves mutual promises to complete the exchange, nor that the parties intend to bind themselves to carry out the agreement. In fact, the law commonly does make this assumption, the house-buying case being generally seen as an exceptional sort of case, justified on special grounds. And most probably the common legal equation of agreements with mutual promises to complete the exchange would be made by many non-lawyers also. But if the equation cannot be made, then it is clear that in cases of agreement without such mutual promises the element of obligation must be supplied from outside, as it were. There must be reasons which lead the social group to decide that when two parties have reached agreement on the terms of an exchange they should (in general) be compelled to carry through the exchange.

How important is this possibility? Might it not be said that these are relatively unusual cases, and that in most circumstances an agreement clearly does involve mutual promises to carry out the exchange? This does not seem to me nearly so clear as is generally assumed. Take the ordinary agreement for a sale *which may indeed actually contain explicit promises*. A promises to B £10 in return for B's cow, and B promises the cow to A in return for the £10. Now, to the modern lawyer, as to the modern man in the street, it is perfectly obvious that we have here a mutual agreement, a contract, a 'deal' in the colloquial idiom. Both parties have given explicit promises. Each party is bound by his promise; and each promise creates an obligation. It all seems so simple. But in truth, it may be too simple. Suppose that A changes his mind after making this agreement, and declines to proceed with it. B will protest that A has broken his promise. But suppose that, in answer to this, A says, in effect, 'I promised you £10 in return for your cow. But you haven't delivered me the cow. So I have not broken my promise.' B may well protest, in reply, that he was perfectly willing to deliver the cow; indeed, he may have actually offered to deliver the cow, and A may have refused to take it. Thus *B* will argue that, if the cow was not delivered, *A* has only himself to blame for that; in consequence, he will repeat his allegation that *A* has broken his promise. In modern law, this would be a perfectly sound position to take. Indeed, a modern lawyer (or man in the street) would feel that the case is so simple that surely there can be no possible defence to the claim. But this is not so. Suppose that, in answer to *B*'s last claim—that he offered to deliver the cow, and *A* refused to take it—*A* replies as follows: 'Yes, it is quite true that I refused to accept your cow, but I was perfectly entitled to do that. I never promised to accept your cow. What I promised was to pay £10 for it, if and when it was delivered. If I had accepted it, I would thus have been bound to pay the £10. But I have not accepted it. My promise does not oblige me to accept it. Ergo, I have not broken my promise.'

B's only possible answer to this argument is to claim that by promising to pay £10 for the cow, *A* was impliedly promising that he would not refuse (? unreasonably) to accept the cow when de-livered. And, once again, to the modern man, lawyer or other-wise, that implication is so obvious, that *A*'s arguments begin to look increasingly specious. But are they? To promise to pay £10 for something if and when it is delivered does not *entail* a promise to accept the delivery of it. There is nothing illogical, or even irrational, in making a promise to pay for some goods or service, once they have been accepted, or received, but to decline to commit oneself in advance to accepting or receiving them. So, on what basis does one decide that *A* must have impliedly prom-ised to accept the cow, when proffered? On what grounds does one make this implication? One straightforward answer seems to be to say that the implication comes from normal understand-ings.[17] When parties exchange promises as in this hypothetical case, the usual understanding would be that both bind themselves at the outset, and that is the source of *A*'s implied promise. No doubt, this is true enough in many simple transactions, such as in the simple sale discussed above, but it is not evident to me that this is the norm, at any rate outside the commercial or busi-ness sphere. In other cases it may well be that there is a distinction between an agreement made today for future performance *because the parties do not want to perform it today,* and an agreement made today for future performance *because the parties cannot perform it*

---

[17] Sidgwick, *Methods*, pp. 437-8.

today. In the first case the whole purpose of making an agreement today is to create an obligation; for if that were not so, there is no obvious reason why the parties should not wait until they want to perform, and then make their exchange. But in the second case, that is not the purpose of the parties at all. What they are trying to do is to make a present exchange, but because that is not immediately practical for one reason or another, they arrange to postpone its performance. In this situation they may well not think about the status of their agreement in the interim, and neither of them may have adverted to the question of what is to happen if one wishes to withdraw.

It seems to me quite possible that this latter is really quite a common type of case, although this is not how things are normally perceived. But in the end, it is an empirical question what the common understanding is when parties make agreements for future performance (in either sense) and what the particular parties have intended. My point is that it is too facile to assume that the law and the moral code merely give effect to common understandings. Those responsible for creating the law (or propagating the moral code) may be motivated at least in part by the desire to encourage or discourage certain types of behaviour, for example, (in this context) fixity of purpose as opposed to changing one's mind, or the economic desirability of completing an exchange when the parties are agreed on the terms of the proposed exchange. So we are driven back to our question, what are the reasons for treating agreements of this kind as creating obligations?

Consider first the simplest case, namely where the parties do intend to bind themselves to future performance, where, that is to say, they have deliberately entered into an agreement today for performance at a later date. Of course, one explanation of this case is to say that the parties intend to bind themselves, and that is all there is to be said. It will be evident that I do not accept this short-cut solution if only because it is by now clear that intention is neither a necessary nor a sufficient condition for the creation of an obligation. But a more basic reason for putting aside this argument here is that it does not really answer the question I am posing. I am seeking an answer to the question posed from an external viewpoint, namely why should mutual executory promises create obligations? What reasons are there for holding that people who make such promises should perform them? It is no answer to these questions to say that mutual promises are obligation-creating acts. The whole question is, why should there be—why should we create a moral system which recognizes—such obligation-creating acts? Obligations normally arise from actions that create or reduce utilities, that is from actions which benefit or harm others. Why should a person who has done neither of these things (or anything else that may, as an act, be thought to create obligations, such as fathering a child) be able to create an obligation just by saying that he has one? The same point can be put in a slightly different way, as follows. Even if we assume that promises are intentionally made in order to create obligations, it only follows that we should recognize this result insofar as we wish to respect *intentions*. To the extent that a society or a moral code does not accept the right of citizens to pursue their own good in their own way, it ceases to be tautological to argue that promises should be kept because that is what promises are *for*.

In the end, therefore, other justifications must be sought for treating agreements or mutual promises as binding, even where it is clear that the parties intended to create obligations on themselves.

The place to start, it may be suggested, is the reason for the whole arrangement. As I have suggested above, if parties have made an agreement today for future performance because they want future performance, then one needs to understand why the parties do not simply wait until the time arrives when they want performance to take place. Why, in other words, do people make advance arrangements of this kind in the first place? The answer surely is that they want to eliminate (or shift) risks of various kinds. Contracts for future performance are often deliberately entered into for the purpose of shifting a risk. For example, X may contract to buy from Y 100 tons of coffee at a fixed price, delivery to be in 12 months time. The purpose of this arrangement is to shift on to Y the possibility of future price increases in coffee above a certain figure. This is a kind of speculation, a bet, but it is likely to have a more useful social or economic purpose than a simple bet. For risk-allocation between business men may be designed to shift risks to those who are better able to evaluate and absorb risks, or even prevent them. In contracts of this kind, the whole purpose of the arrangement requires that it be entered into in advance, and that the parties be held to it even prior to any reliance or receipt of benefits.

Now the making of future contracts in business is, taken as a whole, probably a highly efficient instrument for shifting risks on to those best able to handle them. The aggregate gains to the community as a whole may well be vast, and, to most people, this may be a sufficient economic justification for treating such contracts as legally binding. It is not, of course, an ethical argument; but anyone who insists on searching for some independent ethical justification for treating contracts of this kind as binding, must explain how they differ from bets—unless he is prepared to invest bets with the same degree of moral sanctity.

However, as I have said, this is not the only kind of future contract or agreement. We also have to explain why agreements of a non-commercial character are morally or legally obligatory; and we have to justify our willingness to treat agreements as binding even where it is far from clear that the parties intended to bind themselves to completing the exchange. Agreements of this kind are not designed to shift risks, and although they may be held to have this result, there is no *a priori* reason to suppose that this will be efficient risk-shifting. Other reasons must therefore be sought for treating such agreements as binding.

The first possible argument, which I discussed extensively earlier, is that promises give rise to expectations and that this fact alone is sufficient to justify the obligation. This argument, as we saw earlier, has been extensively used by utilitarians to explain the basis of promissory obligation, but the utilitarians have generally placed more weight on expectations than is necessary. It should by now be clear that only where there is no element of benefit or reliance is it necessary to place the whole case for the binding nature of promises on the expectations they generate. It will also be apparent that, as with reliance, the expectations derive not primarily from the binding force of the promise (which would involve a circular argument) but from the assertion content of the promise. Indeed, where there is a mere agreement without any actual intention to create obligations to complete the exchange, it seems that the fact of the expectations would have to bear the burden of justifying the compulsion to complete the exchange. In cases where the parties would have preferred to complete their exchange on the spot, and have only postponed their performance because they could not do that, it may be that the protection of the parties' expectations derives from the sense that an inchoate exchange ought to be consummated. In this connection it is interesting to note that there are a number of legal rules which treat an inchoate transfer of property (or exchange) *as a promise,* thereby imposing on the transferor an obligation to complete the transfer.

Now it cannot be denied that, if the expectations are justified, (as reliance may be justified) the mere fact of the expectations is some ground for holding the promisor bound by his promise. If the promisor has *no* reason at all for breaking his promise (other than a sheer disinclination to perform) it would seem plain that he has caused a disappointment to the promisee which could have been avoided by not making the promise at all. Prima facie, this is evidently an unnecessary injury, though I have pointed out before that the promisee may not, in the result, be 'worse off' than he was before the promise was made at all. But pure expectations are of limited force in explaining promissory obligation. For the disappointment of expectations is not a particularly serious matter. Life is, after all, full of disappointed expectations. Many of them are unavoidable, or attributable to the disappointed person himself, for instance, in entertaining expectations which are too sanguine, or unwarranted. This is, of course, no argument for denying that it is wrong to disappoint another's expectations when one has aroused them oneself, and where the disappointment *is* avoidable, but it does help to place the matter in perspective. A disappointed expectation is a disappointment—just that, and no more. If the promisor has *any* genuine reason for wishing to resile (or perhaps postpone performance), it will often seem unreasonable to demand performance according to the letter of the promise.

The second explanation is the argument from principle. Promises are liable to be relied upon, and even if a promise has not yet been relied upon, it may come to be relied upon at any time. Moreover, the promisor will often not know whether the promise has been relied upon. In order the better to ensure that relied-upon promises are performed, it may, therefore, be desirable to insist that even unrelied-upon promises are performed. Now this argument, and the objections to it, have already been encountered. It will be, indeed, has been, objected, that this argument from principle assumes that people are very stupid. For it assumes that people will not be able to distinguish relied-upon from unrelied-upon promises. However, I have already suggested that this objection is not fatal to the argument. It is not so much stupidity as self-interest which is the problem. And it is quite wrong to think that an optimal rule must precisely coincide with the goals which the rule is designed to achieve. A little overshooting of the mark is often a small price to pay for a greater number of shots actually on the target.

There is a further complication about wholly executory promises which may illustrate the value of the argument from principle. One of the commonest ways of relying on a promise is to give other promises in turn to third parties. Similarly, with legal contracts, one of the commonest forms of action in reliance is entering into another contract with a third party which depends on the first contract. Now if promises were generally treated as only binding where they have been relied upon, but *not* where they have merely given rise to expectations, cases of this nature would raise difficulties. For it might be urged that the mere making of the second promise or contract—so long as no action in reliance on *that* promise or contract has yet occurred—should not be treated as action in reliance on the first promise or contract. For if the second contract is not binding, neither should the first be. This would evidently raise very serious practical difficulties about knowing when promises have been relied upon and become binding; the argument from principle may be thought to dispose of these difficulties.

A third possible argument is that mutual executory promises are in fact mutually beneficial, even prior to actual performance. If we assume that on average, or in general, promises are more likely to be performed than not, then each party to a mutual executory contract has made an arrangement which is likely to bring him in a benefit. A promise-breaker is thus a free rider who is willing to accept the other party's performance if it is due first, or if it turns out advantageous to do so, but will default on his own promise if performance of that is due first, or if it turns out to be disadvantageous to him. There is therefore a sense in which it is just as unfair to accept another's promise in return for one's own promise, and then to break it, as it would be to accept the actual benefit of the performance of another's promise, and then refuse to perform one's own return promise. This argument has force once the institution of promising is securely established, and so long as promises are very widely performed. But it does not help in cases where it is not clear to what extent promissory commitments are in practice respected.

These answers will seem unsatisfactory to some, I have no doubt. They are vague, not always very forceful, some of them do not apply to all mutual promises, and some (like the argument from principle) depend on accepting that rules do not operate in a logical fashion. But if I am correct, the right conclusion is not to continue the somewhat desperate search for more satisfactory reasons for upholding the binding nature of mutual executory promises. The right conclusion is to recognize that we are prone to think of mutual executory promises as having a more binding character than is in truth warranted by the reasons.

Unilateral Gratuitous Promises

I turn now to examine the case of the unilateral gratuitous promise. I take this to be the case of a promise made, not in fulfilment of any previous obligation derived from other sources, not given in return for any benefits, received or anticipated, and not yet relied upon in any way.

It should perhaps first be said that it may be more difficult than it seems at first sight to exclude unilateral promises which are given as a result of some previously existing obligation. For, on one view, most gratuitous promises are in fact given in circumstances where some other obligation exists. A man promises a treat to his children. This seems to create a wholly new obligation. But does it? Does a man not owe duties to his children? Is he not morally obliged to do what he can to give them pleasures of various sorts? If he promises a particular treat—an outing, or a party for instance—can we not take this as evidence of what, in the circumstances, is a reasonable way of discharging these existing obligations? Of course, the way in which a parent should discharge his duties to his children must depend on a variety of factors, his wealth, his other commitments, his children's aptitudes and tastes, and so on. But once this promise is given, it seems natural to take it as an admission that, having weighed up the various considerations, the father has concluded that this is the best way to discharge his duties.

Much the same could be said of the more extensive duties which a man owes to his fellow men at large. It would surely not be denied that a man owes such duties, and if he promises (say) a donation to a charity, it does not seem difficult to see such a promise as evidence. It is an admission that he recognizes these duties, and a way of quantifying and giving precision to them. Ideas of this kind are many hundred years old, and are to be found in the early history of the common law, as well as in the work of some of the Natural Lawyers.

Now in modern times this way of looking at gratuitous promises has almost vanished. In the law, this may well be because there are so many cases where modern law actually creates a direct legal obligation upon a person to perform these general obligations to his relatives and dependants, and the world at large. It is no longer left to the individual to decide which of them to perform himself. For example, taxation laws are one means by which the able-bodied and fit discharge their duties to succour the sick, the disabled, and the aged. Divorce, separation, and maintenance laws provide a network of rules under which domestic duties can be directly enforced by law, without any need for promises. This does not necessarily preclude parties from making their own agreements and promises, and, indeed, this is still commonly done, but these promises are perhaps seen as ways of forestalling the legal jurisdiction rather than as ways of doing what a person is already obliged to do.

It may be objected that this extensive use of the idea of a pre-existing obligation is too broad to be useful. Many gratuitous promises to do an act of kindness to a friend or relation may, it is said, not be in any real sense obligatory on the promisor prior to the giving of the promise. If that is indeed the case, then the conclusion must surely be that the promise itself makes very little difference to the situation. I have already suggested that, even in the case of mutual executory promises, the search for independent grounds for treating the promises as obligatory is much less satisfying than most people would expect. But of all the reasons I have given for holding that mutual executory promises create obligations, only two have any relevance to the case of unilateral promises. The bare expectation created by the promise is, doubtless, always a factor entitled to some weight. And so, too, it may be argued that the free-rider problem arises, in a very broad and general sort of way, with unilateral promises. I propose to say just a little about each of these.

So far as expectations are concerned, the only point that needs to be made here is that, in the case of gratuitous promises, expectations may sometimes play a role which they do not normally play with bilateral or exchange-promises. For in the bilateral case, each promisor normally looks forward to receiving some benefit from the other in due course; but the gratuitous promisor, by definition, does not. Why then do people make gratuitous promises at all? Why do they not simply wait until they are able to perform their acts of benevolence and then perform them? The answer to that seems to be that (as with bilateral cases) two cases need to be distinguished. First, it may be that the gratuitous promise is made in order to enable the promisee to adjust his own behaviour, i.e. it is made to induce reliance. But secondly, it is sometimes the case that the purpose of making the promise is simply to create expectations, because the promisor himself actually benefits from such expectations. A parent, for instance, may delight in the anticipation of a treat which his children feel when he makes a promise to them. It has also been argued that, even in quite different situations, a promisor gets a benefit from knowing that his promise is, or may be, binding on him, because its value is thereby enhanced to the promisee.[18] The promisor is thus able to achieve the same result by promising less than he might otherwise have had to promise. These are thus cases in which a promisor is able to get some benefit from making even a gratuitous unilateral promise. Perhaps, therefore, such promises should be regarded as more binding than those gratuitous promises which are made in order to induce reliance. Once such reliance occurs, of course, this latter class of promise may become binding simply because of the reliance; but prior to the reliance, the case for regarding promises of this kind as binding will often be very weak.

With regard to the free-rider problem, it may be argued that this arises even with gratuitous promises. For when others make unilateral promises to me, I expect them to be kept; and it would be to take advantage of this social institution if I did not reciprocate when my turn came.

Nevertheless, these arguments seem weak, and the more difficult it is to find any adequate grounds for making the promise in the first place, the weaker do the reasons seem to become. The more gratuitous the promise is, the less it is required by some pre-existing obligation, the less binding it seems to be. If the promise is given for *no* reason at all, nothing that could be called a rational ground, then it would seem that we have finally reached the end of the road. How can such a promise create any sort of an obligation? Is it not relevant to recall that the phrase a *gratuitous* promise means both a promise without reason and a promise without return? Perhaps that is to be unduly cynical. But if the promise is made without any reason at all, it surely becomes a senseless act, not capable in a rational world of creating an obligation at all.

At this stage it is right to remind the reader of some of the

---

[18] See R. A. Posner, in 6 *J. of Legal Studies* 411 (1977).

points made about the law in earlier chapters. For example, in Chapter 1, I pointed out that in the law a promise which is given without any 'consideration' does not create a binding legal obligation. And in law a consideration for a promise is a benefit, an act of detrimental reliance, or a counter-promise. I have also shown in Chapter 2 and elsewhere how important the concept of reciprocity has been in influencing the judicial sense of justice. I have pointed out, too, that the bare expectations created by executory mutual promises, although creating legal obligations, are often not well protected by law. It has generally been thought by lawyers, at least since the late eighteenth century, that the law was out of step with morality in not recognizing the binding force of a gratuitous promise. But it will now be appreciated that there are good reasons for rejecting this view. No doubt the law may have made mistakes in some marginal areas; and no doubt too, lawyers have not paid sufficient attention to the importance of reliance, at least in their articulated versions of contract law. But the general picture I have tried to draw suggests that the grounds for regarding unilateral promises as a source of binding obligations are very weak.

In conclusion, a few words may be spared on the wide gap which this book may have opened up between a legal theory of promising and much modern philosophical work on the theory of promising. It will, I think, be apparent that the philosophical tradition in this sphere is still heavily dominated by writers who reflect liberal values. Liberal values no doubt still have many attractions, but it is simply misleading to think that the moral beliefs of our generation are congruent with these liberal values. In particular, the value of free choice, which underlies the high regard with which the nineteenth-century thinkers viewed the institution of promising, has declined greatly in contemporary society. By contrast, paternalism, which is a negation of the ideal of individual free choice, has become a much more important aspect of social policy. No contemporary lawyer can be unaware of the extent to which changing values have weakened, and in some areas quite destroyed, the belief in freedom of contract which was so prominent a feature of nineteenth-century thought. Any theory of promising which fails to take account of movements in opinion of this magnitude is in danger of ending up as an obsolete theory. Far from explaining the moral basis of promising in any absolute or eternal sense, such theories turn out to be firmly rooted in the ideology of nineteenth-century Western thought.

Index